Communications
in Computer and Information Science 2489

Series Editors

Gang Li ⓘ, *School of Information Technology, Deakin University, Burwood, VIC, Australia*
Joaquim Filipe ⓘ, *Polytechnic Institute of Setúbal, Setúbal, Portugal*
Zhiwei Xu, *Chinese Academy of Sciences, Beijing, China*

Rationale

The CCIS series is devoted to the publication of proceedings of computer science conferences. Its aim is to efficiently disseminate original research results in informatics in printed and electronic form. While the focus is on publication of peer-reviewed full papers presenting mature work, inclusion of reviewed short papers reporting on work in progress is welcome, too. Besides globally relevant meetings with internationally representative program committees guaranteeing a strict peer-reviewing and paper selection process, conferences run by societies or of high regional or national relevance are also considered for publication.

Topics

The topical scope of CCIS spans the entire spectrum of informatics ranging from foundational topics in the theory of computing to information and communications science and technology and a broad variety of interdisciplinary application fields.

Information for Volume Editors and Authors

Publication in CCIS is free of charge. No royalties are paid, however, we offer registered conference participants temporary free access to the online version of the conference proceedings on SpringerLink (http://link.springer.com) by means of an http referrer from the conference website and/or a number of complimentary printed copies, as specified in the official acceptance email of the event.

CCIS proceedings can be published in time for distribution at conferences or as post-proceedings, and delivered in the form of printed books and/or electronically as USBs and/or e-content licenses for accessing proceedings at SpringerLink. Furthermore, CCIS proceedings are included in the CCIS electronic book series hosted in the SpringerLink digital library at http://link.springer.com/bookseries/7899. Conferences publishing in CCIS are allowed to use Online Conference Service (OCS) for managing the whole proceedings lifecycle (from submission and reviewing to preparing for publication) free of charge.

Publication process

The language of publication is exclusively English. Authors publishing in CCIS have to sign the Springer CCIS copyright transfer form, however, they are free to use their material published in CCIS for substantially changed, more elaborate subsequent publications elsewhere. For the preparation of the camera-ready papers/files, authors have to strictly adhere to the Springer CCIS Authors' Instructions and are strongly encouraged to use the CCIS LaTeX style files or templates.

Abstracting/Indexing

CCIS is abstracted/indexed in DBLP, Google Scholar, EI-Compendex, Mathematical Reviews, SCImago, Scopus. CCIS volumes are also submitted for the inclusion in ISI Proceedings.

How to start

To start the evaluation of your proposal for inclusion in the CCIS series, please send an e-mail to ccis@springer.com

Sihem Mesnager · Pantelimon Stănică ·
Sumit Kumar Debnath
Editors

Security and Privacy

3rd International Conference, ICSP 2024
Jamshedpur, India, November 20–21, 2024
Proceedings

Editors
Sihem Mesnager
University of Paris VIII
Saint-Denis, France

Pantelimon Stănică
Naval Postgraduate School
Monterey, CA, USA

Sumit Kumar Debnath
National Institute of Technology
Jamshedpur, Jharkhand, India

ISSN 1865-0929 ISSN 1865-0937 (electronic)
Communications in Computer and Information Science
ISBN 978-3-031-90586-5 ISBN 978-3-031-90587-2 (eBook)
https://doi.org/10.1007/978-3-031-90587-2

© The Editor(s) (if applicable) and The Author(s), under exclusive license
to Springer Nature Switzerland AG 2025

This work is subject to copyright. All rights are solely and exclusively licensed by the Publisher, whether the whole or part of the material is concerned, specifically the rights of translation, reprinting, reuse of illustrations, recitation, broadcasting, reproduction on microfilms or in any other physical way, and transmission or information storage and retrieval, electronic adaptation, computer software, or by similar or dissimilar methodology now known or hereafter developed.
The use of general descriptive names, registered names, trademarks, service marks, etc. in this publication does not imply, even in the absence of a specific statement, that such names are exempt from the relevant protective laws and regulations and therefore free for general use.
The publisher, the authors and the editors are safe to assume that the advice and information in this book are believed to be true and accurate at the date of publication. Neither the publisher nor the authors or the editors give a warranty, expressed or implied, with respect to the material contained herein or for any errors or omissions that may have been made. The publisher remains neutral with regard to jurisdictional claims in published maps and institutional affiliations.

This Springer imprint is published by the registered company Springer Nature Switzerland AG
The registered company address is: Gewerbestrasse 11, 6330 Cham, Switzerland

If disposing of this product, please recycle the paper.

Preface

This volume contains the refereed proceedings of the Third International Conference on Security and Privacy (ICSP 2024), organized by the Department of Mathematics, National Institute of Technology Jamshedpur, India, during November 20–21, 2024. The call for papers for ICSP 2024 included the following topics:

- Cryptography
- Secure cryptographic protocols
- Post-quantum cryptography
- Quantum cryptography
- Blockchain and cryptocurrency
- IoT security and privacy
- Cloud security
- Privacy-preserving technologies
- Biometric security
- Security and privacy of big data
- Cloud and edge computing security
- Access control
- Steganography and steganalysis
- Leakage-resilient cryptography
- Cyber-physical security
- Database security
- Embedded systems security
- Lightweight security
- Authentication and authorization
- Social networks security, privacy, and trust
- Wireless security
- Distributed systems security
- Cyber-physical systems security
- Verification of security protocols
- Machine learning in cybersecurity

The proceedings of the conference contain 13 accepted papers, selected from the 39 submitted papers. All papers were thoroughly refereed by at least three referees. Most of the refereeing was done by members of the program committee. We thank all of them for their help. In addition to the contributed papers, we had seven invited lectures given by Jintai Ding (Tsinghua University, China), Anupam Chattopadhyay (NTU, Singapore), Subhamoy Maitra (Indian Statistical Institute, Kolkata, India), Saibal Kumar Pal (Defense Research & Development Organization, India), Debasish Roy (Government of West Bengal, India), Sourav Mukhopadhyay (Indian Institute of Technology Kharagpur, India), and Ratna Dutta (Indian Institute of Technology Kharagpur, India). In addition, a workshop was organized on the topic "Introduction to Quantum Cryptanalysis with Shor's Algorithm" by Vikas Srivastava (Indian Institute of Technology Madras, India) and Tapaswini Mohanty (Indian Institute of Technology Roorkee, India). Many thanks to all for sharing their expertise. The conference was sponsored by generous funding from DRDO, SERB, and IIT Bombay Trust Lab.

February 2025

Sihem Mesnager
Pantelimon Stanica
Sumit Kumar Debnath

Organization

Program Committee

General Chair

Sihem Mesnager — University of Paris VIII, France

Program Chairs

Pantelimon Stanica — Naval Postgraduate School, USA
Sumit Kumar Debnath — NIT Jamshedpur, India

Technical Program Committee Members

Tapas Pal — Karlsruhe Institute of Technology, Germany
Tanmay Choudhury — Coochbehar Government College, India
Tan Chik How — NUS, Singapore
Daniele Bartoli — University of Perugia, Italy
Chandrashekhar Azad — NIT Jamshedpur, India
Arthur van der Merwe — University of New England, Australia
Dheerendra Mishra — MANIT Bhopal, India
Chunlei Li — University of Bergen, Norway
Arup Kumar Pal — IIT (ISM) Dhanbad, India
Constanza Susana Riera — Western Norway University of Applied Sciences, Norway
Sapna Jyoti Patel — NIT Jamshedpur, India
Meiqin Wang — Shandong University, China
Satya Bagchi — NIT Durgapur, India
Partha Sarathi Roy — University of Wollongong, Australia
Abhishek Kumar — NIT Jamshedpur, India
Kouichi Sakurai — Kyushu University, Japan
Dibyendu Roy — IIIT Vadodara, India
Jaykrushna Sahoo — IIIT Kottayam, India
Shoichi Hirose — University of Fukui, Japan
Bernardo Margi — University of Manchester, UK
Claude Carlet — University of Paris 8, France and University of Bergen, Norway

Venkata Suresh Babu Chilluri	Intuit Inc, USA
Chandramohan Dhasarathan	Thapar University, India
Sushmita Sarkar	NIT Jamshedpur, India
Mostafizar Rahman	University of Hyogo, Japan
Ramprasad Sarkar	IIT Kharagpur, India
Subhranil Dutta	IIT Kharagpur, India
Stuti Kumari	NIT Jamshedpur, India
Jayshree Dey	IIT Kharagpur, India
Ravi Anand	University of Hyogo, Japan
Tapaswini Mohanty	IIT Roorkee, India
Vikas Srivastava	IIT Madras, India
Basudeba Behera	NIT Jamshedpur, India
Harshdeep Singh	DRDO, India
Mriganka Mandal	Indian Statistical Institute Kolkata, India
Kunal Dey	University of Calgary, Canada
Chinmoy Biswas	University of Calgary, Canada
Bhaskar Mondal	NIT Patna, India
Debashish Roy	IIT Kharagpur, India
Saibal Kumar Pal	DRDO, India
Meenakshi Kansal	Rashtriya Raksha University, India
Amit Kumar Singh	Siksha 'O' Anusandhan, India
Kamalesh Acharya	VIT Chennai, India
Prashant Kumar	NIT Jamshedpur, India
Kalika Prasad	Government Engineering College Bhojpur, India
Ghanshyam S. Bopche	NIT Trichy, India
Shi-Feng Sun	Shanghai Jiao Tong University, China
Sabyasachi Dutta	SRM University, India
Chris Mitchell	Royal Holloway, University of London, UK
Paresh Baidya	Siksha 'O'Anusandhan, India
Arpita Maitra	TCG CREST, India
Jason LeGrow	Virginia Polytechnic Institute and State University, USA
Alekha Kumar Mishra	NIT Jamshedpur, India
Luca De Feo	IBM Research Zürich, Switzerland
Jintai Ding	Tsinghua University, China
Bimal Mandal	IIT Jodhpur, India
Dipanwita Roy Chowdhury	IIT Kharagpur, India
J. Srinivas	Jindal Global Business School, India
Subrata Dutta	NIT Jamshedpur, India
Prem Laxman Das	SETS Chennai, India
Santanu Sarkar	IIT Madras, India
Pascal Lorenz	University of Haute Alsace, France

Somnath Kumar	NIT Jamshedpur, India
Sreenivasa Rao Y	NIT Warangal, India
Avishek Adhikari	Presidency University, India
Francesco Regazzoni	University of Amsterdam, The Netherlands
Matthew Stewart	Harvard University, USA
Purushothama B. R.	NITK Surathkal, India
Hiraku Morita	Aarhus University, Denmark
Sriramulu Bojjagani	SRM University, India
Koushlendra Kumar Singh	NIT Jamshedpur, India

Organizing Committee

Chief Patron

Goutam Sutradhar   National Institute of Technology Jamshedpur, India

Chairperson

National Institute of Technology Jamshedpur, India

Chairman

Sourav Das   National Institute of Technology Jamshedpur, India

Convener and Organizing Secretary

Sumit Kumar Debnath   National Institute of Technology Jamshedpur, India

Members (National Institute of Technology Jamshedpur, India)

Tarni Mandal
Ramayan Singh
Sunil Kumar
Raj Nandkeolyar
Shakti Prasad
Ratnesh Kumar Mishra
Rajat Tripathi

Snehasis Kundu
Hari Shankar Prasad
Subha Sarkar
Samiran Chakraborty
Y. Ramu Naidu

Contents

Cryptanalysis and Other Attacks

SIS-Based Signature Schemes and Their Countermeasures: From
Vulnerability to Vigilance 3
   Akanksha Singh, Harish Chandra, and Saurabh Rana

On the Security of AMRIBE, Anonymous Multi-receiver Identity-Based
Encryption 13
   Ramprasad Sarkar, Utkarsh Sahai, and Mriganka Mandal

Algebraic Cryptanalysis and Countermeasures of Lightweight Signature
Scheme Based on Multivariate Quadratic Polynomials 28
   Kuldeep Namdeo, Dheerendra Mishra, and Namita Srivastava

Boolean Functions

Construction of Boolean Functions with $2k$-Valued Walsh Spectrum
and High Nonlinearity 47
   A. U. Zeenath, K. V. Lakshmy, and Chungath Srinivasan

On (Noisy) Simon's (Quantum) Algorithm for Multi-shift Boolean
Functions 62
   Suman Dutta, Aarav Jaiswal, Subhamoy Maitra, and Debasish Roy

Authentication and Authorization, Cyber-physical Systems Security, Privacy-preserving Technologies

Generation of Believable Fake Integral Equations for Cyber Deception 79
   Nilin Prabhaker, Rahul Maurya, Ghanshyam S. Bopche,
   and Michael Arock

A Security and Privacy Model for Automotive 94
   Teodor-Cosmin Curcudel

MAP-ECC: Mutual Authentication Protocol for e-Agriculture Using ECC 109
   Manish Kumar Pandit, Sangram Ray, and Priyanka Das

Blockchain and Cryptocurrency, IoT Security and Privacy, Database Security

Robust Image Steganography: A SLIC and QWT-Based Approach for Secure Data Embedding 127
   Gatram Sravan Kumar, Kamalakanta Sethi, Piyush Joshi, and Padmalochan Bera

A Secure and Decentralized EHR System Using Blockchain and IPFS 142
   Narendra Kumar Ch, Dinesh Kumar, and Amit Prakash

SQL Injection Detection Using Recurrent Neural Networks (RNN) 154
   V. Valli Kumari and Y. Prasanna Kumar

Quantum Cryptography

A Quantum Public Key Cryptographic Scheme Using Entangled States and Grover Operator 171
   Soumen Bajpayee, Sarbani Sen, Prithwish Dey, and Imon Mukherjee

An Efficient and Secure Quantum Group Signature with Applications to Vehicular Ad Hoc Networks 183
   Vikas Srivastava, Tapaswini Mohanty, and Y. Sreenivasa Rao

Author Index 195

Cryptanalysis and Other Attacks

SIS-Based Signature Schemes and Their Countermeasures: From Vulnerability to Vigilance

Akanksha Singh[1], Harish Chandra[1](✉), and Saurabh Rana[2](✉)

[1] Department of Mathematics and Scientific Computing, Madan Mohan Malaviya University of Technology, Gorakhpur 273010, India
hcmsc@mmmut.ac.in
[2] Department of Mathematics (SCSET), Bennett University, Greater Noida 201310, Uttar Pradesh, India
saurabhranapsm@gmail.com

Abstract. Digital signatures are essential to secure digital communications, such as emails, documents, and transactions. Innovative signature techniques are being created to fend off quantum assaults as quantum computing develops. A compact lattice-based protocol that includes lower key and signature sizes was recently presented by Soni et al. However, after analysis, Pursharthi et al. expose a severe weakness, and they find that the signer's key, which is intended for several uses, can be exposed by a single valid message-signature pair. To improve this, she proposed a countermeasure to secure the signature key and claimed that the signature key is now unobtainable even with several legitimate message-signature combinations. Thus, we analyze the Pursharthi et al. technique using cryptanalysis, which suggests that an attacker can obtain the signer's secret key if even one legitimate message-signature pair is available. To address this issue, we provide a countermeasure that guarantees the signing key cannot be obtained even with numerous valid message signature combinations.

Keywords: Signature · Lattice based cryptography · Shortest · Integer Solution problem

1 Introduction

A digital signature is a critical area for encryption and cybersecurity to develop and expand. Digital documents and messages are authenticated, and their integrity is confirmed with the use of these signatures. Secure communication requires the use of digital signature (DS) techniques. Although digital signatures in the random oracle model (ROM) are more effective than those in the standard model (SDM), it might be difficult to create a truly random oracle. Thus, a major area of study continues to be creating DS methods that are provably secure in the SDM. Certain discrete logarithm problems (DLP) and integer factorization problems have been shown to depend on the security of certain DS systems in the literature when it comes to the SDM. In light of the development of Shor's algorithm [22], it may be possible to exploit these strategies with quantum computers. It is therefore crucial to develop DS systems that are resilient to quantum attacks as well as conventional ones.

Inspired by the rapid advancements in quantum computing, researchers are experimenting with creating digital signature schemes that are resistant to quantum assaults. These protocols are sometimes referred to as "post-quantum cryptography" or "quantum-safe cryptography." Cryptography based on multivariate polynomials, isogeny of elliptic curves, and lattice cryptography appear to be promising approaches to creating post-quantum protocols that are safe and secure. The development of quantum safe systems is promising, especially when it comes to the difficulty of issues involving lattices. Strong theoretical security guarantees, a range of feasible cryptographic primitives, and an efficiency level comparable to pre-quantum systems are all provided by lattice-based encryption.

Shortest Integer Solution (SIS) based digital signature systems have gained popularity because of their benefits, which include lower key sizes, fewer communication rounds, less storage needs, and simplicity of implementation. A digital signature scheme based on the SIS problem was recently presented by Soni et al. [23] and their scheme was crptanalyzed by pursharthi et al. [20].

1.1 Related Work

In 1976, Whitfield Diffie and Martin Hellman [15] first proposed the concept of trapdoor-based digital signature protocol. This important finding made it possible to develop the RSA algorithm in 1978 [21], which is still one of the most popular cryptographic techniques for securing data transfers over public networks. Several other digital signature algorithms were developed after the release of RSA [6,14]. ElGamal [8] presented a signature scheme in 1985 that considered the difficulty of the discrete logarithm problem. ElGamal's technique was improved upon over time and applied to a number of domains, such as polynomials over finite fields and Gaussian integers [13]. Johnson et al. [16] introduced the elliptic curve digital signature algorithm (ECDSA) in 1998, offering improved security with reduced key sizes.

ECDSA became widely used in applications such as smart cards, SSL/TLS, and Bitcoin after it achieved rapid popularity and was standardized by NIST in 1999. However, It is important to note that because these signature systems are based largely on factoring hardness (RSA) or the complexity of the discrete log challenge (DSA/ECDSA), they are all susceptible to possible security issues posed by highly scalable quantum computers.

One significant contender for post-quantum encryption is lattice-based cryptography. Using a pre-image sampleable function (PSF), Gentry et al. [9] created the first lattice-based proven secure DS technique in 2008; they showed that their method is secure in ROM. Cash et al. [5] used the lattice delegation approach in 2010 to develop a DS, and their technique was shown to be secure in SDM. Additionally, Boyen [4] presented a lattice-based DS system with a mixing dimension in 2010. Boyen used a unique delegation tool. In SDM, this approach is likewise secure. Nonetheless, both systems [4,5] have sizable verification keys and signatures. Lubashevsky presented lattice signatures devoid of trapdoors in 2012 [18]. This protocol's key and signature are smaller than those of any previous "hash and sign" signature technique. This approach was followed by the presentation of an implementable digital signature protocol by Guneysu et al. [11], who also demonstrated that this scheme is more embedded system optimized than [18]. Additionally, they reduced the signature size by a factor of two as an improvement over [18]. A signature method that alters the rejection sampling technique used in [18] was reported by Ducas et al. [7] in 2013. A bimodal Gauss distribution is used in this new rejection sampling technique to reduce the deviation of the obtained signatures by an asymptotically square root of the factor of security. Based on learning with errors, Bai and Galbraith introduced a new compression strategy in 2014. Xu et al. [25] showed that the Boyen scheme does not meet the requirements of strong unforgeability, and In 2015, Alkim et al. [2] introduced a very efficient and fully secure signature procedure using conventional lattices. They strengthened the proposal of [3] security. The groundbreaking digital signature system was shown by Akleylek et al. [19] in 2016 and is typified by exceptional efficiency and provably secure. In terms of performance, it is comparable to RSA and ECDSA. In a similar manner, in 2018 [12], Gupta and Biswas proposed a lattice-based Elgamal signature scheme on the complexity of the SIS challenge. They demonstrated how their plan offers strong security features, effective execution, and good protection in the contemporary computer environment. Soni et al. [23] recently proposed a signature technique based on SIS with much-reduced signature and key sizes. Developing encryption and signature systems with average case hardness using lattice-based approaches is the fundamental objective of [23], as it guarantees security against quantum assaults both present and future. In a similar manner, recently in 2023, pursharthi [20] inspected their scheme and found that the signer's key is not secure and easily breakable with the help of valid message signature pair and gave a countermeasure.

2 Mathematical Background

This section explores the fundamental features and concepts of the Shortest Integer Solution (SIS) problem, using symbols m, n for integers and q for large prime numbers, and notations Z for set of integers and R for set of real numbers.

Definition 1 (Lattice). *[10] A lattice is defined as a discrete additive subgroup of a vector space. Lattices are defined as follows. Consider a set of linearly independent vectors, $\mathbf{v}_1, \ldots, \mathbf{v}_n$, in an m-dimensional Euclidean space, $\mathbb{R}^m$. The lattice L formed by $\mathbf{v}_1, \mathbf{v}_2, \ldots, \mathbf{v}_n$ is as follows:*

$$L = \left\{ \sum_{i=1}^{n} a_i \mathbf{v}_i : a_i \in \mathbb{Z} \right\}$$

The lattice's size and rank are denoted by the numbers m and n, respectively, and its basis is defined as $[\mathbf{v}_1, \mathbf{v}_2, \ldots, \mathbf{v}_n]$. The minimal distance of the lattice is determined by measuring the length of the shortest nonzero vector $\mathbf{b}$ in the lattice, which is represented as $D_{min}(L) = \min_{\mathbf{b} \in L \setminus \{0\}} ||\mathbf{b}||$.

Definition 2 (q ary Lattice). *[10] If q is any integer modulus then, An integer lattice L that contains Z_q^n and contained in Z^n is known as q ary Lattice.*

Definition 3 (Shortest Vector Problem). *[17] The objective of the Shortest Vector Problem within a lattice $L(B)$ is to find a non-zero vector Bx (where x belongs to Z^n) such that $||Bx||$ is less than or equal to λ_1. Here, λ_1 represents the minimum distance, which is the smallest norm among all non-zero vectors in the lattice, denoted as $\min_{x \in L, x \neq 0} ||x||$.*

Definition 4 (Shortest Integer Solution problem). *[1] The goal is to discover a vector $\mathbf{x} \in \mathbb{Z}^n \setminus \{0\}$ such that $A\mathbf{x} \equiv 0 \mod q$ in the context of an $m \times n$ integral matrix $A \in \mathbb{Z}_q^{m \times n}$ (where $m > n$) with an integer modulus q and a real constant β.*

$$A\mathbf{x} \equiv 0 \mod q \quad and \quad ||\mathbf{x}|| < \beta.$$

Definition 5 (Shortest Independent Vectors Problem (SIVP)). *[24] The SIVP in a lattice $L(B)$ seeks to find n linearly independent lattice vectors with lengths of no more than λ_n. These vectors are denoted as $B\mathbf{x}_1, \ldots, B\mathbf{x}_n$. Here, λ_i is defined as the lowest radius r for which the dimension of the span $\text{span}(B(r) \cap L)$ is at least i, and $B(r)$ indicates the ball centered at zero with radius r.*

3 Pursharthi's Scheme [20]

In their scheme, the following sets of matrices are taken into consideration: All modular matrices of order $m \times n$ are collected in $\mathcal{B} \subset \mathbb{Z}_q^{m \times n}$. $\mathcal{T} \subset \mathbb{Z}_q^n$ is the set of all modular vectors with n tuples. The message space is $\mathcal{P} \subset \mathbb{Z}_q^n$, while the public key space is $\mathcal{P}_u \subset \mathbb{Z}_q^m$. They have not altered the key generating step as part of their countermeasure. There are four phases in this protocol that are detailed below:

- Setup Phase : From $\mathbb{Z}$, pick two big prime integers, m and n, such that n is at least as large as m times the logarithm of q ($n \geq m \log q$), create a hash function $H : \mathbb{Z}_q^{n \times m} \to \mathbb{Z}_q^m$ and assign $\mathbb{Z}_q^{n \times n}$ to the message space.
- Key Generation:
  - Signer selects randomly $B \in \mathcal{B} \subset \mathbb{Z}_q^{m \times n}$ and a vector $t \in \mathcal{T} \subset \mathbb{Z}_q^n$.
  - Computes $Pu = t^T \cdot B^T \in \mathcal{P}_u \subset \mathbb{Z}_q^{1 \times m}$.
  - The public keys B and P_u, as well as the private key t, are established throughout this procedure.

- Signing a message $P \in \mathbb{Z}_q^{n \times n}$.
  - Select two random vectors r, s such that $r = (0, r_1, r_2, \ldots, r_{n-1}) \in \mathbb{Z}_q^n$ as $(r_1, r_2, \ldots, r_{n-1}) \in \mathbb{Z}_q^{n-1}$ and $s \in \mathbb{Z}_q$.
  - Compute $G_1 = sr^T \in \mathbb{Z}_q^{1 \times n}$ and $G_2 = P - G_1^T t^T$.
  - Send $(H(P), (G_1, G_2))$ to the verifier.
- Verification of $(H(P), (G_1, G_2))$:
  - The verifier computes $W = G_1^T . P_u$ and verifies $W \in \mathbb{Z}_q^{n \times m}$.
  - Compute $P_1 . B^T = (G_2 . B^T + W) \mod q$.
  - Verify $H(P_1 . B^T)$ is equal to $H(P . B^T)$ or not.
  - The signature is legitimate if it is confirmed.

4 Cryptanalysis of Pursharthi's Scheme

We have found a weakness in the signature system proposed by Pursharthi et al. Any attacker can obtain message-signature pair since they are publicly available. Let us assume that $(P, (G_1, G_2))$ is a legitimate pair. The signer computes $G_2 = P - G_1^T \cdot t^T$ in the technique outlined. Clearly we can see that,

$$G_2 = P - G_1^T \cdot t^T$$
$$= G_2 - P = -G_1^T \cdot t^T$$
$$= -G_2 + P = G_1^T \cdot t^T$$

Clearly $G_1^T \in \mathbb{Z}_q^{n \times 1}$ as $G_1 \in \mathbb{Z}_q^{1 \times n}$. So, $G_1 . G_1^T \in \mathbb{Z}_q$ and as q is a prime number so clearly its inverse also exist so any adversary calculate signer's secret value t easily, as $t^T = G_3^{-1} . G_1 . (-G_2 + P)$ where $G_3 = G_1 . G_1^T$.

Here, we note that an attacker may determine the signer's secret key from every valid message-signature pair that is accessible.

This assault can be carried out effectively since it just needs the following effective actions to be completed:

- To add the two vectors $-G_2$ and P, do a single addition operation.
- One multiplication operation between vector G_1 and a vector $(-G_2 + P)$ with modulo q.
- Finally onle muliplication operation between (G_3^{-1}) integer modulo q and $G_1 . (-G_2 + P)$

Therefore, we can effectively obtain the secret key of signer and establish a legitimate sign on any message of our choosing using just one valid message-signature pair.

4.1 Toy Example

For better understanding, we took the almost same example that was given in [23], and we tried to show that after applying the Pursharthi [20] scheme, we could again retrieve the secret key. Public parameters taken in for signature generation are $m = 2$, $n = 3$ and $q = 11$. Consider,

$$B = \begin{bmatrix} 5 & 6 & 1 \\ 1 & 0 & 3 \end{bmatrix}$$

and secret key $t = \begin{bmatrix} 4 \\ 9 \\ 3 \end{bmatrix}$. Then the public key is $P_u = (t^T) \cdot B^T = \begin{bmatrix} 0 & 2 \end{bmatrix}$.

The sender signed the message

$$P = \begin{bmatrix} 1 & 2 & 3 \\ 0 & 1 & 0 \\ 0 & 0 & 1 \end{bmatrix}$$

by using $r = \begin{bmatrix} 0 \\ 1 \\ 2 \end{bmatrix}$ and $s = \begin{bmatrix} 5 \end{bmatrix}$.

Now

$$G_1 = s.r^t = \begin{bmatrix} 0 & 5 & 10 \end{bmatrix}$$

and

$$G_2 = \begin{bmatrix} 1 & 2 & 3 \\ 2 & 0 & 7 \\ 4 & 9 & 4 \end{bmatrix}$$

The signature according to is

$$(G_1, G_2) = (s.r^t, P - G_1^T t^T)$$

$$= \left(\begin{bmatrix} 0 & 5 & 10 \end{bmatrix}, \begin{bmatrix} 1 & 2 & 3 \\ 2 & 0 & 7 \\ 4 & 9 & 4 \end{bmatrix} \right)$$

The adversary can extract the secret key t from the message-signature pair $(P, (G1, G2))$ by following these steps:

$$G_2 = P - G_1^T.t^T$$
$$= G_2 - P = -G_1^T.t^T$$
$$\to -G_2 + P = G_1^T.t^T$$
$$-\begin{bmatrix}1 & 2 & 3\\2 & 0 & 7\\4 & 9 & 4\end{bmatrix} + \begin{bmatrix}1 & 2 & 3\\0 & 1 & 0\\0 & 0 & 1\end{bmatrix} = G_1^T.t^T$$
$$= \begin{bmatrix}0 & 0 & 0\\9 & 0 & 4\\7 & 2 & 8\end{bmatrix} = G_1^T.t^T$$
$$\begin{bmatrix}0 & 5 & 10\end{bmatrix}.\begin{bmatrix}0 & 0 & 0\\9 & 0 & 4\\7 & 2 & 8\end{bmatrix} = \begin{bmatrix}0 & 5 & 10\end{bmatrix}.\begin{bmatrix}0\\5\\10\end{bmatrix}.t^T$$
$$= \begin{bmatrix}5 & 9 & 1\end{bmatrix} = 4.t^T$$
$$= (4)^{-1}.\begin{bmatrix}5 & 9 & 1\end{bmatrix} = t^T$$
$$\to t^T = 3.\begin{bmatrix}5 & 9 & 1\end{bmatrix} = \begin{bmatrix}15 & 27 & 3\end{bmatrix} = \begin{bmatrix}4 & 9 & 3\end{bmatrix}$$
$$\to t = \begin{bmatrix}4\\9\\3\end{bmatrix}.$$

5 Our Improved Scheme

Our investigation revealed that the assault was taking place as a result of the signing and setup phases using the wrong settings. We also do little bit changes to the key creation step in our approach. Thus, we concentrate on improving the following aspects of the setup, key creation, signature, and verification stages:

- Setup Phase: Select two integers $m, n \in \mathbb{Z}$, pick a large prime number q such that $n \geq m \log q$, establish a hash function $H : \mathbb{Z}_q^{m \times n} \to \mathbb{Z}_q^m$, and the message space has a dimension of $\mathbb{Z}_q^{m \times n}$.
- Key Generation:
  - In this step signer's choose matrix $B \in \mathcal{B} \subset \mathbb{Z}_q^{m \times n}$ randomly and a vector $t \in \mathcal{T} \subset \mathbb{Z}_q^n$.
  - Computes $P_u = B \cdot t \in \mathcal{P}_u \subset \mathbb{Z}_q^{m \times 1}$.
  - The public keys B and P_u, as well as the private key t, are established throughout this procedure.
- Signing a message $P \in \mathbb{Z}_q^{m \times n}$:
  - Choose r, s randomly, such that $r = (0, r_1, r_2, \ldots, r_{m-1}) \in \mathbb{Z}_q^{1 \times m}$, $s \in \mathbb{Z}_q^{m \times n}$.
  - Compute $G_1 = t.r.s \in \mathbb{Z}_q^{n \times n}$ and $G_2 = P - P_u.r.s \in \mathbb{Z}_q^{m \times n}$.

- Send $(H(P), (G_1, G_2))$ to the verifier.
- Verification of $(H(P), (G_1, G_2))$:
  - The verifier computes $W = BG_1$ and verifies $W \in \mathbb{Z}_q^{m \times n}$.
  - Compute $P_1' = (G_2 + W) \mod q$.
  - Verify $H(P_1') \stackrel{?}{=} H(P)$.
  - The signature is legitimate if it is confirmed.

5.1 Correctness

It is enough to prove that P_1' and P are congruent in order to show the signature technique's feasibility.

$$\begin{aligned} P_1' &= (G_2 + W) \\ &= G_2 + BG_1 \\ &= P - P_u.r.s + B.t.r.s \\ &= P - P_u.r.s + P_u.r.s \\ &= P \end{aligned}$$

6 Security Analysis Discussion

Pursharthi et al. [20] had cryptanalyzed Soni's scheme [23] and provided a countermeasure. They used a zero divisor element r in their countermeasure and used it in the signature $G_1 = sr^T$ and G_2 as $G_2 = P - G_1^T.t^T$. We inspected their scheme and found that their signature scheme is also very weak and can easily broken. Further, we analyzed that whenever signing key (signer's secret key), t is used with valid message then adversary is able to attack and easily compute the signer's secret key. In view of all these, we adopted the idea of zero divisor and suggest a scheme in which signature messages are $G_1 = t.r.s \in \mathbb{Z}_q^{n \times n}$ here $r = (0, r_1, r_2, \ldots, r_{m-1})$, $s \in \mathbb{Z}_q^{m \times n}$ and $G_2 = P - P_u.r.s \in \mathbb{Z}_q^{m \times n}$. No adversary can compute the secret key as the randomness of choice of r and s makes our scheme stronger. We do not use a secret key along with a valid message; it makes our scheme safe, and no one can find the signing key using a valid(message, signature).

Additionally, the advantages of lower key sizes remain, as the key generation procedure is the same as [20,23], and it is resistant to quantum assaults because of the SIS problem on lattices. Our method competes favorably with other lattice-based signature schemes because of the comparable amount of identical matrix operations as shown in [20,23], which also adds to the benefit of storage, key sizes, and computational overhead. With a secured signing key, our countermeasure's signature, represented as (G_1, G_2), where $G_1 \in \mathbb{Z}_q^{n \times n}$ and $G_2 \in \mathbb{Z}_q^{m \times n}$, produces a signature size of $n^2 + mn$, which is marginally bigger than the signature size of [23] and [20]. However, the drawback of a short signature is that collisions are more likely to occur so the signing key is secured in our case. Table 1 compares the sizes of keys and signatures and provides an alternative format.

Table 1. Comparison of the suggested lattice-based signature scheme's performance with earlier works

Scheme	Signing Key	Verification Key	Signature
[23]	n	$nm + m$	$1 + n$
[20]	n	$nm + m$	$n^2 + n$
Proposed Scheme	n	$nm + m$	$n(n + m)$

7 Conclusion

In this work lattice-based digital signature system based on SIS hardness that was published currently is cryptanalyzed thoroughly. This exposes the weakness in the technique, which is that a single valid message-signature pair is sufficient to get the signer's key. Additionally, an approach against this attack is suggested that preserves the scheme's well-established security elements.

These more compact and safe digital signatures can be used in a variety of real-world domains. Also,It might be feasible in the future to reduce the size of digital signatures without sacrificing security.

References

1. Aggarwal, D., Chung, E.: A note on the concrete hardness of the shortest independent vector in lattices. Inf. Process. Lett. **167**, 106065 (2021)
2. Alkim, E., Bindel, N., Buchmann, J., Dagdelen, Ö., Schwabe, P.: Tesla: Tightly-secure efficient signatures from standard lattices. IACR Cryptol. ePrint Arch. **2015**, 755 (2015)
3. Bai, S., Galbraith, S.D.: An improved compression technique for signatures based on learning with errors. In: Benaloh, J. (ed.) CT-RSA 2014. LNCS, vol. 8366, pp. 28–47. Springer, Cham (2014). https://doi.org/10.1007/978-3-319-04852-9_2
4. Boyen, X.: Lattice mixing and vanishing trapdoors: a framework for fully secure short signatures and more. In: International Workshop on Public Key Cryptography, pp. 499–517. Springer (2010)
5. Cash, D., Hofheinz, D., Kiltz, E., Peikert, C.: Bonsai trees, or how to delegate a lattice basis. J. Cryptol. **25**, 601–639 (2012)
6. Davies, D.W.: Applying the RSA digital signature to electronic mail. Computer **16**(02), 55–62 (1983)
7. Ducas, L., Durmus, A., Lepoint, T., Lyubashevsky, V.: Lattice signatures and bimodal gaussians. In: Annual Cryptology Conference, pp. 40–56. Springer (2013)
8. ElGamal, T.: A public key cryptosystem and a signature scheme based on discrete logarithms. IEEE Trans. Inf. Theory **31**(4), 469–472 (1985)
9. Gentry, C., Peikert, C., Vaikuntanathan, V.: Trapdoors for hard lattices and new cryptographic constructions. In: Proceedings of the Fortieth annual ACM Symposium on Theory of Computing, pp. 197–206 (2008)
10. Goldwasser, S., Micciancio, D.: Complexity of lattice problems: a cryptographic perspective (2002)

11. Güneysu, T., Lyubashevsky, V., Pöppelmann, T.: Practical lattice-based cryptography: a signature scheme for embedded systems. In: Prouff, E., Schaumont, P. (eds.) CHES 2012. LNCS, vol. 7428, pp. 530–547. Springer, Heidelberg (2012). https://doi.org/10.1007/978-3-642-33027-8_31
12. Gupta, D.S., Biswas, G.: Design of lattice-based ELGamal encryption and signature schemes using sis problem. Trans. Emerg. Telecommun. Technol. **29**(6), e3255 (2018)
13. Haraty, R.A., El-Kassar, A.N., Shebaro, B.M.: A comparative study of ELGamal based digital signature algorithms. J. Comput. Methods Sci. Eng. **6**(s1), S147–S156 (2006)
14. Harn, L.: Batch verifying multiple RSA digital signatures. Electron. Lett. **34**(12), 1219–1220 (1998)
15. Hellman, M.: New directions in cryptography. IEEE Trans. Inf. Theory **22**(6), 644–654 (1976)
16. Johnson, D.B., Menezes, A.J.: Elliptic curve DSA (ECDSA): an enhanced DSA. In: Proceedings of the 7th Conference on USENIX Security Symposium, vol. 7, pp. 13–23 (1998)
17. Khot, S.: Hardness of approximating the shortest vector problem in lattices. J. ACM (JACM) **52**(5), 789–808 (2005)
18. Pointcheval, D., Johansson, T.: Advances in Cryptology-EUROCRYPT 2012 (2012)
19. Pointcheval, D., Nitaj, A., Rachidi, T.: 8th International Conference on Cryptology in Africa-AFRICACRYPT 2016. In: Africacrypt 2016, no. 9646, Springer Verlag (2016)
20. Pursharthi, K., Mishra, D.: Cryptanalysis with countermeasure on the sis based signature scheme. In: International Conference on Security, Privacy, and Applied Cryptography Engineering, pp. 92–100. Springer (2023)
21. Rivest, R.L., Shamir, A., Adleman, L.: A method for obtaining digital signatures and public-key cryptosystems. Commun. ACM **21**(2), 120–126 (1978)
22. Shor, P.W.: Algorithms for quantum computation: discrete logarithms and factoring. In: Proceedings 35th Annual Symposium on Foundations of Computer Science, pp. 124–134. IEEE (1994)
23. Soni, L., Chandra, H., Gupta, D.S., Keval, R.: Quantum-resistant public-key encryption and signature schemes with smaller key sizes. Clust. Comput. **27**(1), 285–297 (2024)
24. Wang, S.B., Zhu, Y., Ma, D., Feng, R.Q.: Lattice-based key exchange on small integer solution problem. Sci. China Inf. Sci. **57**(11), 1–12 (2014). https://doi.org/10.1007/s11432-014-5147-z
25. Xu, Y., Tian, M., Huang, L., Yang, W., Shen, X.: Improvement of a lattice-based signature scheme. J. Inf. Hiding Multim. Signal Process. **5**(1), 41–46 (2014)

On the Security of **AMRIBE**, Anonymous Multi-receiver Identity-Based Encryption

Ramprasad Sarkar[✉], Utkarsh Sahai, and Mriganka Mandal

Cryptology and Security Research Unit, Indian Statistical Institute Kolkata,
Kolkata 700108, India
{rpsarkar_p,sahai.utkarsh_r,mriganka}@isical.ac.in

Abstract. Anonymous Multi-Receiver Identity-Based Encryption (AMRIBE) is a cryptographic method that enables a sender to efficiently and securely encrypt a common message for a group of receivers while prioritizing the subscribed receivers' outsider and insider anonymity. In 2021, Tseng and Fan [Security and Communication Network] presented an Anonymous Multi-Receiver Identity-Based Encryption (AMRIBE) scheme and asserted that their system provides security against the chosen ciphertext attacks. During our analysis, we investigated the aforementioned security of the AMRIBE scheme and found that it is susceptible to certain Probabilistic Polynomial-Time (PPT) attackers. Through our proposed two attack models, we have demonstrated that their system does not achieve the primary security requirement, which is ciphertext confidentiality in the Multi-Receiver Encryption framework. Additionally, we have shown that any PPT attacker can recover the Master Secret-Key (MSK) of the underlying system by utilizing the KeyExtract Query of some users. To further resolve this issue, in this paper we propose a generic modification technique to improve their scheme and show a pathway to construct a secure AMRIBE. Furthermore, we implemented our proposed two attack models considering a particular case, and the execution time proved that our attack technique can efficiently break their protocol in a short time.

Keywords: Cryptanalysis · Identity-based encryption · Broadcast encryption · Chosen-ciphertext attack security · Anonymity

1 Introduction

Broadcast Encryption (BE) (or Multi-Receiver Encryption (MRE)) is an advanced cryptographic primitive that provides an efficient and secure method to share enciphered digital contents with a group of subscribers through an insecure broadcasting medium in such a way that no one other than the legitimate users can successfully recover the original broadcast contents while the illegitimate users get only negligible information about the broadcast contents even if they collude. This concept of BE was first formally proposed by Fiat et al. [9]. Later,

BE has been intensely and broadly studied [2,3,6,19] as one of the leading primitives for various real-life application scenarios ranging from the pay-TV systems, video conference, distance learning, radio broadcast, distribution of copyrighted materials, etc., to the encrypted data distribution system and many more. A Multi-Receiver Identity-Based Encryption (MRIBE) [1] is an advanced variant of MRE which allows the scheme to bypass the requirement of the Public-Key Infrastructure (PKI). [5,12,14,22]. Identity-Based Broadcast Encryption (IBBE) [5] and MRIBE are the identical variants of traditional BE. The IBBE system can accommodate an arbitrary (or unbounded) number of users. In an IBBE, the required public-key of a user in the system can be generated utilizing only his unique identity (e.g., the user's IP address, employment ID, phone/email address, etc.).

The privacy of the transmitted enciphered broadcast message is the MRIBE's fundamental security property, which means no information about the common broadcast data gets leaked. However, the system can disclose the subscribers' social information, such as identifiers. By using this information, any attacker may retrieve the correct broadcast data. In the real-life practical application scenario, such as the sensitive TV subscription service, hiding the subscribers' set from the attackers is crucial [11,12,15–17]. It is required that the MRIBE networks must be able to protect the subscriber's identity from not only the outsiders but also from the other subscribers.

In 2010, Fan et al. [7] first formulated an anonymous MRIBE scheme to tackle the security and privacy concerns of the subscribers set in the MRIBE framework. Anonymous MRIBE schemes are divided into two classes: Outsider Anonymous MRIBE (OAMRIBE) [4,8,20] and Fully Anonymous MRIBE (FAMRIBE) [7,23,24]. In OAMRIBE, the subscribers set is entirely hidden only from the outsiders. Conversely, information about subscribers set is concealed from outsiders and insiders in the FAMRIBE. In 2012, Kiayias et al. [13] showed that in a fully anonymous scheme, the ciphertext size is at least linear to the total number of system users, and a further reduction in the final ciphertext size is unattainable. In 2021, Tseng et al. [23] presented a fully anonymous multi-receiver identity-based encryption protocol and claimed that their system is adaptive chosen-ciphertext attack secure in the standard security model against any PPT attackers, which is the strongest security notion for MRIBE system. Unfortunately, their claim is untrue in that any PPT attacker can efficiently break their provable security. As a result, achieving *ciphertext confidentiality* is one of the main security goals in any privacy-preserving anonymous MRIBE.

Our Contribution. In this paper, we will show that the AMRIBE scheme of Tseng et al. [23] does not offer the essential security property (i.e., *ciphertext confidentiality*) in BE framework. Accordingly, it cannot withstand the PPT attackers. I have briefly discussed what we have achieved below.

(i) Firstly, in AMRIBE of [23], we show that any unsubscribed recipient can correctly recover the original broadcast data without having a valid decryption privilege. Along the way, our investigation exposed a broader security concern: any PPT attacker can reveal the master secret key (MSK) of

the system. Consequently, this attacker gains the ability to decrypt the encrypted content transmitted within the system solely by utilizing the KeyExtract oracle access for an unsubscribed user during the security game.
(ii) We also present that any PPT attacker can break the *ciphertext confidentiality* game of the AMRIBE scheme regardless of the user's identity length. We exhibit that an attacker can efficiently break the entire AMRIBE scheme of [23] with a non-negligible advantage.
(iii) To validate the effectiveness of our proposed attack techniques, we have implemented them utilizing the standard Pairing-Based Cryptography (PBC) library and analyzed the execution time of the attack models comprehensively. In addition to the implementation, we have provided a graphical representation that visually illustrates the execution time of our attacks.
(iv) Finally, we suggest a generic technique for designing a provably secure AMRIBE scheme.

Organization. The paper is arranged as follows. Essential cryptographic backgrounds are addressed in the subsequent Sect. 2. Section 3 reviews the work of Tseng et al. [23]. Our proposed two attack models, computational complexity and implementation details, are discussed in Sect. 4. Section 5 outlines potential modifications to counter these attacks. Finally, Sect. 6 concludes the paper.

2 Prerequisites

This section will describe some essential cryptographic preliminaries required for our paper's detailed presentation. The notation that is used throughout our article is described in Table 1.

Table 1. Notations

Symbol	Descriptions
λ	System security parameter
$\perp$	Null string
ID_u	Identity of the user u
$|M|$	Length of a message M
$|S|$	number of distinct elements in a set S
$[N]$	Set of all natural numbers from 1 to N
$\delta \in_R \{0,1\}$	Bit δ is chosen at random from the set $\{0,1\}$
IND-MID-CCA	Indistinguishability under full-multi-identity chosen-ciphertext attack
ANON-MID-CCA	Anonymity under full-multi-identity chosen-ciphertext attack

Definition 1 (Type-3 Bilinear Map [21,23]). *A prime order Type-3 Bilinear Mapping, also known as a T3-map, is a fundamental cryptographic construct*

defined over three multiplicative cyclic groups: $\mathbb{G}_1$, $\mathbb{G}_2$, and $\mathbb{G}_T$. These groups all share the same large prime order p. Importantly, $\mathbb{G}_1$ and $\mathbb{G}_2$ are required to be distinct groups such that there exists no isomorphism between them that can be computed efficiently. Assuming that random elements g and $\widetilde{g}$ generate the first source group, $\mathbb{G}_1$ and the second source group, $\mathbb{G}_2$ respectively, a Type-3 Bilinear Mapping is described by a function $e : \mathbb{G}_1 \times \mathbb{G}_2 \to \mathbb{G}_T$, satisfying three key properties:

(i) **Bilinearity:** This property ensures that for all X in $\mathbb{G}_1$, Y in $\mathbb{G}_2$, and random integers $m, n \in \mathbb{Z}_p^*$, the equation $e(X^m, Y^n) = e(X, Y)^{mn}$ holds.

(ii) **Non-degenerate:** The map e must be non-degenerate, i.e., the element $e(g, \widetilde{g})$ should be a non-identity element and hence the generator for the target group $\mathbb{G}_T$.

(iii) **Computability:** The bilinear pairing $e(g, \widetilde{g})$ is required to be efficiently computable within polynomial time.

Then the tuple, $\mathbb{BG} = (p, \mathbb{G}_1, \mathbb{G}_2, \mathbb{G}_T, e)$, is termed as a prime order Type-3 bilinear map (or T3-map) system.

2.1 Type-3 Bilinear Hard Problem

The security of the AMRIBE scheme [23] relies on the Decisional Bilinear Diffie-Hellman Type-3 (DBDH-3) problem, a hard problem that is defined as follows [21,23].

- **Input:** The input instance $\langle Z = (\mathbb{BG}, g, \widetilde{g}, \widetilde{g}^x, g^y, \widetilde{g}^y, g^z, \widetilde{g}^z), U\rangle$, where, x, y and z are random elements chosen from $\mathbb{Z}_p^*$ and U is either $e(g, \widetilde{g})^{xyz}$ or is equal to some random element $W \in \mathbb{G}_T$.
- **Output:** The following two outputs

$$\begin{cases} 0 & \text{if } U = e(g, \widetilde{g})^{xyz} \\ 1 & \text{otherwise} \end{cases}$$

Definition 2 (DBDH-3 Assumption). *The DBDH-3 assumption holds if the advantage $\mathsf{Adv}_{\mathcal{A}}^{DBDH\text{-}3}(1^\lambda)$, which is given below, of any PPT attacker $\mathcal{A}$ in solving the aforementioned hard problem is at most a negligible quantity.*

$$\mathsf{Adv}_{\mathcal{A}}^{DBDH\text{-}3}(1^\lambda) = \big| Pr[\mathcal{A}(Z, U = e(g, \widetilde{g})^{xyz}) = 0] \\ - Pr[\mathcal{A}(Z, U = W) = 0] \big|$$

2.2 Syntax of AMRIBE

An AMRIBE protocol [23] is an interaction model that involves a Private Key Generation Center (PKGC), a broadcaster, and an arbitrary collection of users. It encompasses three PPT algorithms- (Setup, KeyExtract, Encrypt) and one deterministic algorithm Decrypt, which are described below.

- (MPK, MSK) ← Setup(λ): The PKGC takes as input only the system security parameter λ to construct the system master public-key MPK and system master secret-key MSK. It then publishes MPK in the public domain while keeping MSK secret to itself.
- (SK_i) ← KeyExtract(MSK, ID_i): Receiving the MSK and an identity ID_i of a user i as inputs, the PKGC generates a secret-key SK_i for the user i. This SK_i is then securely transmitted to user i.
- (C) ← Encrypt(MPK, D, M): On receiving the input of MPK, a set of identities D representing subscribed users, and a message M, the broadcaster processes this information to generate a ciphertext C, that is subsequently made publicly accessible.
- ($M \vee \bot$) ← Decrypt(C, SK_i): Upon receiving the ciphertext C as input, a decryptor i utilizes its secret key SK_i to attempt decryption. If successful, the decryptor retrieves the correct message M. However, if decryption fails, the decryptor receives a designated symbol $\bot$.

Definition 3 (Correctness of AMRIBE). *The above-mentioned AMRIBE scheme is considered to be correct if for all security parameter λ, all message M, and all user identities $ID_i \in D$ the following holds.*

$$(M) \leftarrow \text{Decrypt}(C, \text{KeyExtract}(\text{MSK}, ID_i)), \qquad (1)$$

where $(C) \leftarrow$ *Encrypt* (MPK, D, M), *and* (MPK, MSK) ← *Setup* (λ).

2.3 Security Notions of AMRIBE

The security framework of the aforementioned AMRIBE scheme is based on the following two security games.

(i) Confidentiality [17,21,23]: This section discusses the security definition for the confidentiality of AMRIBE. Here, the attacker, $\mathcal{A}$, and the challenger, $\mathcal{C}$, play the confidentiality game as detailed below.

- **Setup:** In the setup phase, $\mathcal{C}$ runs the algorithm Setup(λ) to generate the MPK and MSK. It then keeps MSK secret and sends MPK to $\mathcal{A}$.
- **Phase-1:** The attacker $\mathcal{A}$ is allowed to perform several adaptive queries to the challenger $\mathcal{C}$. In return, $\mathcal{C}$ recalls from the following oracles.
  (a) **KeyExtract Query:** The attacker $\mathcal{A}$ makes a KeyExtract Query to $\mathcal{C}$ corresponding to the identity ID_i. The challenger $\mathcal{C}$ runs the algorithm KeyExtract to generate the secret key, SK_i and sends SK_i to $\mathcal{A}$.
  (b) **Decryption Query:** With the ciphertext C and the user identity ID_i, the attacker $\mathcal{A}$ makes a Decryption Query to $\mathcal{C}$. In turn, $\mathcal{C}$ runs the algorithm Decrypt to retrieve the message and sends the decrypted message back to $\mathcal{A}$.

- **Challenge:** The attacker $\mathcal{A}$ submits to $\mathcal{C}$ two messages M_0, M_1 of the same length (i.e., $|M_0| = |M_1|$) and a challenge set of identities $D^* = \{ID_1^*, ID_2^*, \ldots, ID_n^*\}$, for any random positive integer n, with the limitation that no identity from D^* appears in KeyExtract oracle query of **Phase-1**. Then, $\mathcal{C}$ randomly picks $\delta \in_R \{0,1\}$ and produces C^* by running the algorithm Encrypt(MPK, D^*, M_δ). Finally, $\mathcal{C}$ returns the ciphertext C^* to $\mathcal{A}$.
- **Phase-2:** The attacker $\mathcal{A}$ is permitted to make adaptive queries the same as that of in the Phase-1 except for the specific queries, like the KeyExtract with $ID_i \in D^*$ and the Decrypt queries with $(C^*, ID_i \in D^*)$.
- **Guess:** In the guessing phase, the attacker, $\mathcal{A}$ outputs a bit δ' and wins the confidentiality game if the bit $\delta' = \delta$.

The advantage of the attacker $\mathcal{A}$ in the above-mentioned security game for the AMRIBE scheme can be defined as follows.

$$Adv_{\mathcal{A},\text{AMRIBE}}^{\text{IND-MID-CCA}}(\lambda) = \left| \Pr(\delta' = \delta) - \frac{1}{2} \right|$$

Definition 4. *An AMRIBE scheme is considered to be (κ, ε) - adaptive IND-MID-CCA (indistinguishability under full-multi-identity chosen-ciphertext attack) secure if all κ time attackers have at most a non-negligible advantage ε in winning the above IND-MID-CCA game.*

(ii) Anonymity [23]: This part covers the description of the anonymity of the AMRIBE scheme. We examine a game with four main stages that involve the challenger $\mathcal{C}$ and the attacker $\mathcal{A}$.

- **Setup:** In the setup phase, $\mathcal{C}$ runs the algorithm Setup(λ) to generate the MPK and MSK. It then keeps MSK secret and sends MPK to $\mathcal{A}$.
- **Phase-1:** The attacker $\mathcal{A}$ can perform several adaptive queries to $\mathcal{C}$ for the following oracles.
  (a) **KeyExtract Query:** The attacker $\mathcal{A}$ makes an Extract Query to $\mathcal{C}$ corresponding to the identity ID_i. In return, the challenger $\mathcal{C}$ runs the algorithm KeyExtract to generate the secret key, SK_i and sends SK_i to $\mathcal{A}$.
  (b) **Decryption Query:** With the ciphertext C and the user identity ID_i, the attacker $\mathcal{A}$ makes a Decryption Query to $\mathcal{C}$. In turn, $\mathcal{C}$ retrieves the message by running the algorithm Decrypt and sends the decrypted message back to $\mathcal{A}$.
- **Challenge:** The attacker $\mathcal{A}$ submits to $\mathcal{C}$ a message M, a challenge identity set $D^* = \{ID_0^*, ID_1^*\}$ and a set $\{ID_2^*, ID_3^*, \ldots, ID_n^*\}$ of identities for any random positive integer n, with the limitation that no identity from D^* appears in KeyExtract oracle query of Phase-1. Then the challenger, $\mathcal{C}$ randomly picks $\delta \in_R \{0,1\}$ and computes $D_\delta^* = \{ID_\delta^*, ID_2^*, ID_3^*, \ldots, ID_n^*\}$. It then produces the challenge ciphertext C^* by running the algorithm Encrypt(MPK, D_δ^*, M). Finally, $\mathcal{C}$ sends the ciphertext C^* to $\mathcal{A}$.
- **Phase-2:** The attacker $\mathcal{A}$ is permitted to make adaptive queries the same as that of in the Phase-1 except for the specific queries like the KeyExtract with $ID_i \in D^*$ and Decryption queries $(C^*, ID_i \in D^*)$.

- **Guess:** In the guessing phase, $\mathcal{A}$ returns a guess bit δ' and wins the game if the bit $\delta' = \delta$.

The advantage of the attacker in the above security game for the AMRIBE scheme is defined as follows.

$$Adv_{\mathcal{A},\text{AMRIBE}}^{\text{ANON-MID-CCA}}(\lambda) = \left|\Pr(\delta = \delta') - \frac{1}{2}\right|$$

Definition 5. *An AMRIBE scheme is considered to be (κ, ε) - adaptive ANON-MID-CCA (anonymity under full-multi-identity chosen-ciphertext attack) secure if all κ time attackers have at most a non-negligible advantage ε in winning the above ANON-MID-CCA game.*

3 Review of Tseng *et al*'s AMRIBE

This section primarily reviews the work of Tseng *et al.* [23]. Three entities are involved in their scheme: a Private Key Generation Center (PKGC), a data owner (also referred to as a broadcaster), and a set of users. The details of their algorithms are described below.

- Setup(λ): Upon taking the security parameter λ as input, the PKGC first generates a prime order T3-map system $\mathbb{BG} = (p, \mathbb{G}_1, \mathbb{G}_2, \mathbb{G}_T, e)$. Let us assume l to be the length of each user's identity. PKGC then picks random exponents α, β, $\{t_i\}_{i \in [l]}$, x and y from $\mathbb{Z}_p$ to compute $\Omega = e(g, \tilde{g})^{\alpha\beta}$, $\Lambda = e(g, \tilde{g})^{\alpha(\beta-1)}$, $T_i = g^{t_i}$, $\widetilde{T}_i = \tilde{g}^{t_i}$, $\tilde{X} = \tilde{g}^x$, $\tilde{Y} = \tilde{g}^y$. It also picks two collusion-resistant cryptographically secure hash functions $\mathcal{H} : \{0,1\}^* \to \{0,1\}^l$ and $\widetilde{\mathcal{H}} : \{0,1\}^* \to \mathbb{Z}_p$ to set the system master public-secret key pair as follows.

$$\text{MPK} = \left(\mathbb{BG}, g, \Omega, \Lambda, \{T_i\}_{i=1}^l, \tilde{X}, \tilde{Y}, \mathcal{H}, \widetilde{\mathcal{H}}\right)$$

$$\text{MSK} = \left(\tilde{g}, \tilde{g}^\alpha, \{\widetilde{T}_i\}_{i=1}^l\right)$$

Finally, it makes MPK publicly available and keeps MSK secret to itself.

- KeyExtract(MSK, ID_i): The PKGC takes a user's identity ID_i, and MSK as inputs to generate the user i's secret-key, SK_i. It first selects an element r_i randomly from $\mathbb{Z}_p^*$ and computes $\widetilde{\mathcal{F}}_{ID_i} = \prod_{j \in [l]} \widetilde{T}_j^{h_i[j]}$, where $h_i = \mathcal{H}(ID_i)$ is the hash-value of the identity ID_i and $h_i[j]$ represents the j-th bit of $h_i \in \{0,1\}^l$. Finally, the PKGC outputs the secret-key $\text{SK}_i = (d_{i,0}, d_{i,1})$, where

$$d_{i,0} = (\tilde{g})^\alpha \cdot (\widetilde{\mathcal{F}}_{ID_i})^{r_i} \text{ and } d_{i,1} = (\tilde{g})^{r_i}$$

- Encrypt(MPK, D, M): Taking as inputs the system master public-key MPK, a set of user's identities $D = \{ID_i \mid i \in \mathcal{I}_D\}$ with $|\mathcal{I}_D| = L \leq N$ and a message $M \in \mathbb{G}_T$, the broadcaster first randomly picks a value s from $\mathbb{Z}_p^*$ and then computes $\mathcal{F}_{ID_i} = \prod_{j \in [l]} T_j^{h_i[j]}$ for all $i \in \mathcal{I}_D$. Here, N denotes the total number of users in the system and $h_i = \mathcal{H}(ID_i)$ represents the hash value for $ID_i \in D$. It then computes the following ciphertext components.

$$C_0 = M \cdot \Omega^s, \; C_1 = \Lambda^s,$$
$$C_{3,i} = (\mathcal{F}_{ID_i})^s \text{ for all } i \in \mathcal{I}_D,$$
$$C_2 = g^s, \; K = \frac{\Lambda^s}{\Omega^s}$$

It also generates the following two elements

$$\theta = \widetilde{\mathcal{H}}(C_0, C_1, C_2, \{C_{3,i}\}_{i \in \mathcal{I}_D}, K, M),$$
$$\widetilde{\Gamma} = (\widetilde{X} \cdot \widetilde{Y}^\theta)^s$$

Finally, the broadcaster publishes $C = (C_0, C_1, C_2, \{C_{3,i}\}_{i \in \mathcal{I}_D}, \widetilde{\Gamma})$ as the ciphertext.

- Decrypt(C, SK_i): Upon taking as inputs the secret-key $\mathsf{SK}_i = (d_{i,0}, d_{i,1})$ and the ciphertext $C = (C_0, C_1, C_2, \{C_{3,i}\}_{i \in \mathcal{I}_D}, \widetilde{\Gamma})$, a subscribed user i, whose identity is $ID_i \in \{0, 1\}^l$, first recovers the message components by executing the below computations.

$$K' = \frac{e(C_{3,i}, d_{i,1})}{e(C_2, d_{i,0})}, \; M' = \frac{C_0}{C_1} \times K'$$
$$\theta' = \widetilde{\mathcal{H}}(C_0, C_1, C_2, \{C_{3,i}\}_{i \in \mathcal{I}_D}, K, M')$$

It then retrieves the original message as

$$M = \begin{cases} M' & \text{if } e(C_2, \widetilde{X} \cdot \widetilde{Y}^{\theta'}) = e(g, \widetilde{\Gamma}) \\ \bot & \text{otherwise.} \end{cases}$$

4 Our Proposed Attacks

This section describes how can a PPT attacker get the original broadcast message, and we also implement it to examine the runtime of our attack model.

4.1 Attack Model

In the work of [23], the authors have shown that the AMRIBE scheme has achieved *ciphertext confidentiality* in the adaptive IND-MID-CCA security model (cf. Definition4) under the standard Decisional Bilinear Diffie-Hellman Type-3 (DBDH-3) assumption [21,23] (cf. Definition 2). In this section, we show that any PPT attacker $\mathcal{A}$ can recover the original broadcast messages from the challenge ciphertext for an unsubscribed user who does not belong to the subscribed users set by playing the following security game with the AMRIBE challenger $\mathcal{C}$. The same game is considered in the AMRIBE [23] scheme and also described in the Subsect. 2.3. We have divided our proposed attack techniques into two cases depending on the hash value of an unsubscribed user's identity. When the hash value of the unsubscribed user's identity is not equal to 0^l, we consider it as Case-I, and the dual of it is considered as Case-II. Here, 0^l represents a l length bit string of all 0. Applying our attack model for Case-I, the attacker can correctly retrieve the original message with a non-negligible probability. For Case-II, the attacker can expose the MSK component by utilizing the KeyExtractOracle in the confidentiality security game, thereby enabling the recovery of the original broadcast message.

Case-I. To exhibit the attack model for Case-I, we assume that the challenger $\mathcal{C}$ and the PPT attacker $\mathcal{A}$ play the *confidentiality security game* of the AMRIBE scheme (cf. Subsect. 2.3) in the following way.

- $\mathcal{A}$·**Setup:** The attacker $\mathcal{A}$ has access to all components of the MPK from the AMRIBE scheme of Tseng *et al.* [23].
- $\mathcal{A}$·**Phase-1:** The attacker is allowed to issue the KeyExtract Query and Decryption Query polynomially many times to $\mathcal{C}$ as explained in the original game.
- $\mathcal{A}$·**Challenge:** The attacker $\mathcal{A}$ selects two messages M_0, M_1 of the same length (*i.e.*, $|M_0| = |M_1|$). Now, the attacker chooses a subset $S^* = \{h_1, h_2, h_3\}$ from the range of $\mathcal{H}$, where $h_1 = k_1 k_2 \ldots k_{j-2}(1 - k_{j-1})k_j k_{j+1} k_{j+2} \ldots k_l$, $h_2 = k_1 k_2 \ldots k_{j-2} k_{j-1}(1 - k_j)k_{j+1} k_{j+2} \ldots k_l$, $h_3 = k_1 k_2 \ldots k_{j-2}(1 - k_{j-1})k_j(1 - k_{j+1})k_{j+2} \ldots k_l$ are the hash values of some identities of users and sends it to $\mathcal{C}$. Each k_j for $j \in \{1, 2, \ldots, l\}$ is either 0 or 1. In this attack model, the attacker's main goal is to recover the transmitted message. Here, the attacker $\mathcal{A}$ and challenger $\mathcal{C}$ do not need to know about the information of the user's identity (*i.e.*, the information of h_i^{-1}, $i = 1, 2, 3$) as the main encryption algorithm Encrypt of [23] only requires the hash values of the users identities. Thereafter, $\mathcal{C}$ chooses M_δ, where $\delta \in_R \{0, 1\}$ and generates the ciphertext $C^* = \left(C_0^*, C_1^*, C_2^*, C_{3,1}^*, C_{3,2}^*, C_{3,3}^*, \widetilde{\varGamma}^*\right)$ for the set S^*, and send C^* to $\mathcal{A}$. Here, the ciphertext components $C_0^* = M_\delta \cdot \varOmega^s, C_1^* = \varLambda^s, C_2^* = g^s$ and $C_{3,i}^*$ for all $i = 1, 2, 3$ are of the following form,

$$C_{3,1}^* = g^{s\left((1-k_{j-1})t_{j-1} + \sum_{i=1, i \neq (j-1)}^l k_i t_i\right)}$$

$$C_{3,2}^* = g^{s\left((1-k_j)t_j + \sum_{i=1, i \neq j}^l k_i t_i\right)}$$

$$C_{3,3}^* = g^{s\left((1-k_{j-1})t_{j-1} + (1-k_{j+1})t_{j+1} + \sum_{i=1, i \neq \{(j-1),(j+1)\}}^l k_i t_i\right)}$$

- $\mathcal{A}$·**Phase-2:** The attacker $\mathcal{A}$ asks the secret-key of another user, whose hash value is $h_4 = k_1 k_2 \ldots k_{j-2} k_{j-1}(1 - k_j)(1 - k_{j+1})k_{j+2} \ldots k_l$. Observe that this KeyExtract Query is a valid query since $h_4 \notin S^*$. It is worth mentioning that the attacker has the flexibility to choose h_4 in various ways, and we have demonstrated one possible approach: $h_4 = h_1 + h_2 - h_3 \pmod{2}$. Additionally, the attacker does not require knowledge of the identity of the user associated with the hash value h_4 to recover the original message. In return, $\mathcal{A}$ gets the secret-key $\mathsf{SK}_4 = (d_{4,0}, d_{4,1})$ of the user from $\mathcal{C}$, where

$$d_{4,0} = \widetilde{g}^\alpha \cdot \widetilde{g}^{r_4\left((1-k_j)t_j + (1-k_{j+1})t_{j+1} + \sum_{i=1, i \neq \{j,(j+1)\}}^{l} k_i t_i\right)}$$
$$d_{4,1} = \widetilde{g}^{r_4}$$

- $\mathcal{A}$·**Guess:** The attacker $\mathcal{A}$ is now able to produce a new decryption privilege for the user, whose hash value h_4. To decrypt the challenge ciphertext C^*, the attacker executes the following computations

$$C_{3,4}^* = C_{3,1}^* \cdot C_{3,2}^* \cdot \frac{1}{C_{3,3}^*}$$
$$= g^{s\left((1-k_j)t_j + (1-k_{j+1})t_{j+1} + \sum_{i=1, i \neq \{j,(j+1)\}}^{l} k_i t_i\right)}$$

Then, $\mathcal{A}$ can retrieve the intended message correctly by computing the following steps.

$$K = \frac{e\left(C_{3,4}^*, d_{4,1}\right)}{e\left(C_2^*, d_{4,0}\right)} = \frac{1}{e(g, \widetilde{g})^{\alpha s}}$$
$$M_\delta = \frac{C_0^*}{C_1^*} \times K$$

Therefore, the attacker $\mathcal{A}$ can correctly determine δ with a non-negligible advantage.

Case-II. Similar to Case-I, $\mathcal{C}$ and $\mathcal{A}$ play the *confidentiality security game* of the AMRIBE scheme (cf. Subsect. 2.3) in the following way.

- $\mathcal{A}$·**Setup:** Similar as that of in the Case-I.
- $\mathcal{A}$·**Phase-1:** Similar as that of in the Case-I.
- $\mathcal{A}$·**Challenge:** The attacker $\mathcal{A}$ selects two messages M_0, M_1 of the same length (*i.e.*, $|M_0| = |M_1|$) and a subset $S^* = \{h_1, h_2\}$ from the range of $\mathcal{H}$ in such a way that $h_i \neq 000$ for $i = 1, 2$. It then sends all of this to the challenger $\mathcal{C}$. Then, $\mathcal{C}$ chooses a message M_δ, where $\delta \in_R \{0, 1\}$ and encrypts it by running the Encrypt(MPK, S^*, M_δ) algorithm. Here, the attacker does not need to know about the identity of users whose hash values are h_1 and h_2. As the encryption algorithm Encrypt only requires the hash values of the users, the set S^* will work perfectly in the Encrypt algorithm. Finally, the challenger returns the challenge ciphertext $C^* = \left(C_0^*, C_1^*, C_2^*, C_{3,1}^*, C_{3,2}^*, \widetilde{T}^*\right)$ to the attacker.
- $\mathcal{A}$·**Phase-2:** The attacker $\mathcal{A}$ asks the secret-key of an another user ID_5, whose hash value is given by $h_5 = 000$. Observe that this KeyExtract Query is a

valid query since $ID_5 \notin S^*$. In return, $\mathcal{A}$ gets from $\mathcal{C}$ the secret-key $\mathsf{SK}_5 = (d_{5,0}, d_{5,1})$ of the user, where

$$d_{5,0} = \left(\widetilde{g}\right)^\alpha \cdot \left(\widetilde{g}\right)^{0 \cdot r_5} = \left(\widetilde{g}\right)^\alpha,$$
$$d_{5,1} = \left(\widetilde{g}\right)^{r_5}$$

Therefore, the attacker can retrieve the MSK component $\left(\widetilde{g}\right)^\alpha$ of the system by just querying the KeyExtract Oracle. The attacker can use it to recover the correct message.

- $\mathcal{A}$·**Guess:** Now, the attacker can retrieve the correct message by the following computations.

$$K = \frac{1}{e(C_2^*, d_{5,0})}$$
$$M_\delta = \frac{C_0^*}{C_1^*} \times K$$

We emphasize that the attacker can recover the message using only the components C_0, C_1, and C_2 of the ciphertext. More specifically, since this case does not depend on the challenge set S^*, it is easier than the previous Case-I. Therefore, the attacker $\mathcal{A}$ can correctly determine δ with a non-negligible advantage for Case-II also.

Remark 1. Following the *identity-based broadcast encryption* framework of Boneh et al. [3], we can emphasize that the users' information is available to both challengers and adversaries in the above-mentioned *ciphertext confidentiality* security game. Consequently, they also have the hash value of each user, as the cryptographic hash function $\mathcal{H}$ can be easily extracted from the master public key MPK. In the encryption algorithm proposed by [23], the broadcaster solely requires the hash values of the users' identities. Thus, in our attack model, we construct the challenge set using the hash values of the users instead of their actual identities. By adopting this approach, the attacker can recover the transmitted messages without even knowing the users' identities, bypassing the need for the inverse of the predefined hash values. Therefore, both our attack models for Case-I and Case-II are well-defined.

4.2 Analysis for Our Attack Models

This section analyzes and implement[1] the execution time of our proposed two attack models, considering a realistic scenario. We assume that the target set size is $|S^*| = L \ (\leq N)$. Here, N is the total number of system users. Considering the first case, Case-I, it becomes evident that this model necessitates merely two pairing operations and a maximum of N hash computations and product

Table 2. Execution Time for Case-I Attack Model

Number of users	Initialization time	Challenge time	Attack time	Total time
8	0.013366	0.006525	0.002840	0.022731
32	0.013529	0.006554	0.002860	0.022943
128	0.014018	0.006694	0.002841	0.023553
512	0.014054	0.006645	0.002863	0.023562
2048	0.018693	0.006774	0.002936	0.028403

Table 3. Execution Time for Case-II Attack Model

Number of users	Initialization	Challenge time	Attack time	Total time
8	0.010672	0.006360	0.001403	0.018435
32	0.010662	0.006390	0.001502	0.018554
128	0.010613	0.006481	0.001489	0.018583
512	0.010682	0.006286	0.001460	0.018428
2048	0.010690	0.006385	0.001527	0.018602

operations in a worst-case scenario. On the other hand, Case-II takes only two product operations and one pairing operation.

We discuss the implementation details of our proposed attacks for $N = 8$, 32, 128, 512, and 2048. We also note that $N = 2^l$, where l is the length of each user identity. We have used a Dell Laptop to implement our attack models with the following specifications: AMD A9-9400 Radeon processor, 12GB memory, 64-bit Ubuntu 22.04.4 LTS Linux OS with a 42.9 GNOME version with the help of Pairing-Based Cryptography (PBC) library (version 0.5.14) [18]. We have used an elliptic curve pairing group on the supersingular curve $y = x^3 + x$ and type A bilinear pairing.

The implementation details of our proposed attack for Case-I and Case-II of the AMRIBE scheme of Tseng et al. [23] are presented in Tables 1, 2 and Fig. 1. We implemented our attack models for both cases (Case-I and Case-II), considering different total numbers of users: $N = 8, 32, 128, 512$, and 2048. In both the tables and figures, we have considered Initialization time and Attack time, which are described below.

$$\text{Initialization time} = \text{Setup time} + \text{Phase-1 time},$$
$$\text{Attack time} = \text{Phase-2 time} + \text{Guess time}$$

We have shown the execution time of the Initialization, Challenge, and Attack algorithms for Case-I in Table 2 and analyzed it in Fig. 1. The Initialization time

---
[1] https://github.com/lm10ffi/Attack_AMRIBE.

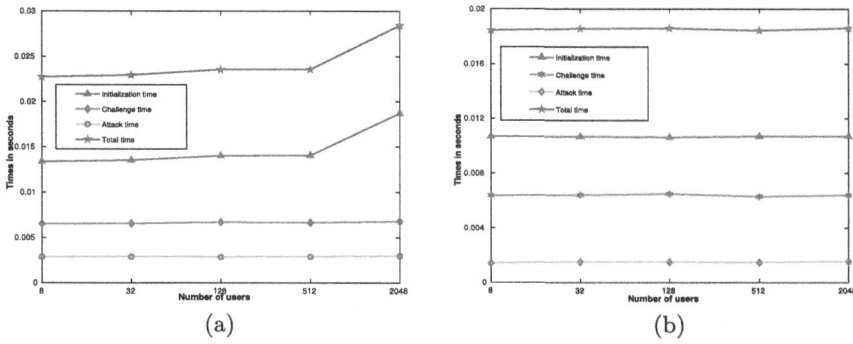

Fig. 1. (a) Time required for our Case-I attack model (b) Time required for our Case-II attack model

and the Total time gradually increase linearly with the total number of system users. Consequently, the running times for these two algorithms only depend on the total number of system users. The running times for another two algorithms, Challenge and Attack, are (almost) constant, which is depicted in Fig. 1.

The execution time of the Initialization, Challenge, and Attack phases for Case-II is presented in Table 3, and its analysis is depicted in Fig. 1b. It is important to note that the attack in Case-II does not rely on the length of the user identity, and therefore, it does not depend on the total number of system users. As seen in Table 3 and Fig. 1b, the Total Time for Case-II remains (almost) constant across different values of N. Specifically, the Total Time is approximately 0.018 seconds, rounded up to three decimal places.

5 Our Proposed Technique to Construct Secure AMRIBE Scheme

In this section, we suggest a technique for designing a secure AMRIBE scheme by mitigating our proposed two attacks. Along the way, we need to modify the main instance of the AMRIBE [23] construction. A generic idea of our proposed technique is described below.

Eliminating IB Framework [10,17]. To mitigate the proposed attacks, the Identity-Based (IB) framework can be omiited from the AMRIBE scheme. Within an IB setup, an attacker $\mathcal{A}$ can query the KeyExtract oracle a polynomial number of times for a chosen set of user identities. For instance, in our attack (cf. Sect. 4), the attacker $\mathcal{A}$ successfully decrypts the broadcast ciphertext by querying the secret keys of unsubscribed users with identities ID_4 and ID_5.

Conversely, in an AMRIBE (without IB framework), $\mathcal{A}$ can make a KeyExtract oracle query for the set of indices $\mathcal{S} \subseteq \{1, 2, \ldots, L\}$, where L is the total number of users of the system. Then, the challenger (secretly) sets a unique identifier corresponding to each index $u \in \mathcal{S}$ and runs the KeyExtract algorithm over the set of identities $\mathcal{ID}_\mathcal{S} = \{ID_u : u \in \mathcal{S}\}$. Therefore, the corresponding set of identities for all the system users is completely anonymous to the adversary $\mathcal{A}$. As a result, if we drop the IB framework from the AMRIBE scheme of Tseng *et al.* [23], then the hybrid AMRIBE scheme can defend our proposed two attacks.

6 Conclusion

In this paper, we reviewed the AMRIBE scheme of Tseng *et al.* [23] and demonstrated its weakness. Our proposed attacks have shown that an unsubscribed user can correctly decrypt the original broadcast message without having a valid decryption privilege. Consequently, we can comment that the work of [23] does not guarantee the crucial security requirement, i.e., the *ciphertext confidentiality*, for BE scheme. We have also discussed a generic modification of their scheme and shown that the hybrid AMRIBE scheme can defend our attacks. However, we have not proposed concrete construction of such a design. Therefore, constructing a fully anonymous identity-based BE scheme with optimal ciphertext size is still an open direction; we can endure it as our future interest.

Acknowledgments. This study was funded by the Science and Engineering Research Board (SERB), Department of Science and Technology (DST), Government of India under File No. EEQ/2023/000164 and the Information Security Education and Awareness (ISEA) Project Phase-III initiatives of the Ministry of Electronics and Information Technology (MeitY) under Grant No. F.No. L-14017/1/2022-HRD.

References

1. Baek, J., Safavi-Naini, R., Susilo, W.: Efficient multi-receiver identity-based encryption and its application to broadcast encryption. In: Vaudenay, S. (ed.) PKC 2005. LNCS, vol. 3386, pp. 380–397. Springer, Heidelberg (2005). https://doi.org/10.1007/978-3-540-30580-4_26
2. Barth, A., Boneh, D., Waters, B.: Privacy in encrypted content distribution using private broadcast encryption. In: International Conference on Financial Cryptography and Data Security, pp. 52–64. Springer (2006)
3. Boneh, D., Gentry, C., Waters, B.: Collusion resistant broadcast encryption with short ciphertexts and private keys. In: Annual International Cryptology Conference, pp. 258–275. Springer (2005)
4. Chen, L., Li, J., Zhang, Y.: Anonymous certificate-based broadcast encryption with personalized messages. IEEE Trans. Broadcast. **66**(4), 867–881 (2020)
5. Delerablée, C.: Identity-based broadcast encryption with constant size ciphertexts and private keys. In: International Conference on the Theory and Application of Cryptology and Information Security, pp. 200–215. Springer (2007)
6. Dodis, Y., Fazio, N.: Public key broadcast encryption for stateless receivers. In: ACM Workshop on Digital Rights Management, pp. 61–80. Springer (2002)
7. Fan, C.I., Huang, L.Y., Ho, P.H.: Anonymous multireceiver identity-based encryption. IEEE Trans. Comput. **59**(9), 1239–1249 (2010)

8. Fazio, N., Perera, I.M.: Outsider-anonymous broadcast encryption with sublinear ciphertexts. In: Fischlin, M., Buchmann, J., Manulis, M. (eds.) PKC 2012. LNCS, vol. 7293, pp. 225–242. Springer, Heidelberg (2012). https://doi.org/10.1007/978-3-642-30057-8_14
9. Fiat, A., Naor, M.: Broadcast encryption. In: Annual International Cryptology Conference, pp. 480–491. Springer (1993)
10. Georgescu, A.: Anonymous lattice-based broadcast encryption. In: Information and Communication Technology-EurAsia Conference, pp. 353–362. Springer (2013)
11. He, K., Weng, J., Liu, J.N., Liu, J.K., Liu, W., Deng, R.H.: Anonymous identity-based broadcast encryption with chosen-ciphertext security. In: Proceedings of the 11th ACM on Asia Conference on Computer and Communications Security, pp. 247–255 (2016)
12. Hur, J., Park, C., Hwang, S.O.: Privacy-preserving identity-based broadcast encryption. Inf. Fusion **13**(4), 296–303 (2012)
13. Kiayias, A., Samari, K.: Lower bounds for private broadcast encryption. In: International Workshop on Information Hiding, pp. 176–190. Springer (2012)
14. Kim, J., Susilo, W., Au, M.H., Seberry, J.: Adaptively secure identity-based broadcast encryption with a constant-sized ciphertext. IEEE Trans. Inf. Forensics Secur. **10**(3), 679–693 (2015)
15. Lai, J., Mu, Y., Guo, F., Susilo, W., Chen, R.: Anonymous identity-based broadcast encryption with revocation for file sharing. In: Liu, J.K., Steinfeld, R. (eds.) ACISP 2016. LNCS, vol. 9723, pp. 223–239. Springer, Cham (2016). https://doi.org/10.1007/978-3-319-40367-0_14
16. Li, X., Yanli, R.: Efficient anonymous identity-based broadcast encryption without random oracles. Int. J. Digit. Crime Forensics (IJDCF) **6**(2), 40–51 (2014)
17. Libert, B., Paterson, K.G., Quaglia, E.A.: Anonymous broadcast encryption: adaptive security and efficient constructions in the standard model. In: Public Key Cryptography–PKC 2012: 15th International Conference on Practice and Theory in Public Key Cryptography, Darmstadt, Germany, May 21-23, 2012. Proceedings 15, pp. 206–224. Springer (2012)
18. Lynn, B.: PBC library-the pairing-based cryptography library, version 0.5. 14. 2013 (2013). https://crypto.stanford.edu/pbc
19. Mandal, M.: Privacy-preserving fully anonymous ciphertext policy attribute-based broadcast encryption with constant-size secret keys and fast decryption. J. Inf. Secur. Appl. **55**, 102666 (2020)
20. Mandal, M., Nuida, K.: Identity-based outsider anonymous broadcast encryption with simultaneous individual messaging. In: Network and System Security: 14th International Conference, NSS 2020, Melbourne, VIC, Australia, November 25–27, 2020, Proceedings 14. pp. 167–186. Springer (2020)
21. Ren, Y., Niu, Z., Zhang, X.: Fully anonymous identity-based broadcast encryption without random oracles. Int. J. Netw. Secur. **16**(4), 256–264 (2014)
22. Sakai, R., Furukawa, J.: Identity-based broadcast encryption. Cryptology ePrint Archive (2007)
23. Tseng, Y.F., Fan, C.I.: Anonymous multireceiver identity-based encryption against chosen-ciphertext attacks with tight reduction in the standard model. Secur. Commun. Netw. **2021**, 1–11 (2021)
24. Tseng, Y.M., Huang, Y.H., Chang, H.J.: CCA-secure anonymous multi-receiver id-based encryption. In: 2012 26th International Conference on Advanced Information Networking and Applications Workshops, pp. 177–182. IEEE (2012)

Algebraic Cryptanalysis and Countermeasures of Lightweight Signature Scheme Based on Multivariate Quadratic Polynomials

Kuldeep Namdeo[✉], Dheerendra Mishra, and Namita Srivastava

Maulana Azad National Institute of Technology, Bhopal 462003, India
imkuldeepak25@gmail.com, dheerendra.m@gmail.com, namitas@manit.ac.in

Abstract. Multivariate Public Key Cryptography (MPKC) is a promising candidate for Post Quantum Cryptography (PQC) that ensures data security, information security, computer system security, and network security against large-scale quantum computers. Among the various threats to MPKC, MinRank attacks are crucial to MPKC, as they attempt to solve the MinRank problem given a public key and can break several multivariate systems. Recent advancements have introduced the rectangular MinRank attack, which breaks the Rainbow signature scheme by altering Rainbow's public keys. This study examines the rank and structural weaknesses of the lightweight signature scheme based on multivariate quadratic equations. In this article, we present the cryptanalysis of the multivariate quadratic polynomial-based digital signature algorithm, called Lite-Rainbow, which is based on the state-of-the-art signature scheme Rainbow, through a rectangular MinRank attack and a simple attack. In addition, we provide countermeasures to overcome the proposed attack on lightweight signature schemes.

Keywords: MQ-Problem · Multivariate Polynomials · Rainbow Signature · MinRank Problem · IP-Problem

1 Introduction

The discrete logarithm problem and prime factorization are two mathematical hardness assumptions that are initially used in the foundations of cryptography. In polynomial time, these classical primitives [24, 25, 33] can be cracked by Peter Shor's quantum algorithm [36]. As a result, these schemes will become antiquated and useless as soon as quantum computers with sufficient power become available. It is possible that the conventional definition of security will not adequately encompass future security ideas. Given the circumstances, cryptographers worldwide are currently engaged in the development of a new set of cryptographic primitives and building blocks that are resistant to attacks utilizing quantum algorithms. This new area of research is referred to as Post

Quantum Cryptography (PQC) [3]. In recent decades, several classes of PQC have emerged, and there has been a significant increase in interest in this area of research. One of the most promising approaches to PQC is multivariate public key cryptography [11].

Cryptosystems with real-world applications are unquestionably one of the main objectives of cryptography. Compared to RSA cryptosystems, Multivariate Public Key Cryptography (MPKC) usually uses much larger keys. However, because multivariate cryptosystems only require basic field operations [13], they often have substantially less computing complexity than RSA and are secure against quantum computers with the right parameter settings. This makes MPKCs appropriate for blockchain technology [34], smart cards, IoT, and low-cost devices. Many workable digital signature schemes based on MPKCs are available, such as MAYO [5], HFEv- [31], Rainbow [15], Unbalanced Oil and Vinegar (UOV) [22], etc. Among all post-quantum cryptographic digital signatures, MPKCs offer the shortest signature (about 120 bits at an 80-bit security level). Because of their exceptional efficiency, one important application for MPKCs is to find new uses for them in scenarios where traditional public key cryptosystems have failed to function efficiently. Although several MPKC-based designs have broken, numerous are nevertheless functional, and new designs are getting increasingly robust. Throughout the last decade or so, the theoretical foundation of multivariate cryptosystems has evolved quickly, so there is plenty of opportunity for these ideas to discover practical applications.

Attacks on MPKCs can be broadly classified into two types: structural attacks and direct algebraic attacks [21]. The goal of a direct algebraic attack is to solve the multivariate polynomial equations system over the finite field directly, using appropriate techniques such as XL algorithms [10], Grobner basis [8], and linearization [14]. In a structural attack, we attempt to determine the structure of the secret affine transformation, or the structure of the public key. Under this classification, there are different attacks like, MinRank attack [37], differential attack [17], subspace differntial attack [12], and Rainbow band seperation attacks [21], Beullens Simple attack [6]. During a few years in the early 2000s, cryptanalysis of different variants of UOV and Rainbow was a vibrant field of study. Among the attacks from this era are the Rainbow Band Separation Attack, the Billet-Gilbert attack, the MinRank attack, the HighRank attack, and the UOV reconciliation attack [7, 16, 19, 22].

After 2015, it appeared that cryptanalysis had steadied, but fresh cryptanalysis was sparked by Rainbow's involvement in the NIST PQC project. A novel algorithm for resolving the MinRank problem was proposed by Bardet et al. during the second round of the NIST project. Although not enough to jeopardize the NIST-submitted parameters, this significantly increased the MinRank attack's efficiency. Baena et al. [1] suggested a more memory-friendly variant of this approach. The study of the Rainbow Band Separation attack was strengthened by Perlner and Smith-Tone [28], who demonstrated that the attack was more effective than previously thought. The Rainbow team decided to raise the parameters as a result. Beullens presented novel threats [6], that break Rainbow's security efficiently. Different variants of Rainbow signature schemes also have been proposed, like IPRainbow [9], Circulant Rainbow [27], CyclicRainbow [29], Lite-Rainbow; a lightweight signature scheme [35] etc.

We have cryptanalyzed the light-weight signature schemes based on multivariate polynomial equations over a finite field [35]. We can obtain the equivalent subspace description that of Rainbow signature scheme and apply Beullens simple attack to retrieve the secret key. We have shown that the lightweight signature scheme shows the rank weakness and finally we have retrieved the key by using Rectangular MinRank attack. Additionally we have provided countermeasures for improving the security of the scheme Lite-Rainbow.

Section 2 presents the basic terms for better understanding of the paper. In Sect. 3 we have given short review of lightweight signature scheme Lite-Rainbow. In Sect. 4 the cryptanalysis of scheme has been done. In Sect. 5 we have provide the analysis and some countermeasures for improving the signature scheme and finally, Sect. 6 concludes the article.

2 Prelminaries

2.1 MQ Problem

The Multivariate Quadratic (MQ) problem involves finding a solution to a system of l multivariate quadratic polynomial equations in r variables over the finite field $\mathbb{K}$. Consider a system of equations given by:

$$p_1 = h_1(y_1, y_2, \ldots, y_r)$$
$$p_2 = h_2(y_1, y_2, \ldots, y_r)$$
$$\vdots$$
$$p_l = h_l(y_1, y_2, \ldots, y_r).$$

The goal is to find the vector $y = (y_1, y_2, \ldots, y_r)$ over the finite field $\mathbb{K}$ that satisfies this system of equations. Each polynomial h_i can be expressed as:

$$h_i(y_1, y_2, \ldots, y_r) = \sum_{1 \leq j \leq k \leq r} \alpha_{ijk} y_j y_k + \sum_{j=1}^{r} \beta_{ij} y_j + \gamma_i$$

where $\alpha_{ijk}, \beta_{ij}, \gamma_i \in \mathbb{K}$. The MQ problem is known to be NP-hard [32].

2.2 IP-Problem

The Isomorphism of Polynomials (IP) problem involves finding two affine transformations S and T such that $P = S \circ F \circ T$, where P and F are multivariate polynomial vectors (not necessarily quadratic) such that every tuple of l- tuples is a polynomial in r- variables. $S \in Aff\ (\mathbb{K}^l)$ and $T \in Aff\ (\mathbb{K}^r)$ are affine transformations, we represent these affine transformations as $S(y) = S'(y) + S_c$

and $T(y) = T'(y) + T_c$, where S' and T' are $l \times l$ and $r \times r$ matrices and S_c and T_c are $l \times 1$ and $r \times 1$ column matrices over the field $\mathbb{K}$ and $y = (y_1, y_2, \cdots, y_r)^T$. IP-Problem is equivalent to MQ-Problem, and it is also an NP-hard problem [32].

2.3 MinRank Problem

Definition 1. MinRank Problem *[20, 26]: Let $H_1, ..., H_v \in \mathbb{K}^{l \times r}$ be v matrices. Then for integer $b > 0$, we have to search the existence of non-trivial linear combination $H = \sum_i c_i H_i$ over the field $\mathbb{K}$ such that rank $(H) = $ rank $(\sum_i c_i H_i) \leq b$.*

The goal of the MinRank attack is to learn about the private key (S, F, T), beginning with the function S. Following that, the main methods to solve it are Kernel attack, Kipnis-Shamir modelling, minor modelling, and support minors modelling [2]. Limination can be used to ascertain the constant and linear coefficients of F. The main methods to solve it are Kernel attack, Kipnis-Shamir modelling, minor modelling, and support minors modelling [2]. The MinRank problem is transformed into an instance of the MQ problem using modelling techniques. One can employ the support-minors algorithm of Bardet et al. [2] for retrieving the key. By employing linearization and sparse linear algebra techniques, this procedure converts the rank condition into a significant sparse system of bilinear equations that can be solved efficiently.

3 Lightweight Signature Schemes Based on Multivariate Quadratic Equations: Lite-Rainbow

The rainbow signature scheme, which relies on multivariate quadratic equations, has been considered as a viable option for ensuring secure communications in the era of post-quantum cryptography since 2005. The speed of this method is significantly faster than conventional public-key signatures such as RSA and ECDSA, yet its key size is considerably larger than that of the classical methods. The lightweight variations of Rainbow, called Lite-Rainbow-0 and Lite-Rainbow-1, are created by substituting small random seeds for some of a public key or secret key using a pseudo-random number generator [35]. In comparison to Rainbow, the public key and secret key of Lite-Rainbow-0 and Lite-Rainbow-1 have been decreased by 71% and 99.8%, respectively. Lite-Rainbow is based on Rainbow signature scheme. The construction of Lightweight Rainbow is described below:

Define three integers D_1, D_2, and D as:

$$D_1 := \frac{v_1 \cdot (v_1 + 1)}{2} + o_1 \cdot v_1$$

where v_1 represents the number of nonzero quadratic terms in the central polynomials of the first layer.

$$D_2 := v_2 \cdot (v_2 + 1)$$

where v_2 denotes the number of nonzero quadratic terms in the central polynomials of the second layer.

$$D := \frac{r \cdot (r+1)}{2}$$

where r signifies the total number of quadratic terms in the public polynomials.

The lightweight Rainbow use a special blockwise ordering of monomials and the lexicographical ordering for inside the blocks as in [30]. A public key is $P = S \circ F \circ T$, where F is a central map, and two invertible linear maps $T : \mathbb{K}^r \to \mathbb{K}^r$ and $S : \mathbb{K}^l \to \mathbb{K}^l$ given by $r \times r$ matrix $T = (t_{ij})$ and $l \times l$ matrix $S = (s_{ij})$, respectively. For simplicity, we use two invertible linear maps S and T instead of invertible affine maps.

Now, suppose $Q = F \circ T$ and $P = S \circ Q$. Suppose coefficient of monomial $x_i x_j$ that is $q_{ij}^{(k)}$ corresponds to k-th component of Q. Now,

$$q_{ij}^{(k)} = \sum_{r'=1}^{r} \sum_{s'=r'}^{r} \alpha_{ij}^{r's'} \cdot f_{r's'}^{(k)}; k = 1, 2, \cdots, l.$$

where

$$\alpha_{ij}^{r's'} = \begin{cases} t_{r'i} \cdot t_{s'i}, i = j \\ t_{r'i} \cdot t_{s'i} + t_{r'j} \cdot t_{s'i}, otherwise \end{cases}$$

Now, because of the unique structure of F, terms can be reduced as follows:

$$q_{ij}^{(k)} = \begin{cases} \sum_{r'=1}^{r} \sum_{s'=r'}^{r} \alpha_{ij}^{r's'} \cdot f_{r's'}^{(k)}; k = 1, 2, \cdots, o_1 \\ \sum_{r'=1}^{r} \sum_{s'=r'}^{r} \alpha_{ij}^{r's'} \cdot f_{r's'}^{(k)}; k = o_1 + 1, \cdots, l. \end{cases}$$

Now, the matrix $\tilde{A}$ is defined as:

$$\tilde{A} = \begin{cases} \alpha_{ij}^{r's'}, (1 \leq r' \leq v_2, r' \leq s' \leq r) \\ \alpha_{ij}^{r's'}, (1 \leq i \leq j \leq r). \end{cases}$$

Now, matrix $\tilde{A}$ can be divided into 6 parts $\begin{bmatrix} A_{11} & A_{12} & A_{13} \\ A_{21} & A_{22} & A_{23} \\ A_{31} & A_{32} & A_{33} \end{bmatrix}$. The matrix constructed by D rows and columns of $\tilde{A}$ is given by $A = \begin{bmatrix} A_{11} & A_{12} \\ A_{21} & A_{22} \end{bmatrix}$. The coefficient of P, Q, F can be written as elements in matrices P', Q', F' respectively, with associated monomial ordering. P, Q, R are the matices that consist of initial D_2 columns of matrices P', Q', F', respectively. Consequently we consider the matrices P'', F'' that are consisted of initial D columns of P', F'.respectively. Now, we will obtain $P'' = S \cdot F'' \cdot \tilde{A}$. Now, we obtain below relation:

$$P = S \cdot Q \implies Q = \tilde{S} \cdot P = \begin{bmatrix} S'_{11} & S'_{12} \\ S'_{21} & S'_{22} \end{bmatrix} \cdot \begin{bmatrix} P_{11} & P_{12} \\ P_{21} & P_{22} \end{bmatrix}$$

where $\tilde{S} = S^{-1}$ and $P_{l \times D_2}, \tilde{S}_{l \times l}, Q_{l \times D_2}$ matrices and S'_{11} is $o_1 \times o_1$ submatrix of $\tilde{S}$.

$$Q = F \cdot A = \begin{bmatrix} Q_{11} & Q_{12} \\ Q_{21} & Q_{22} \end{bmatrix} = \begin{bmatrix} F_{11} & 0 \\ F_{21} & F_{22} \end{bmatrix} \cdot \begin{bmatrix} A_{11} & A_{12} \\ A_{21} & A_{22} \end{bmatrix},$$

where
$$F \in \mathbb{K}^{l \times D_2}, \quad F_{11} \in \mathbb{K}^{o_1 \times D_1},$$

and $A_{D_2 \times D_2}$ is a submatrix of $\tilde{A}$ and A_{11} is a $D_1 \times D_1$ submatrix of A.

Now, consider the linear parts of P', Q', and F', denoted as P_L, Q_L, and F_L respectively. Then we have

$$P_L = S \cdot Q_L, Q_L = \tilde{S} \cdot P_L = \begin{bmatrix} S'_{11} & S'_{12} \\ S'_{21} & S'_{22} \end{bmatrix} \cdot \begin{bmatrix} P_{L11} & P_{L12} \\ P_{L21} & P_{L22} \end{bmatrix} = \begin{bmatrix} Q_{L11} & Q_{L12} \\ Q_{L21} & Q_{L22} \end{bmatrix}$$

$$Q_L = F_L \cdot T = \begin{bmatrix} Q_{L11} & Q_{L12} \\ Q_{L21} & Q_{L22} \end{bmatrix} = \begin{bmatrix} F_{11} & 0 \\ F_{21} & F_{22} \end{bmatrix} \cdot \begin{bmatrix} T_{11} & T_{12} \\ T_{21} & T_{22} \end{bmatrix}$$

Finally we obtained $P' = (P, P_R, P_L, P_C)$ and $F' = (F, F_L, F_C)$, this represents public polynomials and central polynomial respectively.

The whole secret key (S, F, T) of Lite Rainbow-0 is obtained by using a random seed. Therefore, in contrast to Rainbow, it must retrieve the whole secret key in order to sign. For positive integers λ, κ, let $G : \{0,1\}^\lambda \to \{0,1\}^\kappa$ be an adequately secure Pseudo Random Number Generator that generates random numbers. Now, P_{11}, P_{21}, P_{22} are corresponding to quadratic part and $P_{L11}, P_{L21}, P_{L22}$ corresponds to linear part, and PC is corresponds to constant and represented in matrix P' in the construction of Lite Rainbow-1 and are also generated by Pseudo Random Number Generator. Now, the Lite-Rainbow follows the basic steps of Key Generation, Signature Generation and Signature Verification [35].

4 Cryptanalysis of Lite-Rainbow

The security of Rainbow signature scheme and other signature schemes, that are using Rainbow or UOV structure is dependent not only on the MQ problem, but also on the IP - problem, and the MinRank problem. Consequently the formal security proofs become more complex as a result. MinRank attack is very powerful in MPKCs, this can break several schemes. A multi-layered version of the UOV scheme, Rainbow is immune to all MinRank attacks because it lacks the MinRank problem's structure. Beullens proposed new form of MinRank attack in case Rainbow, called Rectangular MinRank attack, that decreases the security of Rainbow by transforming the public key of Rainbow. Another attack on Rainbow is Beullens' Simple attack that breaks completely Rainbow efficiently. We are employing the Rectangular MinRank attack and Simple attack on Lite-Rainbow for recovering the key. The attacks are very efficient and recover the secret key in significant time. The security of the underlying consideration for Lite-Rainbow is based on following lemma:

Lemma 1. *The Isomorphism of Polynomials (IP) problem, when using bijective affine transformations $S \in \mathrm{GL}_l(\mathbb{K})$ and $T \in \mathrm{GL}_r(\mathbb{K})$, can be polynomially reduced to the IP problem, where $\mathrm{GL}_r(\mathbb{K})$ and $\mathrm{GL}_l(\mathbb{K})$ are representing the general linear groups.*

The author has claimed that this transformation does not change the security of MQ-Problem. But the rank weakness is still not protected by this equivalent conversion of isomorphism of polynomial problem and hence we can retrieve the key by employing rectangular MinRank attack. On the other hand the subspace description is corresponding to the variable classification depends on number of oil variables, vinegar variables, so it is also not much affected by this conversion. Therefore by employing simple attack, we transform Lite-Rainbow into equivalent UOV problem and retrieve the key efficiently for all suggested parameter sets in [35]. The lightweight signature scheme does not match the security level with any parameter set that has been claimed. Next sections show the cryptanalysis of Lite-Rainbow.

4.1 Rectangular MinRank Attack

We are employing the Rectangular MinRank attack [4] on Lite-Rainbow, since Lite-Rainbow has the same central polynomial as of Rainbow and the PRNG has been used for generating the coefficient of polynomials. We can obtained the subspace description of Lite-Rainbow as follows:

The Lite-Rainbow signature can be described in equivalent subspace form (as of Rainbow) [4] by the following parameters:

- $q = |\mathbb{K}|$
- $r = $ number of unknowns,
- $l = $ number of polynomials in P,
- $o_2 = Dim(O_2) = Dim(W)$, where O_2 and W are the subspaces of $\mathbb{K}_q^r$ and $\mathbb{K}_q^l$ respectively.

The multivariate quadratic map $P : \mathbb{K}_q^r \rightarrow \mathbb{K}_q^l$ be the public key and (O_1, O_2, W) be the secret key and having the following relations:

1. $O_2 \subset O_1 \subset \mathbb{K}_q^r$ and $W \subset \mathbb{K}_q^l$,
2. $Dim(O_2) = Dim(W) = o_2$ and $Dim(O_1) = l$,
3. $P(o_2) = 0$ and $P'(x, o_2) \in W$, $\forall o_2 \in O_2$,
4. $P(o_1) \in W$, $\forall o_1 \in W$.

P is uniformly over all P satisfying the above conditions on (O_2, O_2, W). The public key is generated by selecting $O_2 \subset O_1 \subset \mathbb{K}_q^r$ and $W \subset \mathbb{K}_q^l$ with appropriate dimension. This is known as the Rainbow subspace description. The traditional description and subspace description of Rainbow are both similar. The subspace description provides the structure of the Rainbow in a very nice manner.

Algebraic Cryptanalysis and Countermeasures 35

Algorithm 1. Rectangular MinRank Attack on Lite-Rainbow

1: **Input**: Public key polynomial map $P : \mathbb{K}_q^r \to \mathbb{K}_q^l$ and dimensions o_2, r, l
2: **Output**: A vector $o \in \mathbb{K}_q^r$ such that $o \in O_2$, and secret key recovery
3: **Step 1: Subspace Description of Lite-Rainbow**
4: Let $q = |\mathbb{K}|$, r be the number of unknowns, l be the number of polynomials.
5: Define subspaces $O_2 \subset O_1 \subset \mathbb{K}_q^r$ and $W \subset \mathbb{K}_q^l$.
6: $Dim(O_2) = Dim(W) = o_2$ and $Dim(O_1) = l$.
7: $\mathcal{P}$ is uniformly over all P satisfying the conditions on (O_2, O_1, W).
8: **Step 2: Rectangular Matrix Formulation**
9: Choose a basis $\{e_1, e_2, \ldots, e_r\}$ of $\mathbb{K}_q^r$.
10: **for** each $1 \leq i \leq r$ **do**
11:    Compute $L_i = \begin{bmatrix} P'(e_1, e_i) \\ \vdots \\ P'(e_r, e_i) \end{bmatrix}$ where P' is bilinear.
12: **end for**
13: Let $o = (o_1, o_2, \ldots, o_r) \in \mathbb{K}_q^r$ be an unknown vector.
14: Form $\sum_{i=1}^{r} o_i L_i = \begin{bmatrix} P'(e_1, o) \\ \vdots \\ P'(e_r, o) \end{bmatrix}$.
15: **Step 3: Solving MinRank Problem**
16: Solve for $o = (o_1, \ldots, o_r)$ such that the rank of $\sum_{i=1}^{r} o_i L_i \leq Dim(W) = o_2$.
17: Use the Bardet et al. algorithm to solve the MinRank problem for this condition.
18: Identify a coordinate vector $o = (o_1, \ldots, o_r)$ such that $o \in O_2$ with high probability.
19: **Step 4: Elimination of Matrices**
20: Eliminate $o_2 - 1$ matrices from the linear combination and reduce the rank of the remaining matrices.
21: After elimination, ensure the span of $r - o_2 + 1$ matrices contains at least one non-zero matrix.
22: This reduction lowers the cost of solving the MinRank problem.
23: **Step 5: Recovering the Secret Key**
24: Once $o_2 \in \mathbb{K}_q^r$ is obtained, attack Lite-Rainbow by breaking the equivalent UOV scheme.
25: Retrieve the secret key by solving the UOV system.
26: **Return**: The vector o and the secret key.

Now, Consider a basis $\{e_1, e_2, \cdots, e_r\}$ of $\mathbb{K}_q^r$ and r rectangular matrices $L_i \in \mathbb{K}_q^{r \times l}$ such that

$$L_i = \begin{bmatrix} P'(e_1, e_i) \\ \vdots \\ P'(e_r, e_i) \end{bmatrix}, \forall 1 \leq i \leq r.$$

where P is public polynomials and P' is bilinear. Now, for a vector $o \in \mathbb{K}_q^r$, we obtain $\sum_{i=1}^{r} o_i L_i = \begin{bmatrix} P'(e_1, o) \\ \vdots \\ P'(e_r, o) \end{bmatrix}$ having the rank $\rho \leq Dim(W) = o_2$, since all the rows are elements of subspace W.

Now, for $r \times l$ matrices corresponding to the public polynomials, there exist a linear combinations of these matrices such that $\rho(\sum_{i=1}^{r} o_i L_i) \leq Dim(W)$. This is one equivalence of MinRank Problem. Now, we can solve this MinRank problem by using algorithm of Bardet et al. and find coordinate vector $o = (o_1, \cdots, o_r) \in \mathbb{K}_q^r$ satisfying $\rho(\sum_{i=1}^{r} o_i L_i) \leq Dim(W) = o_2$. Consequently, suppose o is such vector then with high probability $o \in O_2$.

Now, each $o \in \mathbb{K}_q^r$ can provide such linear combination. Hence we can eliminate $o_2 - 1$ matrices and after this the span of $r - o_2 + 1$ matrices also contains atleast one matrix that is non-zero. In such a way, we can reduce the cost of solving MinRank problem by eliminating the matrices from linear combination.

Finally, when we obtain $o_2 \in \mathbb{K}_q^r$, the whole problem of attacking Lite-Rainbow is equivalent to break a UOV signature scheme and we can easily retrieve the key. Algorithm 1 shows the steps for exececution of attack.

4.2 Simple Attack

Now, suppose $pk = P$ and $sk = (O_2, O_1, W)$ are the public key and secret key of Rainbow. Let $x \in \mathbb{K}_q^r$ and $o_2 \in O_2$ then $P'(x, o_2) \in W$. Now consider the linear differential map

$$D_x : \mathbb{K}_q^r \to \mathbb{K}_q^l : y \mapsto P'(x, y),$$

then D_x maps O_2 to W. The restriction $D_{x|O_2}$ is uniformly linear. The probability of having the kernel vector into O_2 of D_x is the probability for the matrix $A \in \mathbb{K}_q^{o_2 \times o_2}$ to be singular, i.e. $1 - \prod_{i=0}^{o_2-1}(1 - q^{i-o_2}) \sim 1/q$ for significantly larger q. Now, let $0 \neq x$ randomly and suppose $ker(D_x) \cap O_2 \neq \{0\}$. Now, as $P(o) = 0, \forall o \in O_2$, so we solve for o in $ker(D_x) \cap O_2$ such that $D_x = 0$ and $P(o) = 0$. This is the system of l linear homogeneous and l quadratic homogeneous equations with r unknown of o. We can use l linear homogeneous equations to eliminate l variables from l quadratic homogeneous equations. Then, we obtained an equation system with l equations and $r-l$ unknown. Now, consider a matrix $B \in \mathbb{K}_q^{r \times (r-l)}$ such that columns of B are the elements of the basis of $ker(D_x)$. Now, we have to solve $\tilde{P}(y) = 0$ such that $\tilde{P}(y) = \tilde{P}(By)$.

Case 1. In case of field of odd characteristic, $\tilde{P}$ is equivalent to a random homogeneous quadratic system with l equations and $r-l$ unknowns. This obtained system can be solved efficiently by the XL algorithm if exists with $3\binom{r-l+1+d}{d}^2 \binom{r-l+1}{2}^2$ field operations, where d be the operating degree of XL algorithm is least integer such that the coefficient of t^d term in the power series expansion of $\frac{(1-t^2)^l}{(1-t)^r}$ is non-positive.

Case 2. In case of field of even characteristic, $\tilde{P}(x,x) = 2P(x) \equiv 0$ and consequently $x \in ker(D_x)$. Hence, the rank is not equal in both systems,i.e., XL and some random systems of homogeneous quadratic equations. This implies that adversary $\mathcal{A}$ has idea about $\tilde{y} \in \mathbb{K}_q^{r-l}$ satisfying $B(\tilde{y}) = x$ and $\tilde{P}(\tilde{y} + y) = \tilde{P}(\tilde{y}) + \tilde{P}(y), \forall y \in \mathbb{K}_q^{r-l}$. This is not true generally in the case of random P. Now, consider a subspace $Y \subset \mathbb{K}_q^{r-l}$ such that $Dim(Y) = r - l - 1$ and $<\tilde{y}> + Y = \mathbb{K}_q^{r-l}$ and $\tilde{y} \notin Y$. Since $y = \sqrt{\alpha}\tilde{y} + y'$ satisfies $\tilde{P}(y) = 0$, because $\tilde{P}(\sqrt{\alpha}\tilde{y} + y') = \alpha \tilde{P}(\tilde{y}) + \tilde{P}(y') = 0$, hence we have to only find $\tilde{y} \in Y$ such that $\tilde{P}(y') = \alpha \tilde{P}(\tilde{y}), \alpha \in \mathbb{K}_q$, because $\sqrt{\alpha}$ exists, if $char(\mathbb{K}) = 2$. Now, in order to find $y' \in Y$, we solve $\bar{P} = \tilde{p}_1 a_i - \tilde{p}_i a_1, 2 \le i \le l, a = \tilde{P}(\tilde{y})$ and $a_1 \ne 0$. Hence, we can obtain the solution if it exists efficiently with $3\binom{r-l-2+d}{d}^2 \binom{r-l}{2}^2$ field operations. where d be the operating degree of XL algorithm is the least integer such that the coefficient of t^d term in the power series expansion of $\frac{(1-t^2)^{l-1}}{(1-t)^{l-r-1}}$ is non-positive.

If we obtained any element from O_2, then Lite-Rainbow is reduced into UOV instances having $l' = l - o_2$ equations and $r'' = r - o_2$ unknowns. Now, compute $< P'(o, e_1), \cdots, P'(o, e_r) > \subset W$, for $o \in O_2$. Consider $P_1 : \mathbb{K}_q^r \to \mathbb{K}_q^{l-o_2}$ and $P_1 : \mathbb{K}_q^r \to \mathbb{K}_q^{o_2}$ and V that maps W onto last o_2 coordinates of $\mathbb{K}_q^l$ such that

$$V \circ \mathcal{P}(x) = \begin{cases} P_1(x) \\ P_2(x) \end{cases},$$

where $P_1(x)$ contains initial $l - o_2$ coordinates and $P_2(x)$ contains last o_2 coordinates of $V \circ P$ Now, we can find O_2, which is the $ker(o \mapsto \begin{pmatrix} P_1'(e_1, o) \\ \vdots \\ P_1'(e_r, o) \end{pmatrix})$, since $P'(x, o) \in W, \forall x \in \mathbb{K}_q^r$, with high probablity.

Suppose U, that maps last o_2 coordinates of $\mathbb{K}_q^l$ onto O_2 such that

$$V \circ P \circ U(x) = F(x) = \begin{cases} F_1(x) \\ F_2(x) \end{cases},$$

where $F_1(x)$ contains initial $l - o_2$ coordinates and $F_2(x)$ contains last o_2 coordinates of $V \circ P \circ U$. Suppose a vector y having initial $r - o_2$ coordinates zero, then $U(y) \in O_2$, Therefore $F_1(x+y) = F_1(x) + P_1'(U(x), U(y)) + P(U(y)) = F_1(x)$. Also $F_1(U^{-1}O_1) = 0$, since $P(O_1) \in W$. Hence, if we omit the last o_2 coordinates, then F_1 is reduced into an UOV instance's public key with $r'' = r - o_2$ unknowns and oil subspace O such that $Dim(O) = l' = l - o_2$. Now, to obtain P^{-1} is similar to obtaining F^{-1}, because the adversary $\mathcal{A}$ have idea about the difference of P and F and the problem of obtaining F^{-1} can be reduced to obtaining F_1^{-1}. we can easily deduce this. For this suppose, we wish to get x satisfying $F_1(x) = t_1$ and $F_2(x) = t_2$, where $t = (t_1, t_2)$. Then

Algorithm 2. Simple Attack on Lite-Rainbow

1: **Input**: Public key P, parameters (q, r, l, o_2)
2: **Output**: Secret key (O_1, O_2, W)
3: **Step 1: Compute D_x**
4: Randomly choose a non-zero vector $x \in \mathbb{K}_q^r$
5: Compute the differential matrix $D_x : \mathbb{K}_q^r \to \mathbb{K}_q^l$, where $D_x(y) = P'(x, y)$ maps O_2 to W
6: Restrict D_x to O_2: $D_{x|O_2}$
7: Determine $ker(D_x)$, which is the solution to the linear homogeneous system
8: **Step 2: Solve for $ker(D_x) \cap O_2$**
9: Assume $ker(D_x) \cap O_2 \neq \{0\}$.
10: Solve a system of l linear and l quadratic homogeneous equations with r unknowns and find $o \in O_2$ such that $P(o) = 0$
11: Use the l linear equations to eliminate l variables, reducing the system to l quadratic homogeneous equations in $r - l$ unknowns
12: **Step 3: Use XL Algorithm**
13: Construct a matrix $B \in \mathbb{K}_q^{r \times (r-l)}$ whose columns form a basis of $ker(D_x)$
14: Define a new system $\tilde{P}(y) = \tilde{P}(By)$ and solve $\tilde{P}(y) = 0$ using the XL algorithm
15: **Case 1: Field of Odd Characteristic**
16: $\tilde{P}$ is a random homogeneous quadratic system with l equations and $r - l$ unknowns
17: Use XL algorithm to solve the system, requiring $3 \binom{r-l+1+d}{d}^2 \binom{r-l+1}{2}^2$ field operations, where d is the operating degree
18: **Case 2: Field of Even Characteristic**
19: $\tilde{P}(x, x) = 2P(x) \equiv 0$, meaning that $x \in ker(D_x)$
20: Solve for $y' \in Y \subset \mathbb{K}_q^{r-l}$ such that $\tilde{P}(y') = \alpha \tilde{P}(\tilde{y})$, where $\alpha \in \mathbb{K}_q$ and $\sqrt{\alpha}$ exists
21: Solve the system using $3 \binom{r-l-2+d}{d}^2 \binom{r-l}{2}^2$ field operations, where d is the least integer such that the coefficient of t^d in the power series expansion of $\frac{(1-t^2)^{l-1}}{(1-t)^{l-r-1}}$ is non-positive
22: **Step 4: Retrieve O_2**
23: If any element is obtained from O_2, reduce Lite-Rainbow to a UOV instance with $l' = l - o_2$ equations and $r'' = r - o_2$ unknowns
24: Compute $< P'(o, e_1), \ldots, P'(o, e_r) > \subset W$ for $o \in O_2$
25: **Step 5: Reduce to UOV Instance**
26: Consider the maps $P_1 : \mathbb{K}_q^r \to \mathbb{K}_q^{l-o_2}$ and $P_2 : \mathbb{K}_q^r \to \mathbb{K}_q^{o_2}$
27: Define a map $V \circ P(x) = \begin{cases} P_1(x) \\ P_2(x) \end{cases}$ where $P_1(x)$ contains the initial $l - o_2$ coordinates and $P_2(x)$ contains the last o_2 coordinates
28: Find O_2 as the kernel of the map $o \mapsto \begin{pmatrix} P_1'(e_1, o) \\ \vdots \\ P_1'(e_r, o) \end{pmatrix}$, since $P'(x, o) \in W, \forall x \in \mathbb{K}_q^r$
29: **Step 6: Solve UOV Instance Using Kipnis-Shamir Attack**
30: Use the Kipnis-Shamir attack to solve the reduced UOV instance with r'' unknowns and l' equations
31: Recover O_1 by solving for the secret key using $q^{r''-2l'} \cdot \text{poly}(r'')$ field operations
32: **Step 7: Return the Secret Key**
33: Once O_1 and O_2 are retrieved, the full secret key (O_1, O_2, W) is obtained
34: **Return** the secret key (O_1, O_2, W)

- By using any attack method of UOV, we can find x satisfying $F_1(x) = t_1$ such that $(r'', l') = (r - o_2, l - o_2)$.
- Since $F_2(x + o) = F_2(x) + F_2'(x, o)$ is linear in o, therefore we can solve efficiently the system of linear equation $F_2(x+o) = t_2$ having o_2 unknowns and equations for $o \in \mathbb{K}_q{}^r$ that is having initial $r - o_2$ coordinates zero.
- Now, $F_1(x + o) = F_1(x) = t_1$, since F is dependent only on initial $r - o_2$ unknowns. Hence, $x + o$ is the solution.

Now, since F_1 is an instance of UOV with parameter (r'', l'), therefore we can recover O_1 and consequently the key efficiently by Kipnis-Shamir attack in time $q^{r''-2l'}.poly(r'')$ for NIST parameter set SL1 and we can forge signature for SL3 and SL5 by XL algorithm without recovering O_1 effectively.

Now, an adversary can take advantage of the simple attack and easily retrieve its own signing key or secret key. This attack method is very efficient and retrieves the secret key for all suggested parameters for Lite-Rainbow. Now, consider the NIST parameter set SL1 such that $q = 16, r = 96, l = 64, o_2 = 32$. Now, for retrieving O_2 and W, we have to find the solution of a homogeneous quadratic system with $l-1 = 63$ equations and $r-l-1 = 31$ unknowns. The computational cost is $2^{52.3}$ field operations. Now, we will solve approximately 15.06 equation systems. Suppose one $\mathbb{K}_{16}$- operation requires 36 gates, therefore, in this case, the complete computational cost for retrieving O_2 and W is $2^{52.3} \times 15.06 \times 36 \sim 2^{61.4}$. When we retrieve O_2 and W, the Lite-Rainbow instance is equivalent to the UOV instance with $l' = 32$ equation and $r'' = 64$ unknowns. Hence, we can efficiently obtain O_1 using the Kipnis-shamir attack [23] in polynomial time. Hence, the overall computational complexity for retrieving the secret key is $\sim 2^{61.4}$. An adversary $\mathcal{A}$ can retrieve the secret keys of Lite-Rainbow in both cases, i.e. in the cases of Lite Rainbow-0 and Lite Rainbow-1. Algorithm 2 shows the steps for execution of attack.

5 Countermeasures

Optimizing parameters, using randomization strategies, creating secure keys, and applying algorithmic hardening are all necessary to protect a lightweight Rainbow signature scheme from different types of attacks. Enhancing the rainbow structure's, field size, and layer count is the first step in optimizing its parameters. To greatly increase the complexity of possible attacks, for example, one can choose a larger finite field, such $\mathbb{K}_{2^{16}}$, rather than $\mathbb{K}_{2^8}$. A multi-layer scheme considerably complicates matters for attackers when it is upgraded from a two-layer one. In other words, each layer of the Rainbow scheme has a distinct affine transformation performed to it, making it more difficult for attackers to identify patterns. This can be achieved by applying a secret affine transformation on the public key polynomials. The public key's structure can also be hidden by adding random noise, as long as the noise is small enough to prevent it from interfering with the verification of valid signatures.

Therefore, the construction of secure keys is crucial. Ensuring that the randomness used in key generation comes from a cryptographically secure random number generator (CSPRNG) requires the use of high-entropy sources. Regular upgrading and key replacement also aid in avoiding prolonged exposure to possible vulnerabilities. Algorithmic hardening adds an extra degree of protection by applying cryptographic hash functions, like SHA-256, to the inputs and outputs of public key polynomials. In the context of parameter optimization, tangible approaches include using a 3-layer Rainbow structure and increasing the finite field size to $\mathbb{K}_{2^{16}}$. The cryptographic strength of $\mathcal{H}$ determines the features of the transformed polynomial $P'(x) = \mathcal{H}(P(x))$, if $\mathcal{H}$ is a hash function. The original polynomial cannot be retrieved by an adversary in significant time. A further way to improve security is to incorporate components from other cryptographic hard problems, like linear codes.

By employing a larger and more complicated base field and changing parameters to make low-rank solutions more difficult to discover, it is required to increase the minimum rank of the matrices involved in order to counteract specific attacks such as the rectangular min-rank attack. To break up the regularity that min-rank attack take advantage of, introduce random perturbations to the polynomial coefficients. Simple algebraic attacks, on the other hand, are not feasible unless the system of equations is sufficiently complex and overrefined. It's also beneficial to apply secure masking techniques to obscure the system architecture. Additionally, applying a layer-splitting technique, where variables in specific layers are obscured, complicates Beullens' key reconstruction efforts. Inspired by the VDOO [18] technique, integrating a "diagonal layer" into the oil-and-vinegar structure enhances resistance to Intersection attacks by adding complexity. VDOO has three main advantages over existing UOV schemes and Rainbow: security, efficiency, and flexibility. The diagonal layer of the UOV framework shows how VDOO improves efficiency without sacrificing security. In addition to offering EUF-CMA protection, VDOO successfully repels all active threats. It performs well compared to NIST-standardized post-quantum signatures, achieving an astonishingly shortest signature size of 96 bytes with proper parameter choice (NIST SL-I).

Hence by employing these techniques and the same architecture that lite-Rainbow has been used for decreasing the key sizes, we can obtained a probable secure and lightweight signature scheme based on MQ-problem.

6 Conclusion

In this work, we used Beullens' simple attack and the rectangle min-rank attack to examine the lightweight Rainbow signature scheme and found several serious security flaws. To address these, we suggested a number of countermeasures, including hidden affine transformations, random modifications, higher-rank matrices, and improved parameter selection. The scheme is strengthened against attacks by these steps. Finding the ideal settings that strike a compromise between security and efficiency, researching novel attack techniques, and making sure the scheme remains safe from quantum computing threats are all crucial for future research. Moreover, multivariate signature schemes will be made even more secure and user-friendly by merging them with other cryptographic techniques, creating quick and safe implementations for real-world use—especially on low-resource devices—and collaborating with standards organizations to improve and validate the scheme in practical settings.

The cryptanalysis of the Lite-Rainbow signature scheme, a lightweight protocol based on the multivariate quadratic (MQ) problem, has revealed vulnerabilities when subjected to rectangular MinRank and simple attacks. These findings highlight the importance of continuous scrutiny of cryptographic schemes, particularly those designed for resource-constrained environments, to ensure their robustness against emerging threats.

Future research in multivariate public key cryptography should focus on developing countermeasures to enhance the resilience of MQ-based schemes against known and emerging attacks. Additionally, exploring new MQ-based schemes, improving their efficiency, and ensuring their suitability for post-quantum cryptography are critical areas of interest. Practical implementations in various environments will also be essential to validating these schemes' security and performance in real-world scenarios.

References

1. Baena, J., Briaud, P., Cabarcas, D., Perlner, R., Smith-Tone, D., Verbel, J.: Improving support-minors rank attacks: applications to GeMSS and rainbow. In: Annual International Cryptology Conference, pp. 376–405. Springer (2022)
2. Bardet, M., et al.: Improvements of algebraic attacks for solving the rank decoding and MinRank problems. In: Moriai, S., Wang, H. (eds.) ASIACRYPT 2020. LNCS, vol. 12491, pp. 507–536. Springer, Cham (2020). https://doi.org/10.1007/978-3-030-64837-4_17
3. Bernstein, D.J., Lange, T.: Post-quantum cryptography. Nature **549**(7671), 188–194 (2017)
4. Beullens, W.: Improved cryptanalysis of UOV and rainbow. In: Annual International Conference on the Theory and Applications of Cryptographic Techniques, pp. 348–373. Springer (2021)
5. Beullens, W.: Mayo: practical post-quantum signatures from oil-and-vinegar maps. In: International Conference on Selected Areas in Cryptography, pp. 355–376. Springer (2021)
6. Beullens, W.: Breaking rainbow takes a weekend on a laptop. In: Annual International Cryptology Conference, pp. 464–479. Springer (2022)
7. Billet, O., Gilbert, H.: Cryptanalysis of rainbow. In: De Prisco, R., Yung, M. (eds.) SCN 2006. LNCS, vol. 4116, pp. 336–347. Springer, Heidelberg (2006). https://doi.org/10.1007/11832072_23
8. Buchberger, B.: Ein algorithmus zum auffinden der basiselemente des restklassenringes nach einem nulldimensionalen polynomideal. Ph. D. Thesis, Math. Inst., University of Innsbruck (1965)
9. Cartor, R., Cartor, M., Lewis, M., Smith-Tone, D.: Iprainbow. In: International Conference on Post-Quantum Cryptography, pp. 170–184. Springer (2022)
10. Courtois, N., Klimov, A., Patarin, J., Shamir, A.: Efficient algorithms for solving overdefined systems of multivariate polynomial equations. In: International Conference on the Theory and Applications of Cryptographic Techniques, pp. 392–407. Springer (2000)

11. Dey, J., Dutta, R.: Progress in multivariate cryptography: systematic review, challenges, and research directions. ACM Comput. Surv. **55**(12), 1–34 (2023)
12. Ding, J., Deaton, J., Vishakha, Yang, B.Y.: The nested subset differential attack: a practical direct attack against luov which forges a signature within 210 minutes. In: Annual International Conference on the Theory and Applications of Cryptographic Techniques, pp. 329–347. Springer (2021)
13. Ding, J., Gower, J.E., Schmidt, D.S.: Multivariate public-key cryptosystems. In: International conference on the Algebra and its application, pp. 79–94. Springer (2005)
14. Ding, J., Hu, L., Nie, X., Li, J., Wagner, J.: High order linearization equation (hole) attack on multivariate public key cryptosystems. In: International Workshop on Public Key Cryptography, pp. 233–248. Springer (2007)
15. Ding, J., Schmidt, D.: Rainbow, a new multivariable polynomial signature scheme. In: International Conference on Applied Cryptography and Network Security, pp. 164–175. Springer (2005)
16. Ding, J., Yang, B.-Y., Chen, C.-H.O., Chen, M.-S., Cheng, C.-M.: New differential-algebraic attacks and reparametrization of rainbow. In: Bellovin, S.M., Gennaro, R., Keromytis, A., Yung, M. (eds.) ACNS 2008. LNCS, vol. 5037, pp. 242–257. Springer, Heidelberg (2008). https://doi.org/10.1007/978-3-540-68914-0_15
17. Fouque, P.A., Granboulan, L., Stern, J.: Differential cryptanalysis for multivariate schemes. In: Annual International Conference on the Theory and Applications of Cryptographic Techniques, pp. 341–353. Springer (2005)
18. Ganguly, A., Karmakar, A., Saxena, N.: Vdoo: A short, fast, post-quantum multivariate digital signature scheme. In: International Conference on Cryptology in India, pp. 197–222. Springer (2023)
19. Goubin, L., Courtois, N.T.: Cryptanalysis of the TTM cryptosystem. In: Okamoto, T. (ed.) ASIACRYPT 2000. LNCS, vol. 1976, pp. 44–57. Springer, Heidelberg (2000). https://doi.org/10.1007/3-540-44448-3_4
20. Hogben, L.: Minimum rank problems. Linear Algebra Appl. **432**(8), 1961–1974 (2010)
21. Ikematsu, Y., Nakamura, S., Takagi, T.: Recent progress in the security evaluation of multivariate public-key cryptography. IET Inf. Secur. **17**(2), 210–226 (2023)
22. Kipnis, A., Patarin, J., Goubin, L.: Unbalanced oil and vinegar signature schemes. In: International Conference on the Theory and Applications of Cryptographic Techniques, pp. 206–222. Springer (1999)
23. Kipnis, A., Shamir, A.: Cryptanalysis of the oil and vinegar signature scheme. In: Krawczyk, H. (ed.) CRYPTO 1998. LNCS, vol. 1462, pp. 257–266. Springer, Heidelberg (1998). https://doi.org/10.1007/BFb0055733
24. Koblitz, N.: Elliptic curve cryptosystems. Math. Comput. **48**(177), 203–209 (1987)
25. Kravitz, D.W.: Digital signature algorithm. uS Patent 5,231,668. Accessed 27 Jul 1993
26. Nakamura, S., Wang, Y., Ikematsu, Y.: Analysis on the MinRank attack using Kipnis-Shamir method against rainbow. Cryptology ePrint Archive (2020)
27. Peng, Z., Tang, S.: Circulant rainbow: a new rainbow variant with shorter private key and faster signature generation. IEEE Access **5**, 11877–11886 (2017)
28. Perlner, R., Smith-Tone, D.: Rainbow band separation is better than we thought. Cryptology ePrint Archive (2020)
29. Petzoldt, A., Bulygin, S., Buchmann, J.: Cyclicrainbow–a multivariate signature scheme with a partially cyclic public key. In: Progress in Cryptology-INDOCRYPT 2010: 11th International Conference on Cryptology in India, Hyderabad, India, December 12-15 2010. Proceedings 11, pp. 33–48. Springer (2010)

30. Petzoldt, A., Bulygin, S., Buchmann, J.: Selecting parameters for the rainbow signature scheme. In: Sendrier, N. (ed.) PQCrypto 2010. LNCS, vol. 6061, pp. 218–240. Springer, Heidelberg (2010). https://doi.org/10.1007/978-3-642-12929-2_16
31. Petzoldt, A., Chen, M.S., Yang, B.Y., Tao, C., Ding, J.: Design principles for HFEv-based multivariate signature schemes. In: Advances in Cryptology–ASIACRYPT 2015: 21st International Conference on the Theory and Application of Cryptology and Information Security, Auckland, New Zealand, November 29–December 3 2015, Proceedings, Part I 21, pp. 311–334. Springer (2015)
32. RGarey, M., Johnson, D.: Computers and intractability, a guide to the theory of NP-completeness (1979)
33. Rivest, R.L., Shamir, A., Adleman, L.: A method for obtaining digital signatures and public-key cryptosystems. Commun. ACM **21**(2), 120–126 (1978)
34. Shen, R., Xiang, H., Zhang, X., Cai, B., Xiang, T.: Application and implementation of multivariate public key cryptosystem in blockchain (short paper). In: Collaborative Computing: Networking, Applications and Worksharing: 15th EAI International Conference, CollaborateCom 2019, London, UK, August 19–22 2019, Proceedings 15, pp. 419–428. Springer (2019)
35. Shim, K.-A., Park, C.-M., Baek, Y.-J.: Lite-rainbow: lightweight signature schemes based on multivariate quadratic equations and their secure implementations. In: Biryukov, A., Goyal, V. (eds.) INDOCRYPT 2015. LNCS, vol. 9462, pp. 45–63. Springer, Cham (2015). https://doi.org/10.1007/978-3-319-26617-6_3
36. Shor, P.W.: Polynomial-time algorithms for prime factorization and discrete logarithms on a quantum computer. SIAM Rev. **41**(2), 303–332 (1999)
37. Wang, Y., Ikematsu, Y., Nakamura, S., Takagi, T.: Revisiting the MinRank problem on multivariate cryptography. In: You, I. (ed.) WISA 2020. LNCS, vol. 12583, pp. 291–307. Springer, Cham (2020). https://doi.org/10.1007/978-3-030-65299-9_22

Boolean Functions

Construction of Boolean Functions with $2k$-Valued Walsh Spectrum and High Nonlinearity

A. U. Zeenath[1], K. V. Lakshmy[2](✉), and Chungath Srinivasan[2]

[1] Department of Mathematics, Amrita School of Physical Sciences,
Amrita Vishwa Vidyapeetham, Coimbatore 641112, India
au_zeenath@cb.students.amrita.edu
[2] TIFAC CORE in Cyber Security, Amrita School of Engineering,
Amrita Vishwa Vidyapeetham, Coimbatore 641112, India
{kv_lakshmy,c_srinivasan}@cb.amrita.edu

Abstract. Highly nonlinear balanced Boolean functions are of the essential primary cryptographic primitives in symmetric design. The Walsh transform serves as a crucial tool for understanding the cryptographic characteristics of Boolean functions. This paper introduces a method for constructing a class of Boolean functions with at most $2k$ values in their Walsh spectrum and exhibiting high nonlinearity, using the Maiorana-McFarland bent function. The cryptographic properties and distribution of Walsh coefficients are thoroughly examined for this category of Boolean functions, specifically focusing on the case where $k = 4$. Additionally, a subclass is developed within the aforementioned set of Boolean functions, where the Hamming weight of each member equals its nonlinearity, which is achieved through the imposition of certain constraints during the construction. Boolean functions serve as essential building blocks for constructing binary linear codes, with Reed-Muller codes and Kerdock codes emerging as prominent examples within this domain. This method generates a class of functions which can be used for construction of binary linear codes.

Keywords: Boolean function · Walsh transform · Nonlinearity · Correlation immunity · Resiliency · Maiorana-McFarland class bent functions · $2k$-valued Walsh spectrum

1 Introduction

Boolean functions are the major building blocks of symmetric cryptographic systems. The functions with good cryptographic features such as balancedness, high nonlinearity, high algebraic degree, optimal algebraic immunity and correlation immunity are used for designing S-boxes, nonlinear filters, and combiners, as each of these cryptographic properties essentially strengthens the cryptographic design against specific cryptanalytic attacks [16,19]. To resist the linear attacks, the underlying Boolean functions used in the ciphers should have high nonlinearity and to resist algebraic attack introduced by Meier et al., it should have high algebraic immunity. Siegenthaler in 1985 introduced a new concept called correlation immunity with reference to correlation attacks. Hence, a secure design should have a good order of correlation immunity along with the aforementioned immunities. It is important to note that there is some trade-off among the cryptographic properties.

The highest possible nonlinearity of an n-variable Boolean function is $2^{n-1} - 2^{\frac{n}{2}-1}$. The bent functions, introduced by O. Rothaus in 1976 [1], achieved maximum possible nonlinearity, however they can exist only for even n. These functions have several research interests [20] due to their simple definition, interesting combinatorial characteristics, and various applications in coding theory and cryptography. Although bent functions have the maximum nonlinearity, they are not balanced, making them unfit for direct use in cryptography. As a consequence, cryptographers began searching for new classes of balanced Boolean functions with good nonlinearity for both odd and even numbers of variables.

Partially bent functions, a new class of Boolean functions, were identified by Carlet in 1993 [3]. These functions are balanced and can have high nonlinearity. Even though the functions in this class have the desirable properties like high nonlinearity, balancedness, resiliency and propagation characteristics it has nonzero linear structures. This motivated Zheng et al. [4] to determine other class of Boolean functions called plateaued functions as good candidates for designing cryptographic functions. An n-variable Boolean function f is said to be plateaued if its Walsh transform takes only three different values namely $0, \pm\lambda$, where λ is a positive integer, called amplitude of the plateaued function. Plateaued functions with amplitude $\lambda = \frac{2^{n+s}}{2}$ are called s-plateaued functions. It has been shown in [2] the nonlinearity of an s-plateaued function is $2^{n-1} - 2^{\frac{n-s}{2}-1}$.

Rotation symmetric Boolean functions are a class of Boolean functions that remain invariant under cyclic permutations of their input variables. In recent years, rotation symmetric Boolean functions have received significant attention due to their widespread applications in cryptography ([13,18]). Rotation symmetric Boolean functions (RSBFs) were first introduced by Pieprzyk and Qu in 1999 [17]. They have been used as integral components in hashing algorithms to optimize the implementation of cryptographic hash functions, aiming to enhance efficiency and security in information security protocols. A special character of RSBFs is that its Walsh transform values are same in an orbit formed by all cyclic rotation of one input variable. Let g_n be the number of distinct orbits, then the Walsh spectrum of a RSBF contains at most g_n different values. Construction and enumeration of rotation symmetric Boolean functions with good cryptographic properties are important research areas in cryptography [23].

Identifying Boolean functions based on the number of different Walsh coefficients is a nontrivial exercise. Erdener Uyan [5] partially solved the problem of enumerating Boolean functions with specified number of particular Walsh coefficients in their Walsh spectrum. Xiwang Cao, Lei Hu [15] proposed a new method for constructing new balanced Boolean functions with at most five valued Walsh spectra and high nonlinearity. They proved that the Walsh spectrum values of these functions are divisible by $2^{\frac{n}{2}}$ and nonlinearity is greater than or equal to $2^{n-1} - 3 \cdot 2^{\frac{n}{2}-1}$. This nonlinearity is close to the maximum nonlinearity. Guangkui Xu et al. in 2015 [7] discovered several new classes of Boolean functions whose Walsh spectrum contains few values. They constructed these Boolean functions by adding linear functions with the known classes of bent functions. In [8], Sun Zhejiang and Hu Lei determined a class of functions whose spectrum contains four different Walsh transform values. Wengang Jin et al. [9] extended the work to Boolean functions having six different Walsh coefficients.

Inspired by above research on Boolean functions characterized by a limited number of Walsh transform values, we derive a general method for constructing new class of Boolean functions having high nonlinearity and whose Walsh spectrum has at most $2k$ different values. We illustrate this approach by providing a class of functions with at most eight-values in its Walsh spectrum. Additionally, we determine the distribution of their Walsh spectrum and investigate the cryptographic properties of this class of functions. Given a Boolean function f, the *Hamming weight* $wt(f)$ and the nonlinearity N_f are well known to be important in designing functions that are useful in cryptography. Boolean functions having nonlinearity same as its *Hamming weight* are one of the interesting research topic in cryptography [24]. Additionally, we derive a necessary and sufficient condition for Boolean functions to possess a nonlinearity equal to their *Hamming weight*.

The notations and basic concepts about Boolean functions are given in Sect. 2. In Sect. 3, we describe our method for constructing Boolean functions with at most $2k$ values in their Walsh spectrum and determined their cryptographic properties. We illustrate this approach by providing a family of Boolean functions with at most eight different Walsh coefficients in their spectrum. Additionally, we determine the distribution of their Walsh coefficients and investigate the cryptographic significance of this family of Boolean functions. Cryptographic characteristics and uses of this family of Boolean functions are described in Sect. 4. In Sect. 5, we discuss a subclass of these Boolean functions which have the same weight and nonlinearity. We conclude the paper with Sect. 6.

2 Preliminaries

We recall the necessary background knowledge of Boolean functions in this section. Let $\mathbb{F}_2 = \{0,1\}$ be the finite field with two elements and $\mathbb{F}_2^n$ be the n-dimensional vector space over $\mathbb{F}_2$. A map f from $\mathbb{F}_2^n \to \mathbb{F}_2$ is called a Boolean function. Boolean functions are usually defined by its truth table, which is the sequence of bits of length 2^n composed of outputs of all vectors in $\mathbb{F}_2^n$. The inner product of two vectors $\boldsymbol{x} = (x_1, x_2, ..., x_n)$ and $\boldsymbol{y} = (y_1, y_2, ..., y_n) \in \mathbb{F}_2^n$ is defined as

$$x \cdot y = \bigoplus_{i=1}^{n} x_i y_i$$

Given an n-variable Boolean function f on $\mathbb{F}_2^n$, it can be uniquely represented by a multivariate polynomial over $\mathbb{F}_2$ of the form

$$f(x_1, x_2, \ldots, x_n) = \bigoplus_{v \in \mathbb{F}_2^n} a_v x_1^{v_1} \ldots x_n^{v_n}; v = (v_1, v_2, \ldots, v_n)$$

This representation is called Algebraic Normal Form (ANF) of f, and the algebraic degree of f is defined as the global degree of this polynomial, indicated by $deg(f)$. i.e.,

$$deg(f) = max\{wt(v) : a_v \neq (0, \ldots, 0)\},$$

where $wt(v)$ is the number of ones occurred in v. The set of all n-variable Boolean functions is denoted by $\mathcal{B}_n$. The n-variable Boolean functions of the form $f(x) = a_0 \oplus a_1 x_1 \oplus a_2 x_2 \oplus \cdots \oplus a_n x_n$ with $a_i \in \mathbb{F}_2 : 0 \leq i \leq n$; are called the affine functions. The set of all n-variable affine functions is denoted as $\mathcal{A}_n$. The affine functions with zero constant terms are called linear functions. The collection of all n-variable linear functions is represented as $\mathcal{L}_n$. The number of $x \in \mathbb{F}_2^n$ such that $f(x) = 1$ is defined as the *Hamming weight* of the Boolean function f, denoted by $wt(f)$. The support of a Boolean function f, denoted by $supp(f)$ is defined as the set $\{x \in \mathbb{F}_2^n : f(x) = 1\}$. It is clear that the *Hamming weight* of a Boolean function f is the cardinality of the set $supp(f)$. A Boolean function f is balanced if its truth table contains equal number of 0's and 1's, i.e., $|supp(f)| = 2^{n-1}$.

For two Boolean functions $f, g \in \mathcal{B}_n$, the *Hamming distance* between them is defined by $d(f, g) = wt(f \oplus g)$. The nonlinearity of a Boolean function $f \in \mathcal{B}_n$ is defined as the minimum *Hamming distance* between f and the set of all affine functions $\mathcal{A}_n$, denoted by N_f. The Walsh transform of $f(x)$ (denoted as W_f) is an integer valued function from $\mathbb{F}_2^n$ and it defined as

$$W_f(\alpha) = \sum_{y \in \mathbb{F}_2^n} (-1)^{f(y) \oplus \alpha \cdot y}$$

For a Boolean function f, the set $\{W_f(x_1, x_2, \ldots, x_n) : (x_1, x_2, \ldots, x_n) \in \mathbb{F}_2^n\}$ of length 2^n is defined as the Walsh spectrum of f. Each component $W_f(\alpha)$ of a Boolean function f is called a Walsh coefficient of f. The Walsh transform is a common technique for understanding the properties of Boolean functions. The nonlinearity of a Boolean function can be defined in terms of Walsh transform values [21]. Let f be a Boolean function, then its nonlinearity in terms of Walsh transform is defined as

$$N_f = 2^{n-1} - \frac{1}{2} \max_{x \in \mathbb{F}_2^n} |W_f(x)| \tag{1}$$

We can characterize balanced Boolean functions by their Walsh coefficient at $(0, 0, \ldots, 0)$, i.e., an n-variable Boolean functions f is balanced if and only if

$W_f(\mathbf{0},\mathbf{0},\ldots,\mathbf{0}) = 0$. Let $\mathbf{0}_n$ and $\mathbf{1}_n$ denote the all 0's and all 1's vectors of $\mathbb{F}_2^n$ respectively. The Walsh spectrum of bent function contains only two values, $\pm 2^{\frac{n}{2}}$. Bent functions occur in pairs. Let $f \in \mathcal{B}_n$ is a bent function, then the dual $\tilde{f}$ of f, defined by,

$$W_f(\omega) = (-1)^{\tilde{f}(\omega)} 2^{\frac{n}{2}}$$

is also bent. A Boolean function $f \in \mathcal{B}_n$ is m^{th} order correlation immune if it is statistically independent of any m of its input variables. Correlation immunity is a security measure to analyze the resistance of a Boolean function against the correlation attack on stream ciphers. The famous Xiao-Massey characterization [22] of mth order correlation immune Boolean function is that, $W_f(\omega) = 0$ for all $\alpha \in \mathbb{F}_2^n$ with $1 \leq wt(\alpha) \leq m$. A balanced Boolean function of mth order correlation immunity is called m-resilient Boolean function.

3 Boolean Functions with $2k$-Valued Walsh Spectrum

Let $g(\mathbf{x})$ be an n-variable ($n = 2m \geq 6$) bent function. For any $k-1$ distinct vectors $\mathbf{x}_1, \mathbf{x}_2, \ldots, \mathbf{x}_{k-1} \in \mathbb{F}_2^n \backslash \{\mathbf{0}_n\}$, we define the Boolean function $G(\mathbf{x})$ by

$$G(\mathbf{x}) = \begin{cases} g(\mathbf{x}) & \text{if } \mathbf{x} \in \mathbb{F}_2^n \backslash \{\mathbf{0}_n, \mathbf{x}_1, \mathbf{x}_2, \ldots, \mathbf{x}_{k-1}\} \\ g(\mathbf{x}) \oplus 1 & \text{if } \mathbf{x} \in \{\mathbf{0}_n, \mathbf{x}_1, \mathbf{x}_2, \ldots, \mathbf{x}_{k-1}\} \end{cases} \quad (2)$$

Lemma 1. *The Walsh coefficient of $G(\mathbf{x})$ at $\alpha = (\alpha_1, \alpha_2, \ldots, \alpha_n) \in \mathbb{F}_2^n$ is given by*

$$W_G(\alpha) = W_g(\alpha) - 2[(-1)^{g(\mathbf{0}_n)} + \sum_{i=1}^{k-1} (-1)^{g(\mathbf{x}_i) \oplus \alpha \cdot \mathbf{x}_i}]$$

Proof. Let $M = \{\mathbf{0}_n, \mathbf{x}_1, \mathbf{x}_2, \ldots, \mathbf{x}_{k-1}\}$. From the definition of Walsh transform,

$$W_G(\alpha) = \sum_{\mathbf{x} \in \mathbb{F}_2^n} (-1)^{G(\mathbf{x}) \oplus \alpha \cdot \mathbf{x}}$$

$$= \sum_{\mathbf{x} \in \mathbb{F}_2^n \backslash M} (-1)^{g(\mathbf{x}) \oplus \alpha \cdot \mathbf{x}} + \sum_{\mathbf{x} \in M} (-1)^{g(\mathbf{x}) \oplus 1 \oplus \alpha \cdot \mathbf{x}}$$

$$= \sum_{\mathbf{x} \in \mathbb{F}_2^n} (-1)^{g(\mathbf{x}) \oplus \alpha \cdot \mathbf{x}} - 2 \sum_{\mathbf{x} \in M} (-1)^{g(\mathbf{x}) \oplus \alpha \cdot \mathbf{x}}$$

$$= W_g(\alpha) - 2[(-1)^{g(\mathbf{0}_n)} + \sum_{i=1}^{k-1} (-1)^{g(\mathbf{x}_i) \oplus \alpha \cdot \mathbf{x}_i}]$$

Theorem 1. *Let g be an n-variable bent function. Then the function $G(\mathbf{x})$ defined in (2) will have at most $2k$ distinct values in its Walsh spectrum.*

Proof. For any $\alpha \in \mathbb{F}_2^n$, let $\varepsilon = \tilde{g}(\alpha)$, where $\tilde{g}$ be the dual of g, $\varepsilon \in \{0,1\}$ and $b_i = \alpha \cdot x_i \oplus g(x_i)$, for $i = 1, 2, ..., k-1$. Let $\beta = (b_1, b_2, ..., b_{k-1})$, then based on Lemma 1 and the definition of $\tilde{g}$, the Walsh coefficients of $G(x)$ in (2) is given by,

$$W_G(\alpha) = \begin{cases} (-1)^\varepsilon 2^m - 2\,(k - 2\,wt(\beta)) & ;\ g((0,0,\ldots,0)) = 0 \\ (-1)^\varepsilon 2^m - 2\,(k - 2\,(wt(\beta)+1)) & ;\ otherwise \end{cases}$$

where $0 \leq wt(\beta) \leq k-1$, hence the Walsh spectrum contains at most $2k$ distinct values.

The complement of a bent function is again a bent function. Therefore, without loss of generality, here we choose a bent function g which satisfies $g(\mathbf{0}_n) = 0$.

Definition 1. *[21] Consider $\mathbb{F}_2^n$ as $\mathbb{F}_2^m \times \mathbb{F}_2^m = \{(u,v) : u,v \in \mathbb{F}_2^m\}$, where $n = 2m$. Let σ be an arbitrary permutation on the set $\mathbb{F}_2^m$ and h be an arbitrary m-variable Boolean function. The function f defined by $f(u,v) = u \cdot \sigma(v) \oplus h(v)$ is an n-variable bent function. The set of all n-variable bent functions this form is called Maiorana-McFarland class ($\mathcal{MM}$-class) bent functions. The dual of $f(u,v)$ is $\tilde{f}(u,v) = v \cdot \sigma^{-1}(u) + h(\sigma^{-1}(u))$, where σ^{-1} is the inverse of σ.*

3.1 Construction

Let $g(x,y)$ be an n-variable ($n = 2m$) $\mathcal{MM}$-class bent function. Let $S = \{(\mathbf{0}_m, \mathbf{0}_m), (x_1, y_1), ..., (x_{k-1}, y_{k-1})\}$ be a subset of $\mathbb{F}_2^m \times \mathbb{F}_2^m$. Then by Theorem 1, the function $G(x, y)$ defined by,

$$G(x,y) = \begin{cases} g(x,y) & \text{if } (x,y) \in \mathbb{F}_2^m \times \mathbb{F}_2^m \backslash S \\ g(x,y) \oplus 1 & \text{if } (x,y) \in S \end{cases} \quad (3)$$

will have at most $2k$ distinct values in its Walsh spectrum.

3.2 Cryptographic Properties

The Walsh transform is used for analyzing and understanding the cryptographic properties of Boolean functions. We discuss cryptographic properties of the Boolean function $G(x,y)$ in (3) and its applications in this section.

Recall that the characterization of balanced function in terms of Walsh transform is that the Walsh coefficient at zero is zero. According to Theorem 1, the spectrum of $G(x,y)$ at $(u,v) \in \mathbb{F}_2^m \times \mathbb{F}_2^m$ in (3) can take only the values from the set $\{(-1)^\varepsilon 2^m - 2\,(k - 2\,wt(\beta)) : 0 \leq wt(\beta) \leq k-1\}$, here $\beta = (b_1, b_2, ..., b_{k-1})$ and $b_i = (u,v) \cdot (x_i, y_i) \oplus g(x_i, y_i)$.

If $0 \in \{(-1)^\varepsilon 2^m - 2\ (k-2\ wt(\boldsymbol{\beta})) : 0 \leq wt(\boldsymbol{\beta}) \leq k-1\}$ then $(-1)^\varepsilon 2^m - 2\ (k-2\ wt(\boldsymbol{\beta})) = 0$; or $k - 2wt(\boldsymbol{\beta}) = (-1)^\varepsilon 2^{m-1}$; for some $\boldsymbol{\beta}$. Hence k must be even and $wt(\boldsymbol{\beta}) = \frac{k-(-1)^\varepsilon 2^{m-1}}{2}$. Since the balanced functions have spectrum value zero at zero, we must have k even.

4 Boolean Functions with Eight-Valued Walsh Spectrum

To illustrate the proposed method, we present an example demonstrating its application in deriving a class of Boolean functions with at most eight values in their Walsh spectrum.

4.1 Construction

Let $g(\boldsymbol{x}, \boldsymbol{y})$ be an n-variable ($n = 2m$) $\mathcal{MM}$ class bent function and define $G(x, y)$ by,

$$G(\boldsymbol{x}, \boldsymbol{y}) = \begin{cases} g(\boldsymbol{x}, \boldsymbol{y}) & \text{if } (\boldsymbol{x}, \boldsymbol{y}) \in \mathbb{F}_2{}^m \times \mathbb{F}_2{}^m \setminus \{(\boldsymbol{0}, \boldsymbol{0}), (\boldsymbol{a}, \boldsymbol{b}), (\boldsymbol{p}, \boldsymbol{q}), (\boldsymbol{r}, \boldsymbol{s})\} \\ g(\boldsymbol{x}, \boldsymbol{y}) \oplus 1 & \text{if } (\boldsymbol{x}, \boldsymbol{y}) \in \{(\boldsymbol{0}, \boldsymbol{0}), (\boldsymbol{a}, \boldsymbol{b}), (\boldsymbol{p}, \boldsymbol{q}), (\boldsymbol{r}, \boldsymbol{s})\} \end{cases}$$
(4)

Here $\boldsymbol{a}, \boldsymbol{b}, \boldsymbol{p}, \boldsymbol{q}, \boldsymbol{r}$ and $\boldsymbol{s} \in \mathbb{F}_2^m$ with $\{\boldsymbol{b}, \boldsymbol{q}, \boldsymbol{s}\}$ is linearly independent. Then $G(\boldsymbol{x}, \boldsymbol{y})$ is Boolean function with at most eight values in its Walsh spectrum and it follows from Lemma 1 that the Walsh spectrum of $G(\boldsymbol{x}, \boldsymbol{y})$ is $\{(-1)^\varepsilon 2^m - 8, (-1)^\varepsilon 2^m - 4, (-1)^\varepsilon 2^m, (-1)^\varepsilon 2^m + 4\}$. For the function $G(\boldsymbol{x}, \boldsymbol{y})$, we have the following theorem, which provides insight into the distribution of its Walsh spectrum.

Theorem 2. *Let $g(\boldsymbol{x}, \boldsymbol{y}) = \boldsymbol{x} \cdot \sigma(\boldsymbol{y}) \oplus h(\boldsymbol{y})$ is an n-variable $\mathcal{MM}$-bent function and let $h(\boldsymbol{0}_m) = 0$ and $\sigma(\boldsymbol{0}_m) = 0$. Then the number of occurrence of each Walsh coefficients of $G(\boldsymbol{x}, \boldsymbol{y})$ is of the form $2^{n-4} + \alpha\ 2^{m-1} + \mu\ 2^{m-2} + \gamma\ 2^{m-3}$, where α, μ and $\gamma \in \{-1, 0, 1\}$.*

Proof. By Lemma (1) and Eq. (3), to find out the distribution of Walsh coefficients of $G(\boldsymbol{x}, \boldsymbol{y})$, we have to determine the number of $(\boldsymbol{u}, \boldsymbol{v}) \in \mathbb{F}_2^m \times \mathbb{F}_2^m$ such that (y_1, y_2, y_3) span $\mathbb{F}_2^3$, where $y_1 = (\boldsymbol{u}, \boldsymbol{v}) \cdot (\boldsymbol{a}, \boldsymbol{b}) \oplus g(\boldsymbol{a}, \boldsymbol{b})$; $y_2 = (\boldsymbol{u}, \boldsymbol{v}) \cdot (\boldsymbol{p}, \boldsymbol{q}) \oplus g(\boldsymbol{p}, \boldsymbol{q})$; $y_3 = (\boldsymbol{u}, \boldsymbol{v}) \cdot (\boldsymbol{r}, \boldsymbol{s}) \oplus g(\boldsymbol{r}, \boldsymbol{s})$. Let N be the number of $(\boldsymbol{u}, \boldsymbol{v}) \in \mathbb{F}_2^n$ such that $W_G(\boldsymbol{u}, \boldsymbol{v}) = 2^m - 8$. And let $\varepsilon = \tilde{g}(\boldsymbol{u}, \boldsymbol{v}) = 0$. Since $h(\boldsymbol{0}_m) = \sigma(\boldsymbol{0}_m) = 0$, we only need to enumerate the solutions of the following system of equations:

$$\begin{cases} \sigma^{-1}(\boldsymbol{u}) \cdot \boldsymbol{v} = h(\sigma^{-1}(\boldsymbol{u})) \\ \boldsymbol{b} \cdot \boldsymbol{v} = \boldsymbol{a} \cdot \sigma(\boldsymbol{b}) + h(\boldsymbol{b}) + \boldsymbol{a} \cdot \boldsymbol{u} \\ \boldsymbol{q} \cdot \boldsymbol{v} = \boldsymbol{p} \cdot \sigma(\boldsymbol{q}) + h(\boldsymbol{q}) + \boldsymbol{p} \cdot \boldsymbol{u} \\ \boldsymbol{s} \cdot \boldsymbol{v} = \boldsymbol{r} \cdot \sigma(\boldsymbol{s}) + h(\boldsymbol{s}) + \boldsymbol{r} \cdot \boldsymbol{u} \end{cases}$$
(5)

To determine the number of solutions for the given system of equations, we will divide our analysis into the following distinct cases.

Case 1: $\sigma^{-1}(u) = 0_m$ i.e., $u = 0_m$, Eq. 5 reduced to

$$\begin{cases} b \cdot v = a \cdot \sigma(b) + h(b) \\ q \cdot v = p \cdot \sigma(q) + h(q) \\ s \cdot v = r \cdot \sigma(s) + h(s) \end{cases} \quad (6)$$

Since b, q and s are linearly independent, the above system has 2^{m-3} solutions. Therefore, $N = 2^{m-3}$.

Case 2: If $\sigma^{-1}(u) \in \{b, q, s\}$, then also we get $N = 2^{m-3}$ using the proof similar to the **Case 1**.

Case 3: $\sigma^{-1}(u) \in \{b+q, q+s, b+s\}$. Suppose $\sigma^{-1}(u) = b+q$. i.e., $u = \sigma(b+q)$, then the system in (5) will change to

$$\begin{cases} (b+q) \cdot v = h(b+q) \\ b \cdot v = a \cdot \sigma(b) + h(b) + a \cdot \sigma(b+q) \\ q \cdot v = p \cdot \sigma(q) + h(q) + p \cdot \sigma(b+q) \\ s \cdot v = r \cdot \sigma(s) + h(s) + r \cdot \sigma(b+q) \end{cases} \quad (7)$$

Then the system has 2^{m-3} solution if $h(b+q) = a \cdot \sigma(b) + h(b) + a \cdot \sigma(b+q) + p \cdot \sigma(q) + h(q) + p \cdot \sigma(b+q)$ and zero otherwise. Similarly if $\sigma^{-1}(u) = q+s$, then the system has 2^{m-3} solutions if $h(q+s) = p \cdot \sigma(q) + h(q) + p \cdot \sigma(q+s) + r \cdot \sigma(s) + h(s) + r \cdot \sigma(q+s)$ and zero otherwise. If $\sigma^{-1}(u) = b+s$, then also the system has 2^{m-3} solutions if $h(b+s) = a \cdot \sigma(b) + h(b) + a \cdot \sigma(b+s) + r \cdot \sigma(s) + h(s) + r \cdot \sigma(b+s)$ and zero otherwise.

Case 4: $\sigma^{-1}(u) = b+q+s$, then there are 2^{m-3} solutions if $h(b+q+s) = a \cdot \sigma(b) + h(b) + a \cdot u + p \cdot \sigma(q) + h(q) + p \cdot u + r \cdot \sigma(s) + h(s) + r \cdot u$ and zero solutions otherwise.

Case 5: If $\sigma^{-1}(u) \notin \{0_m, b, q, s, b+q, b+s, q+s, b+q+s\}$, then $\sigma^{-1}(u)$ is linearly independent to $\{b, q, s\}$. Therefore, the system has 2^{m-4} solutions, and thus $N = 2^{m-4}(2^m - 8) = 2^{n-4} - 2^{m-1}$.

Similarly, we can determine the distribution of Walsh coefficients of the function $G(x, y)$. We summarize the Walsh spectrum distribution in the Tables (1, 2, 3). Throughout this paper, we have taken

$$x_1 = h(b+q) - [a \cdot \sigma(b) + h(b) + a \cdot \sigma(b+q) + p \cdot \sigma(q) + h(q) + p \cdot \sigma(b+q)]$$
$$x_2 = h(q+s) - [p \cdot \sigma(q) + g(q) + p \cdot \sigma(q+s) + r \cdot \sigma(s) + h(s) + r \cdot \sigma(q+s)]$$
$$x_3 = h(b+s) - [a \cdot \sigma(b) + h(b) + a \cdot \sigma(b+s) + r \cdot \sigma(s) + h(s) + r \cdot \sigma(b+s)]$$
$$A = a \cdot \sigma(b) + h(b) + a \cdot \sigma(b+q+s) + p \cdot \sigma(q) + h(q) + p \cdot \sigma(b+q+s) +$$
$$r \cdot \sigma(s) + h(s) + r \cdot \sigma(b+q+s)$$

Table 1. Walsh spectrum distribution of $(-1)^\varepsilon\, 2^m - 8$ and $(-1)^\varepsilon\, 2^m + 4$

$W_G(u,v)$	(x_1,x_2,x_3)	$h(b+q+s) = A$	$h(b+q+s) \neq A$
$(-1)^\varepsilon 2^m - 8$	(0,0,0)	$2^{n-4} + (-1)^\varepsilon\, 2^{m-1}$	$2^{n-4} + (-1)^\varepsilon\, [3.2^{m-3}]$
	(0,0,1)	$2^{n-4} + (-1)^\varepsilon\, [3.2^{m-3}]$	$2^{n-4} + (-1)^\varepsilon\, 2^{m-2}$
	(0,1,0)	$2^{n-4} + (-1)^\varepsilon\, [3.2^{m-3}]$	$2^{n-4} + (-1)^\varepsilon\, 2^{m-2}$
	(0,1,1)	$2^{n-4} + (-1)^\varepsilon\, 2^{m-2}$	$2^{n-4} + (-1)^\varepsilon\, 2^{m-3}$
	(1,0,0)	$2^{n-4} + (-1)^\varepsilon\, [3.2^{m-3}]$	$2^{n-4} + (-1)^\varepsilon\, 2^{m-2}$
	(1,0,1)	$2^{n-4} + (-1)^\varepsilon\, 2^{m-2}$	$2^{n-4} + (-1)^\varepsilon\, 2^{m-3}$
	(1,1,0)	$2^{n-4} + (-1)^\varepsilon\, 2^{m-2}$	$2^{n-4} + (-1)^\varepsilon\, 2^{m-3}$
	(1,1,1)	$2^{n-4} + (-1)^\varepsilon\, 2^{m-3}$	2^{n-4}
$(-1)^\varepsilon 2^m + 4$	(0,0,0)	2^{n-4}	$2^{n-4} + (-1)^\varepsilon\, 2^{m-3}$
	(0,0,1)	$2^{n-4} - (-1)^\varepsilon\, 2^{m-3}$	2^{n-4}
	(0,1,0)	$2^{n-4} - (-1)^\varepsilon\, 2^{m-3}$	2^{n-4}
	(0,1,1)	$2^{n-4} - (-1)^\varepsilon\, 2^{m-2}$	$2^{n-4} - (-1)^\varepsilon\, 2^{m-3}$
	(1,0,0)	$2^{n-4} - (-1)^\varepsilon\, 2^{m-3}$	2^{n-4}
	(1,0,1)	$2^{n-4} - (-1)^\varepsilon\, 2^{m-2}$	$2^{n-4} - (-1)^\varepsilon\, 2^{m-3}$
	(1,1,0)	$2^{n-4} - (-1)^\varepsilon\, 2^{m-2}$	$2^{n-4} - (-1)^\varepsilon\, 2^{m-3}$
	(1,1,1)	$2^{n-4} + (-1)^\varepsilon\, [-3.2^{m-3}]$	$2^{n-4} - (-1)^\varepsilon\, 2^{m-2}$

Walsh Spectrum Distribution of $(-1)^\varepsilon 2^m - 4$:
We know $W_G(u,v) = (-1)^\varepsilon 2^m - 4$ when $(y_1,y_2,y_3) \in \{(1,0,0),(0,1,0),(0,0,1)\}$. To determine the distribution of each Walsh coefficients, we consider the three cases shown in Table 2.

Walsh Spectrum Distribution of $(-1)^\varepsilon\, 2^m$:
Next, we know $W_G(u,v) = (-1)^\varepsilon\, 2^m - 4$ when $(y_1,y_2,y_3) \in \{(1,1,0),(0,1,1),(1,0,1)\}$. To determine the distribution of each Walsh coefficients, here also we consider the three cases shown in Table 3.

4.2 Nonlinearity

Boolean functions are integral to the design of various cryptographic algorithms. A key criterion in their selection is nonlinearity, which significantly influences the security and effectiveness of these algorithms.

Theorem 3. *The nonlinearity N_G of $G(x,y)$ can take only the values $2^{n-1} - 2^{m-1} - 2$ and $2^{n-1} - 2^{m-1} - 4$, where $G(x,y)$ is the function defined by Construction 4.1.*

Proof. Note that for any n-variable Boolean functions h,
$$\max_{x \in \mathbb{F}_2^n} |W_h(x)| \geq 2^{\frac{n}{2}} \text{ (Theorem 3 of [10])}.$$

Table 2. Walsh spectrum distribution of $(-1)^\varepsilon 2^m - 4$

(x_1,x_2,x_3)	$h(b+q+s) = A$ and $\varepsilon \in \{0,1\}$		
	$(y_1,y_2,y_3) = (1,0,0)$	$(y_1,y_2,y_3) = (0,1,0)$	$(y_1,y_2,y_3) = (0,0,1)$
(0,0,0)	2^{n-4}	2^{n-4}	2^{n-4}
(0,0,1)	$2^{n-4} + (-1)^\varepsilon\, 2^{m-3}$	$2^{n-4} - (-1)^\varepsilon\, 2^{m-3}$	$2^{n-4} + (-1)^\varepsilon\, 2^{m-3}$
(0,1,0)	$2^{n-4} - (-1)^\varepsilon\, 2^{m-3}$	$2^{n-4} + (-1)^\varepsilon\, 2^{m-3}$	$2^{n-4} + (-1)^\varepsilon\, 2^{m-3}$
(0,1,1)	2^{n-4}	2^{n-4}	$2^{n-4} + (-1)^\varepsilon\, 2^{m-2}$
(1,0,0)	$2^{n-4} + (-1)^\varepsilon\, 2^{m-3}$	$2^{n-4} + (-1)^\varepsilon\, 2^{m-3}$	$2^{n-4} - (-1)^\varepsilon\, 2^{m-3}$
(1,0,1)	$2^{n-4} + (-1)^\varepsilon\, 2^{m-2}$	2^{n-4}	2^{n-4}
(1,1,0)	2^{n-4}	$2^{n-4} + (-1)^\varepsilon\, 2^{m-2}$	2^{n-4}
(1,1,1)	$2^{n-4} + (-1)^\varepsilon\, 2^{m-3}$	$2^{n-4} + (-1)^\varepsilon\, 2^{m-3}$	$2^{n-4} + (-1)^\varepsilon\, 2^{m-3}$
(x_1,x_2,x_3)	$h(b+q+s) \neq A$ and $\varepsilon \in \{0,1\}$		
	$(y_1,y_2,y_3) = (1,0,0)$	$(y_1,y_2,y_3) = (0,1,0)$	$(y_1,y_2,y_3) = (0,0,1)$
(0,0,0)	$2^{n-4} + (-1)^\varepsilon\, 2^{m-3}$	$2^{n-4} + (-1)^\varepsilon\, 2^{m-3}$	$2^{n-4} + (-1)^\varepsilon\, 2^{m-3}$
(0,0,1)	$2^{n-4} + (-1)^\varepsilon\, 2^{m-2}$	2^{n-4}	$2^{n-4} + (-1)^\varepsilon\, 2^{m-2}$
(0,1,0)	2^{n-4}	$2^{n-4} + (-1)^\varepsilon\, 2^{m-2}$	$2^{n-4} + (-1)^\varepsilon\, 2^{m-2}$
(0,1,1)	$2^{n-4} + (-1)^\varepsilon\, 2^{m-3}$	$2^{n-4} + (-1)^\varepsilon\, 2^{m-3}$	$2^{n-4} + (-1)^\varepsilon\, [3.2^{m-3}]$
(1,0,0)	$2^{n-4} + (-1)^\varepsilon\, 2^{m-2}$	$2^{n-4} + (-1)^\varepsilon\, 2^{m-2}$	2^{n-4}
(1,0,1)	$2^{n-4} + (-1)^\varepsilon\, [3.2^{m-3}]$	$2^{n-4} + (-1)^\varepsilon\, 2^{m-3}$	$2^{n-4} + (-1)^\varepsilon\, 2^{m-3}$
(1,1,0)	$2^{n-4} + (-1)^\varepsilon\, 2^{m-3}$	$2^{n-4} + (-1)^\varepsilon\, [3.2^{m-3}]$	$2^{n-4} + (-1)^\varepsilon\, 2^{m-3}$
(1,1,1)	$2^{n-4} + (-1)^\varepsilon\, 2^{m-2}$	$2^{n-4} + (-1)^\varepsilon\, 2^{m-2}$	$2^{n-4} + (-1)^\varepsilon\, 2^{m-2}$

If $\max_{x \in \mathbb{F}_2^n}|W_h(x)| = 2^{\frac{n}{2}}$, then by Parseval's equality, $|W_h(a)| = 2^{\frac{n}{2}}$ for all $a \in \mathbb{F}_2^n$, which shows that h is a bent function.

Now consider the function $G(x,y)$ defined by Construction 4.1. Suppose that $\max_{x \in \mathbb{F}_2^n}|W_G(x)| = 2^m$ (where $m = \frac{n}{2}$), then $G(x,y)$ is a bent function. Since, G is constructed by complementing the values of a bent function g at zero and another three different nonzero inputs, hence distance between g and G, $d(g, G) = 4$. Which contradicts the fact that the minimal possible distance between two distinct n-variable bent functions is equal to 2^m [11]. Thus, $\max_{x \in \mathbb{F}_2^n}|W_G(x)| > 2^m$ and the Walsh coefficients of $G(x,y)$ belongs to the set $\{(-1)^\varepsilon 2^m - 8, (-1)^\varepsilon 2^m - 4, (-1)^\varepsilon 2^m, (-1)^\varepsilon 2^m + 4\}$. So, the $\max_{x \in \mathbb{F}_2^n}|W_G(x)|$ should be either $2^m + 8$ or $2^m + 4$. Then by definition of nonlinearity in Eq. (1), it is very clear that N_G is either $2^{n-1} - 2^{m-1} - 2$ or $2^{n-1} - 2^{m-1} - 4$.

Remark 1. By this construction we get a class of Boolean functions with nonlinearity either $2^{n-1} - 2^{m-1} - 2$ or $2^{n-1} - 2^{m-1} - 4$, which is close to the maximum possible nonlinearity $2^{n-1} - 2^{m-1}$.

Table 3. Walsh spectrum distribution of $(-1)^\varepsilon 2^m$

(x_1, x_2, x_3)	$h(\boldsymbol{b}+\boldsymbol{q}+\boldsymbol{s}) = A$ and $\varepsilon \in \{0,1\}$		
	$(y_1, y_2, y_3) = (1,1,0)$	$(y_1, y_2, y_3) = (0,1,1)$	$(y_1, y_2, y_3) = (1,0,1)$
(0,0,0)	2^{n-4}	2^{n-4}	2^{n-4}
(0,0,1)	$2^{n-4} + (-1)^\varepsilon 2^{m-3}$	$2^{n-4} + (-1)^\varepsilon 2^{m-3}$	$2^{n-4} - (-1)^\varepsilon 2^{m-3}$
(0,1,0)	$2^{n-4} + (-1)^\varepsilon 2^{m-3}$	$2^{n-4} + (-1)^\varepsilon 2^{m-3}$	$2^{n-4} + (-1)^\varepsilon 2^{m-3}$
(0,1,1)	$2^{n-4} + (-1)^\varepsilon 2^{m-2}$	2^{n-4}	2^{n-4}
(1,0,0)	$2^{n-4} - (-1)^\varepsilon 2^{m-3}$	$2^{n-4} + (-1)^\varepsilon 2^{m-3}$	$2^{n-4} + (-1)^\varepsilon 2^{m-3}$
(1,0,1)	2^{n-4}	$2^{n-4} + (-1)^\varepsilon 2^{m-2}$	2^{n-4}
(1,1,0)	2^{n-4}	2^{n-4}	$2^{n-4} + (-1)^\varepsilon 2^{m-2}$
(1,1,1)	$2^{n-4} + (-1)^\varepsilon 2^{m-3}$	$2^{n-4} + (-1)^\varepsilon 2^{m-3}$	$2^{n-4} + (-1)^\varepsilon 2^{m-3}$
(x_1, x_2, x_3)	$h(\boldsymbol{b}+\boldsymbol{q}+\boldsymbol{s}) \neq A$ and $\varepsilon \in \{0,1\}$		
	$(y_1, y_2, y_3) = (1,1,0)$	$(y_1, y_2, y_3) = (0,1,1)$	$(y_1, y_2, y_3) = (1,0,1)$
(0,0,0)	$2^{n-4} - (-1)^\varepsilon 2^{m-3}$	$2^{n-4} - (-1)^\varepsilon 2^{m-3}$	$2^{n-4} - (-1)^\varepsilon 2^{m-3}$
(0,0,1)	2^{n-4}	2^{n-4}	$2^{n-4} - (-1)^\varepsilon 2^{m-2}$
(0,1,0)	2^{n-4}	$2^{n-4} - (-1)^\varepsilon 2^{m-2}$	2^{n-4}
(0,1,1)	$2^{n-4} + (-1)^\varepsilon 2^{m-3}$	$2^{n-4} - (-1)^\varepsilon 2^{m-3}$	$2^{n-4} - (-1)^\varepsilon 2^{m-3}$
(1,0,0)	$2^{n-4} + (-1)^\varepsilon 2^{m-2}$	2^{n-4}	2^{n-4}
(1,0,1)	$2^{n-4} - (-1)^\varepsilon 2^{m-3}$	$2^{n-4} + (-1)^\varepsilon 2^{m-3}$	$2^{n-4} - (-1)^\varepsilon 2^{m-3}$
(1,1,0)	$2^{n-4} - (-1)^\varepsilon 2^{m-3}$	$2^{n-4} - (-1)^\varepsilon 2^{m-3}$	$2^{n-4} + (-1)^\varepsilon 2^{m-3}$
(1,1,1)	2^{n-4}	2^{n-4}	2^{n-4}

We know that a Boolean function to be useful in a cryptographic application, it is usually necessary that the function has high nonlinearity. Various research has been dedicated to construct Boolean functions with high nonlinearity. Even though bent functions possess maximum nonlinearity, due to the lack of balancedness make them improper for direct use in the cryptographic systems. A number of researches has been done for identifying and constructing balanced Boolean functions with maximum nonlinearity. In [14], Dobbertin constructed balanced Boolean functions in even n variables with nonlinearity $2^{n-1} - 2^{\frac{n}{2}} + nlb(\frac{n}{2})$, where $nlb(\frac{n}{2})$ is the maximum nonlinearity of balanced Boolean functions in $\frac{n}{2}$ variables. Also, Dobbertin conjectured that

$$nlb(n) \leq 2^{n-1} - 2^{\frac{n}{2}} + nlb(\frac{n}{2})$$

For $n = 8$, according to Dobbertin conjecture, the maximum nonlinearity of a balanced Boolean function is 118. From our construction, we derived Boolean functions with nonlinearity 118 and 116. Unfortunately, they are not balanced. To make them balanced, we have to extend the support of G, while keeping nonlinearity intact. From definition of nonlinearity, it is clear that for an 8-

variable balanced Boolean function f has nonlinearity, $N_f = 118$ iff $-20 \leq W_f(\omega) \leq 20$, for all $\omega \in \mathbb{F}_2^n$.
For $\boldsymbol{x} \in \mathbb{F}_2^n$, define $l_{\boldsymbol{\omega}}(\boldsymbol{x}) = \boldsymbol{\omega} \cdot \boldsymbol{x}$.

Now,

$$W_f(\boldsymbol{\omega}) = \sum_{\boldsymbol{x} \in \mathbb{F}_2^n} (-1)^{f(\boldsymbol{x})+\boldsymbol{\omega} \cdot \boldsymbol{x}}$$

$$= \sum_{\boldsymbol{x} \in \mathbb{F}_2^n} 1 - -2[f(\boldsymbol{x}) \oplus (l_{\boldsymbol{\omega}}(\boldsymbol{x}))]$$

$$= 2^n - 2 \sum_{\boldsymbol{x} \in \mathbb{F}_2^n : f(\boldsymbol{x}) \neq l_{\boldsymbol{\omega}}(\boldsymbol{x})} 1$$

$$= 2^n - 2wt\,[f(\boldsymbol{x}) \oplus (l_{\boldsymbol{\omega}}(\boldsymbol{x}))]$$

Also, we have for any two n-variable Boolean functions g and h,

$$wt(g \oplus h) = wt(g) + wt(h) - 2\,wt(g.h)$$

Here $(g.h)(\boldsymbol{x}) = g(\boldsymbol{x})h(\boldsymbol{x})$, the usual multiplication. Using the above result, we have

$$W_f(\boldsymbol{\omega}) = 2^n - 2[wt(f) + wt(l_{\boldsymbol{\omega}}(\boldsymbol{x})) - 2wt(f.l_{\boldsymbol{\omega}})]$$
$$= 2^n - 2[2^{n-1} + 2^{n-1} - 2wt(f.l_{\boldsymbol{\omega}})]$$
$$= 4wt(f.l_{\boldsymbol{\omega}}) - 2^n$$

Then, for the case of $n = 8$ the inequality; $-20 \leq W_f(\omega) \leq 20$ becomes,

$$59 \leq wt(fl_{\boldsymbol{\omega}}) \leq 69 \qquad (8)$$

The inequality in Eq. (8) is already derived by Maitra et al. with a different approach in [25].

Remark 2. For this construction, we used three linearly independent vectors from $\mathbb{F}_2^m$, thus we can construct $(2^m - 1)(2^m - 2)(2^m - 4)$ Boolean functions with at most eight values in its Walsh spectrum.

5 Boolean Functions with Same Weight and Non-linearity

We define a sub-class of Boolean functions having same weight and nonlinearity from the class of Boolean functions with at most eight values in their Walsh spectrum.

Proposition 1. *Let f be an n-variable Boolean function. Then weight and non-linearity of f are equal if and only if the $\max_{\boldsymbol{a} \in \mathbb{F}_2^n} |W_f(\boldsymbol{a})|$ is attained at zero.*

Proof. Suppose that $\max\limits_{a \in F_2^n}|W_f(a)|$ attained at zero.
By definition,

$$W_f(0) = \sum_{x \in F_2^n}(-1)^{f(x)}$$

$$= \sum_{x \in F_2^n : f(x)=0}(-1)^{f(x)} - wt(f(x))$$

$$= [2^n - wt(f(x))] - wt(f(x))$$

$$= 2^n - 2\ wt(f(x))$$

We've nonlinearity, $N_f = 2^{n-1} - \frac{1}{2}\max\limits_{a \in F_2^n}|W_f(a)|$.
By our assumption,

$$N_f = 2^{n-1} - \frac{1}{2}W_f(0)$$

$$= 2^{n-1} - \frac{1}{2}(2^n - 2\ wt(f(x)))$$

$$= wt(f(x)).$$

Conversely suppose that, weight and non-linearity of the function f are same. Then,

$$2^{n-1} - \frac{1}{2}\max\limits_{a \in F_2^n}|W_f(a)| = wt(f(x))$$

$$2^{n-1} - wt(f(x)) = \frac{1}{2}\max\limits_{a \in F_2^n}|W_f(a)|$$

$$2^n - 2\ wt(f(x)) = \max\limits_{a \in F_2^n}|W_f(a)|$$

$$W_f(0) = \max\limits_{a \in F_2^n}|W_f(a)|$$

From the entire class of Boolean functions, it is highly intriguing to explore the subset of functions that satisfy the condition of weight equaling nonlinearity. It is evident that considerable effort has been dedicated to designing and enumerating Boolean functions with identical weight and nonlinearity.

Remark 3. Using Proposition 1, we can find a class of Boolean functions having same weight and nonlinearity from our derived set of Boolean functions in 4.

Theorem 4. *Let f be a bent Boolean function from Maiorana-McFarland class and*

$$F(u, v) = \begin{cases} f(u, v) & if\ (u, v) \in \mathbb{F}_2^m \times \mathbb{F}_2^m \setminus \{(0, 0), (a, b), (p, q), (r, s)\} \\ f(u, v) + 1 & if\ (u, v) \in \{(0, 0), (a, b), (p, q), (r, s)\} \end{cases}$$

Where a, b, p, q, r and $s \in \mathbb{F}_2^m$ with $\{b, q, s\}$ is linearly independent. Then weight and non-linearity of $F(u, v)$ are same if and only if $\tilde{f}(0) = 1$ and $f(0) = f(a, b) = f(p, q) = f(r, s) = 0$.

In the literature, we can see that various cryptographic applications of Boolean functions can be analyzed by their Walsh spectrum characterizations. Here, we'll look at an important application of the constructed class of Boolean functions using their Walsh spectrum. Linear codes have applications in secret sharing and two-party computation. Cunsheng Ding [12] proved that we can construct $[n_f, n]$ linear codes from an n-variable Boolean function f with weight n_f whenever, $W_f(\boldsymbol{a}) + 2n_f \neq 0$ for all $\boldsymbol{a} \in \mathbb{F}_2^n \backslash \{0\}$. By the definition of $G(\boldsymbol{x}, \boldsymbol{y})$ in (4), we have $n_G \in \{2^{n-1} - 2^{\frac{n}{2}-1} + 4, \ 2^{n-1} - 2^{\frac{n}{2}-1}, \ 2^{n-1} - 2^{\frac{n}{2}-1} + 1, \ 2^{n-1} - 2^{\frac{n}{2}-1} - 1\}$, and thus it is obvious that $W_G(\boldsymbol{a}) + 2n_G \neq 0$ for all $\boldsymbol{a} \in \mathbb{F}_2^n \backslash \{0\}$. So, the function $G(\boldsymbol{x}, \boldsymbol{y})$ can be used to construct $[n_G, n]$ linear codes.

6 Conclusion

In this paper, we have constructed a class of Boolean functions with at most $2k$-values in its Walsh spectrum by utilizing a bent function selected from the $\mathcal{MM}$-class. Investigations into their cryptographic properties have been carried out. To illustrate the effectiveness of our approach, we provide a detailed example showing its application in deriving a class of $(2^m - 1)(2^m - 2)(2^m - 4)$ Boolean functions with at most eight values in its Walsh spectrum. Throughout our analysis, we examined the distributions of their Walsh spectra as well as their cryptographic properties. We made the observation that these functions satisfy the sufficient condition for constructing binary linear codes. As a result, this particular class of Boolean functions holds significant potential in the construction of secret-sharing schemes. Moreover, we have constructed a Boolean function subclass that exhibits equal weight and nonlinearity.

Acknowledgment(s). The first author acknowledges Council of Scientific and Industrial Research for financial support. (File No. 09/1034(0004)/2018-EMR-I).

Disclosure statement. The authors declare that they do not have any conflict of interest/ competing interests.

References

1. Oscar, S.R. : On "bent" functions. J. Comb. Theory, Ser. A **20**(3), 300–305 (1976)
2. Carlet, C., Prouff, E.: On plateaued functions and their constructions. In: Johansson, T. (ed.) FSE 2003. LNCS, vol. 2887, pp. 54–73. Springer, Heidelberg (2003). https://doi.org/10.1007/978-3-540-39887-5_6
3. Carlet, C.: Partially-bent functions. Des., Codes Crypt. **3**, 135–145 (1993)
4. Zheng, Y., Zhang, X.M.: Plateaued functions. In: Information and Communication Security: Second International Conference, ICICS'99, Sydney, Australia, November 9–11 1999. Proceedings 2, 284–300 (1999)
5. Uyan, E., Çalık, Ç., Doğanaksoy, A.: Counting Boolean functions with specified values in their Walsh spectrum. J. Comput. Appl. Math. **259**, 522–528 (2014)

6. Ke, P., Chen, Z.: Boolean functions with few Walsh transform values. In: 10th International Workshop on Signal Design and Its Applications in Communications (IWSDA), pp. 1–5. IEEE (2022)
7. Xu, G., Cao, X., Xu, S.: Several classes of Boolean functions with few Walsh transform values. Appl. Algebra Eng., Commun. Comput. **28**, 155–176 (2017)
8. Sun, Z., Hu, L.: Boolean functions with four-valued Walsh spectra. J. Syst. Sci. Complex. **28**(3), 743–754 (2015)
9. Jin, W., Du, X., Sun, Y., Fan, C.: Boolean functions with six-valued Walsh spectra and their application. Crypt. Commun. **13**, 393–405 (2021)
10. Tokareva, N.: Bent Functions: Results and Applications to Cryptography. Academic Press (2015)
11. Kolomeec, N., Pavlov, A.: Bent functions on the minimal distance. In: IEEE Region 8 International Conference on Computational Technologies in Electrical and Electronics Engineering (SIBIRCON), pp. 145–149. IEEE (2010)
12. Ding, C.: Linear codes from some 2-designs. IEEE Trans. Inf. Theory **61**(6), 3265–3275 (2015)
13. Lakshmy, K.V., Sethumadhavan, M., Cusick, T.W.: Counting rotation symmetric functions using Polya's theorem. Discr. Appl. Math., 162–167 (2014)
14. Dobbertin, H.: Construction of bent functions and balanced Boolean functions with high nonlinearity. In: International Workshop on Fast Software Encryption, pp. 61–74. Springer (1994)
15. Cao, X., Hu, L.: Two Boolean functions with five-valued Walsh spectra and high nonlinearity. Int. J. Found. Comput. Sci. **26**(5), 537–556 (2015)
16. Srinivasan, C., Pillai, U.U., Lakshmy, K.V., Sethumadhavan, M.: Cube attack on stream ciphers using a modified linearity test. J. Discr. Math. Sci. Crypt. **18**(3), 301–311 (2015)
17. Pieprzyk, J., Qu, C.: Fast hashing and rotation-symmetric functions. J. Univ. Comput. Sci. **5**(1), 20–31 (1999)
18. Cusick, T.W., Lakshmy, K.V., Sethumadhavan, M.: Affine equivalence of monomial rotation symmetric Boolean functions: a pólya's theorem approach. J. Math. Crypt. **10**(3-4), 145–156 (2016)
19. Neethu, R., Sindhu, M., Srinivasan, C.: XUBA: an authenticated encryption scheme. In: Data Engineering and Intelligent Computing: Proceedings of IC3T 2016, pp. 647–655 (2018)
20. Nelson, J., Srinivasan, C., Lakshmy, K.V.: An algorithm for constructing support of bent functions by extending a set. Int. J. Math., Eng. Manage. Sci. **8**(5), 1040 (2023)
21. Cusick, T.W., Stanica, P.: Cryptographic Boolean Functions and Applications. Academic Press (2015)
22. Xiao, G.Z., Massey, J.L.: A spectral characterization of correlation-immune combining functions. IEEE Trans. Inf. Theory **34**(3), 569–571 (1988)
23. Zeeanth, A.U., Lakshmy, K.V., Cusick, T.W., Sethumadhavan, M.: Construction and Enumeration of balanced rotation symmetric Boolean functions. Discr. Appl. Math. **357**, 197–208 (2024)
24. Cusick, T.W.: Simple proof for nonlinearity of majority function. Discr. Appl. Math. **297**, 55–59 (2021)
25. Maitra, S., Mandal, B., Roy, M.: Modifying bent functions to obtain the balanced ones with high nonlinearity. In: International Conference on Cryptology in India, pp. 449–470. Springer (2022)

On (Noisy) Simon's (Quantum) Algorithm for Multi-shift Boolean Functions

Suman Dutta[1], Aarav Jaiswal[2], Subhamoy Maitra[1(✉)], and Debasish Roy[3]

[1] Applied Statistics Unit, Indian Statistical Institute, Kolkata, India
sumand.iiserb@gmail.com, subho@isical.ac.in
[2] Modern High School International, Kolkata, India
aaravjaiswal2007@gmail.com
[3] CER, Department of Mathematics, Indian Institute of Technology, Kharagpur, India
debasish.roy@maths.iitkgp.ac.in

Abstract. Given a Boolean function, $f : \{0,1\}^n \to \{0,1\}^n$ with the promise that $f(x) = f(y)$ if and only if $x \oplus y \in \{0^n, s\}$ for all $x, y \in \{0,1\}^n$ and an unknown non-zero bit string $s \in \{0,1\}^n$, Simon's quantum algorithm (1994) determines s using $O(n)$ many queries to the oracle U_f. In this paper, we revisit (Bonnetain, Latincrypt 2021) the Boolean functions having more than one (2^k many) shifts and present an exact count of such functions, with relevant characterization. The characterization was known for $k = 1$ (May et al., CT-RSA 2021), that we generalize here for any k. This characterization is important towards analysing such functions in a noisy quantum environment (Noisy Intermediate Scale Quantum, NISQ), as this formulation presents an efficiently computable form. This reduces the propagation of error due to small depth. Finally, we devise strategies for recovering the shift space for Boolean functions, which almost satisfy the conditions for being used as Simon's oracle, except for a few input point(s), termed as near-Simon functions.

Keywords: Quantum Cryptography · Boolean functions · Cryptanalysis · NISQ · Simon's Algorithm

1 Introduction

Quantum computing is an emerging field of studies that utilizes the unique properties of quantum mechanics to process and analyze data more effectively, providing faster and more efficient solutions to complex problems that are impossible for classical computers. Over the past few decades, the domain of quantum algorithms has evolved rapidly. One of the most notable discoveries is Shor's factoring algorithm [6], which has implications for the security of public-key cryptography in the post-quantum era. Other quantum algorithms, such as Grover's search algorithm [3], Deutsch-Jozsa algorithm [2], and Simon's hidden shift-finding algorithm [7], have also contributed significantly to the cryptanalysis of symmetric-key cryptography. In this paper, we revisit Simon's hidden shift-finding algorithm in a more general setup and explore its functionality in different scenarios.

Given oracle access of an unknown Boolean function, $f : \{0,1\}^n \to \{0,1\}^n$ with the promise that $f(x) = f(y)$ if and only if $x \oplus y \in S \equiv \{0,s\}$ for all $x, y \in \{0,1\}^n$ and an unknown bit string $s \in \{0,1\}^n$, Simon's algorithm finds s using $\mathcal{O}(n)$ many queries to the oracle. The observed bit-patterns $y \in \{0,1\}^n$ obtained from running Simon's algorithm are uniformly distributed over the subspace $S^\perp$, satisfying $y \cdot s = 0$. However, an erroneous quantum machine may produce bit-patterns y that do not satisfy this condition, leading to errors in determining the hidden shift.

Implementing Simon's algorithm in an erroneous quantum machine to recover the corresponding subspace requires more queries to the oracle, and the essential scenario is thoroughly analyzed in [5]. They put forward various strategies to mitigate errors, including an efficient implementation of the quantum oracle for any given Simon function. They further showed that determining the hidden shift space is as challenging as the Learning Parity with Noise (LPN) problem. Additionally, they estimated the number of queries required to detect the hidden shift s by executing the Simon algorithm on an erroneous quantum device.

Our current initiative analyses the error mitigation techniques provided in [5] for the higher dimensional shift space. We try to determine the hidden shift space S, with the minimum number of queries to the corresponding quantum oracle, followed by classical post-processing. In the simplest form of Simon's algorithm, the shift space consists of $\{0,s\}$, where the dimension of the shift space is 1. Here, we revisit the instance where a Boolean function has more than one shift, in particular 2^k many. Given a Boolean function f, the collection of all the shifts forms a k-dimensional subspace under the vector space $\{0,1\}^n$. The observed bit-patterns $y \in \{0,1\}^n$ from running Simon's algorithm on a noise-free quantum device are uniformly distributed over $S^\perp$, an $(n-k)$ dimensional subspace of $\{0,1\}^n$.

We further analyze the Boolean functions, which deviate from a Simon function only at a few points. We call them the near-Simon functions. We analyze such functions and carefully observe the results from running Simon's algorithm in noise-free and noisy quantum devices. We further implement all the available error mitigation techniques and try to determine the underlying shift space (to the closest Simon function) for the given near-Simon function.

Depending on the shift structure of the underlying Simon function and the noise level of the corresponding quantum device, the implementation of Simon's algorithm can be broadly divided into four sub-categories as follows.

- An exact Simon function implemented on a noise-free quantum device - covered in [7].
- An exact Simon function implemented in a noisy quantum device - the Boolean functions with one-dimensional shift space have been covered in [5], and the Boolean functions with multi-dimensional shift space have been covered in this paper using the Qiskit backend "FakeMelbourne()", which takes

care of the simulation of noise. This is to be done as our main motivation in this paper is to understand the practical situations where noise will play an important role and introduce errors during the execution of the algorithms.
- A near-Simon function implemented on a noise-free quantum device - this has also been covered in our current initiative using the 'qasm_simulator' provided by Qiskit.
- A near-Simon function being implemented in a noisy quantum device - partly covered here, and the detail analysis has been put as a future research possibility.

The last scenario, where one is unsure whether the underlying Boolean function is an exact or a near-Simon function, and the corresponding device is in a NISQ device, is the most anticipated one that requires further research. Now let us outline the organization of this paper.

Organization and Contribution. In Sect. 2, we proceed with the preliminaries. The next one (Sect. 3) is the first contributory section where we characterize the Boolean functions having 2^k many hidden shifts and provide an exact count of such functions. We also provide the formulation of an efficiently computable Simon function (oracle), which has a minimum circuit depth and causes the least error during circuit implementation, reducing the overall error while running Simon's algorithm. In Sect. 4, we deal with the Boolean functions, which almost satisfy the condition for being used as an oracle while running Simon's algorithm, except for a few points. We call them the near Simon functions and analyze the observed bit-patterns from running Simon's algorithm over such functions. This is important as during the implementation of Boolean functions in a quantum machine, noise may be introduced and the function may not behave perfectly. Section 5 concludes the paper with a brief summary and future research possibilities in this direction.

In our paper, we use the 'qasm_simulator' from Qiskit as a noise-free quantum device. However, due to the unavailability of the 'ibmq_16_melbourne' as mentioned in [5], we employed the 'FakeMelbourne()' simulator as a substitute, which accurately simulates the behaviour of the 'ibmq_16_melbourne' device.

2 Preliminaries

Let $\mathbb{F}_2 = \{0,1\}$ be a prime field of characteristic 2 and $\mathbb{F}_2^n \equiv \{x = (x_1, \ldots, x_n) : x_i \in \mathbb{F}_2, \forall 1 \leq i \leq n\}$ denotes the vector space of dimension n over $\mathbb{F}_2$. Further, $\mathbb{F}_2^n$ forms an Abelian group with respect to the bit-wise XOR operation where the identity element is given by 0^n, and every element $x \in \mathbb{F}_2^n$ is its own inverse. Let $S \subseteq \mathbb{F}_2^n$ be a subspace of dimension k over $\mathbb{F}_2$, then the following hold. (i) S forms a subgroup under $\mathbb{F}_2^n$ (in the next part of the paper, we will be using the terms subgroup and subspace interchangeably), (ii) the cardinality of S is given by $|S| = 2^k$, and (iii) any k linearly independent elements from S is sufficient to reconstruct S, known as the basis of the subspace S. Moreover, the orthogonal complement of S over $\mathbb{F}_2^n$, defined as $S^\perp = \{y \in \mathbb{F}_2^n : y \cdot s = 0, \forall s \in S\}$ where $y \cdot s = \sum_{i=1}^n y_i s_i \mod 2$. It is direct to observe that $S^\perp$ forms a subspace over $\mathbb{F}_2^n$. In this regard, we have the following results from [8].

Fact 1 *Let $\mathbb{F}_2^n$ be an n-dimensional vector space with well-defined inner product, and let S be a subspace of $\mathbb{F}_2^n$, then $\dim(S) + \dim(S^\perp) = \dim(\mathbb{F}_2^n) = n$ where $\dim(V)$ denotes the dimension of the vector space V.*

Assuming S to be a k-dimensional subspace over $\mathbb{F}_2^n$, we have $\dim(S^\perp) = n - k$, and the cardinality of $S^\perp$ is given by $|S^\perp| = 2^{n-k}$. Further, any $(n-k)$ many linearly independent vectors from $S^\perp$ is sufficient to reconstruct the complete subspace, $S^\perp$, known as the basis of the subspace $S^\perp$.

An n-input n-output Boolean function is a mapping, $f : \mathbb{F}_2^n \to \mathbb{F}_2^n$, and the number of such functions is given by $2^{n \cdot 2^n}$. Given an unknown n-input n-output Boolean function f, the quantum oracle (denoted by U_f) is defined as $U_f : \mathbb{F}_2^{2n} \to \mathbb{F}_2^{2n}$ such that $U_f |x\rangle |a\rangle = |x\rangle |a \oplus f(x)\rangle$. For $a = 0^n$, the functioning of U_f is shown in Fig. 1, where the mathematical formulation is given by $U_f |x\rangle |0^n\rangle = |x\rangle |f(x)\rangle$. Moreover, any superposition state, $\sum_{x,y} \alpha_{x,y} |x\rangle |y\rangle$, can also be used as an input to the oracle U_f and the corresponding output follows.

$$U_f\left(\sum_{x,y} \alpha_{x,y} |x\rangle |y\rangle\right) = \sum_{x,y} \alpha_{x,y} |x\rangle |y \oplus f(x)\rangle.$$

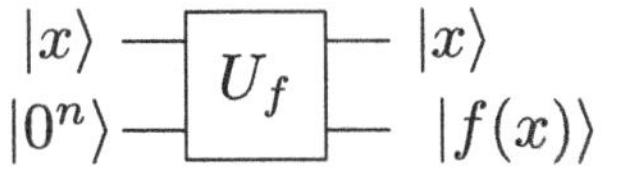

Fig. 1. Quantum oracle of a Boolean function f.

Given oracle access of a Boolean function $f : \mathbb{F}_2^n \to \mathbb{F}_2^n$ and the promise that there exists $s \in \mathbb{F}_2^n$ such that for all $x, y \in \mathbb{F}_2^n$, $f(x) = f(y)$ holds if and only if $x \oplus y \in S = \{0^n, s\}$, then the Simon's algorithm computes s using $\mathcal{O}(n)$ many queries to the quantum oracle U_f. It is direct to observe that a Boolean function f satisfying the above criterion maps two distinct n-length bit-patterns to a single, unique n-length bit-pattern; hence, f is a 2-to-1 Boolean function, known as the Simon function where $S = \{0^n, s\}$ is the underlying (1-dimensional) shift space with the hidden shift s.

We now provide a brief description of Simon's algorithm.

Simon's Algorithm. The algorithm begins with an n-qubit query register initialized to $|0\rangle^n$ and another n-qubit initialized to $|0\rangle^n$ to store the functional outputs. The n-qubit Hadamard gate, H^n is then applied on the query register to produce an equal superposition of all possible n-qubit states, $\frac{1}{\sqrt{2^n}} \sum_{x \in \{0,1\}^n} |x\rangle$

leading to quantum parallelization. The superposition is then fed to the oracle U_f as an input, and the outcome is as follows.

$$|0\rangle^n |0\rangle^n \xrightarrow{H^n \otimes I} \frac{1}{\sqrt{2^n}} \sum_{x \in \{0,1\}^n} |x\rangle |0\rangle^n \xrightarrow{U_f} \frac{1}{\sqrt{2^n}} \sum_{x \in \{0,1\}^n} |x\rangle |f(x)\rangle.$$

Finally, the query register is measured on the Hadamard basis, producing the quantum state

$$\frac{1}{\sqrt{2^n}} \sum_{x \in \{0,1\}^n} |x\rangle |f(x)\rangle \xrightarrow{H^n \otimes I} \frac{1}{2^n} \sum_{y \in \{0,1\}^n} \left(|y\rangle \otimes \left(\sum_{x \in \{0,1\}^n} (-1)^{x \cdot y} |f(x)\rangle \right) \right)$$

where the probability of observing any bit-pattern $y \in \{0,1\}^n$ is given by

$$\mathcal{P}(|y\rangle) = \left\| \frac{1}{2^n} \sum_{x \in \{0,1\}^n} (-1)^{x \cdot y} |f(x)\rangle \right\|^2. \quad (1)$$

Further simplification shows that the observed bit-patterns $y \in \mathbb{F}_2^n$ are uniformly distributed over the subspace $S^\perp$, individually satisfying the equation $y \cdot s = 0$. Given $f : \mathbb{F}_2^n \to \mathbb{F}_2^n$ with the promise that $f(x) = f(y)$ for all $x, y \in \mathbb{F}_2^n$ if and only if $x \oplus y \in S$, where $\dim(S) = k$, then, by repeating the above subroutine $\mathcal{O}(n)$ times, one obtains $n - k$ linearly independent $y \in \mathbb{F}_2^n$, which is sufficient to determine the hidden shift space S since the dimension of $S^\perp$ over $\mathbb{F}_2^n$ is $n - k$. The corresponding quantum circuit for implementing Simon's algorithm is shown in Fig. 2.

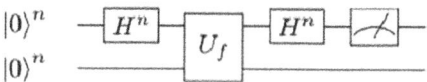

Fig. 2. Quantum circuit for the implementation of Simon's algorithm.

Next, we present the mathematical structure of an efficiently computable Simon function (from [5]) having the minimum circuit depth in oracle implementation, which helps reduce the overall error while running Simon's algorithm in a noisy quantum device.

Definition 1 ([5]). *Let $s \in \mathbb{F}_2^n \setminus \{0^n\}$, and let $i \in [0, 1, \ldots, n-1]$ with $s_i = 1$. Then the Boolean function $f_s : \mathbb{F}_2^n \to \mathbb{F}_2^n$ such that $x \mapsto x \oplus x_i \cdot s$ is a (1)-Simon function with the 1-dimensional shift space $\{0^n, s\}$.*

Moreover, any 1-Simon function, f is of the form $P \circ f_s$, for some bijection $P : \mathbb{F}_2^n \to \mathbb{F}_2^n$.

Example 1. Let $f : \{0,1\}^4 \to \{0,1\}^4$ be Boolean function with shift, $s = 0101$. Considering $i = 2$, we have $s_i = 1$. Following Definition 1, the efficiently computable Boolean function f_s is constructed as

$$f_s(x_3, x_2, x_1, x_0) = x \oplus x_2 \cdot s = (x_3, x_2, x_1, x_0) \oplus (0, x_2, 0, x_2) = x_3, 0, x_1, (x_0 \oplus x_2).$$

In Sect. 3, we further extend the formulation for efficiently computable k-Simon function (see Definition 2), that reduce the circuit-depth of a Simon-oracle to tackle the error caused while running Simon's algorithm in a noisy quantum machine.

In the preceding discussion, we assumed that the dimension of the hidden subspace (subgroup) S is 1, denoted as $|S| = 2$. However, this concept can be expanded to encompass any $k \leq n$-dimensional subspace (S) of $\mathbb{F}_2^n$, where $|S| = 2^k$. If $S_b = \{s_1, s_2, \ldots, s_k\} \subseteq \mathbb{F}_2^n$ represents the basis of subspace S, then the condition $f(x) = f(y)$, $\forall x, y \in \mathbb{F}_2^n$ if and only if $x \oplus y \in S_b$ is equivalent to the condition $f(x) = f(y)$, $\forall x, y \in \mathbb{F}_2^n$ if and only if $x \oplus y \in S$. Essentially, $S = \{\bigoplus s_i : s_i \in S_b\}$ forms a subgroup of $\mathbb{F}_2^n$ where the group operation is bit-wise XOR and $\forall x \in \mathbb{F}_2^n$, $f(x) = f(x \oplus \bigoplus_i s_i)$ for all $s_i \in S_b$, i.e., f becomes a 2^k-to-1 Boolean function. Additionally, when the dimension of S is n, f becomes a constant Boolean function and when the dimension of S is 0, $f : \mathbb{F}_2^n \to \mathbb{F}_2^n$ becomes a permutation.

Definition 2. *Let $f : \mathbb{F}_2^n \to \mathbb{F}_2^n$ be a Boolean function and S be a k-dimensional subspace (subgroup) of $\mathbb{F}_2^n$ such that f satisfies the following condition: $f(x) = f(y)$ if and only if $x \oplus y \in S$ for all $x, y \in \mathbb{F}_2^n$. Then the Boolean function f is called a k-Simon function, and the underlying subspace S is called the k-shift space of f.*

Given oracle access of a k-Simon function $f : \mathbb{F}_2^n \to \mathbb{F}_2^n$ and the underlying k-dimensional shift space (subgroup) $S \subseteq \mathbb{F}_2^n$ such that for all $x, y \in \mathbb{F}_2^n$, $f(x) = f(y)$ if and only if $x \oplus y \in S$, then the Simon's algorithm can be used to find a basis for the subgroup S using $\mathcal{O}(n)$ many queries to the quantum oracle U_f. While running the Simon's algorithm, upon measurement of the query register from the Simon-circuit as in Fig. 2, the probability of observing a bit-pattern $y \in \mathbb{F}_2$ is given by

$$\mathcal{P}(|y\rangle) = \|\frac{1}{2^n} \sum_{x \in \{0,1\}^n} (-1)^{x \cdot y} |f(x)\rangle\|^2 \text{ (from Eq. 1)}.$$

Let the output set is denoted by $A \subseteq \mathbb{F}_2^n$. Therefore, for each element $z \in A$, there are 2^k many pre-images, i.e., $f(x) = f(x \oplus s_i) = z$ for all $s_i \in S$. Hence, the above expression turns out to be

$$\mathcal{P}(|y\rangle) = \|\frac{1}{2^n} \sum_{z \in A} \sum_{s_i \in S} (-1)^{(x \oplus s_i) \cdot y} |z\rangle\|^2$$

$$= \|\frac{1}{2^n} \sum_{z \in A} (-1)^{x \cdot y} \sum_{s_i \in S} (-1)^{s_i \cdot y} |z\rangle\|^2$$

$$= \|\frac{1}{2^n} \sum_{z \in A} (-1)^{x \cdot y} \prod_{s_i \in S_b} \left(1 + (-1)^{s_i \cdot y}\right) |z\rangle\|^2.$$

Here, $\mathcal{P}(|\mathbf{y}\rangle)$ will be non-zero if and only if $(1+(-1)^{s_i \cdot y})$ is non-zero, i.e., when $s_i \cdot y = 0$ for all $s_i \in S_b$. In that case, $\prod_{s_i \in S_b}(1+(-1)^{s_i \cdot y}) = 2^k$ and the corresponding probability is given by

$$\mathcal{P}(|y\rangle) = \|\frac{1}{2^n}\sum_{z \in A}(-1)^{x \cdot y}2^k |z\rangle\|^2 = \|\frac{1}{2^{n-k}}\sum_{z \in A}(-1)^{x \cdot y}|z\rangle\|^2 = \frac{|A|}{2^{2(n-k)}} = \frac{1}{2^{n-k}}.$$

Since $|S^\perp| = 2^{n-k}$, the observed bit-patterns $y \in \mathbb{F}_2^n$ are uniformly distributed over the subspace $S^\perp$. If k is known, $(n-k)$ many linearly independent bit-patterns $y_1, y_2, \ldots, y_{n-k} \in \mathbb{F}_2^k$ satisfying $y_i \cdot s = 0, \forall s \in S$ forms a basis of S, which is sufficient to determine the complete unknown shift space S. Otherwise, $(n-1)$ many such bit-patterns are observed (some of them are not linearly independent), and the null-space of $Y = \begin{pmatrix} y_1 & y_2 & \ldots & y_{n-1} \end{pmatrix}^T$ is determined by obtaining the row-reduced-echelon-form of Y, keeping in mind that the row operations are done over $\mathbb{F}_2$. For the detailed calculations, one may refer to [1,7] and the references therein.

The following section examines the properties of k-Simon functions in a noisy quantum environment and investigates the process of error reduction to identify the hidden subspace $S \subseteq \mathbb{F}_2^n$ using the minimum possible queries to the oracle U_f.

3 Characterization of k-Simon Functions

In [5], a class was defined towards efficient implementation of 1-Simon function (Definition 1). The understanding was to obtain circuits with the minimum circuit depth so that the error during the computation can be reduced in noisy environment. This idea is extended in this section for any k-Simon function (Definition 3). Thus the different error mitigation techniques suggested in [5] can be applied in these cases too.

In the simplest form of Simon's quantum algorithm, it is assumed that the dimension of the hidden shift space is 1. Therefore, in order to determine the hidden shift s from an unknown n-input n-output Boolean function, one requires $n-1$ many linearly independent $y \in \mathbb{F}_2^n$ satisfying $y \cdot s = 0$, since $\dim(S^\perp) = n-1$. This can be further extended for Boolean functions having hidden shift space (subgroup) S of dimension $k (\leq n)$ where the observed bit-patterns $y \in \mathbb{F}_2^n$ from running the Simon's algorithm are uniformly distributed over $S^\perp$, an $(n-k)$-dimensional subspace of $\mathbb{F}_2^n$.

We now present some combinatorial results regarding n-input n-output k-Simon functions as follows.

Theorem 1. *Let $f : \mathbb{F}_2^n \to \mathbb{F}_2^n$ be a Boolean function and S be a k-dimensional subspace (subgroup) of $\mathbb{F}_2^n$ such that for all $x, y \in \mathbb{F}_2^n$, $f(x) = f(y)$ if and only if $x \oplus y \in S$. Then the number of such k-Simon function is given by*

$$\frac{(2^n - 1)(2^n - 2) \ldots (2^n - 2^{k-1})}{(2^k - 1)(2^k - 2) \ldots (2^k - 2^{k-1})} \times {}^{2^n}P_{2^{n-k}}.$$

Proof. The number of k linearly independent vectors in $\mathbb{F}_2^n$ can be determined as follows. Choose the first vector in $2^n - 1$ many ways; the second linearly independent vector in $2^n - 2$ ways; the third linearly independent vector in $2^n - 2^2$ ways, and so on. So this count becomes $\left[(2^n - 1)(2^n - 2)\ldots(2^n - 2^{k-1})\right](k!)^{-1}$. Now, multiple such bases can lead to the same vector space. The number of bases that a k-dimensional subspace has, is given by $k!\left[(2^k - 1)(2^k - 2)\ldots(2^k - 2^{k-1})\right]^{-1}$. Therefore, the number of distinct k-dimensional subspace (choice for S) is given by

$$\frac{(2^n - 1)(2^n - 2)\ldots(2^n - 2^{k-1})}{(2^k - 1)(2^k - 2)\ldots(2^k - 2^{k-1})}.$$

Once we fix the k-dimensional shift space S, the size of the output space is fixed by 2^{n-k} many bit-patterns, which is chosen from 2^n many different patterns of $\mathbb{F}_2^n$. There are exactly $^{2^n}P_{2^{n-k}}$ many ways to do that. Hence, the number of k-Simon functions is given by the number of different subspace of dimension k times the number of choices of the output space for a fixed S, given by

$$\frac{(2^n - 1)(2^n - 2)\ldots(2^n - 2^{k-1})}{(2^k - 1)(2^k - 2)\ldots(2^k - 2^{k-1})} \times {}^{2^n}P_{2^{n-k}}.$$

□

For the most basic case when $k = 1$, the number of such (1)-Simon function is given by $(2^n - 1)\,{}^{2^n}P_{2^{n-1}}$. Thus, for $n = 1, 2, 3, 4, \ldots$, the number of such 1-Simon functions are given by 2, 36, 11760, 7783776000, ... and so on. Similarly, the number of 2-Simon functions for $n = 2, 3, 4, \ldots$ is given by 4, 392, 1528800, ..., and so on. Table 1 gives the count of n-input n-output k-Simon functions for different values of n and k. Since $k = n$ implies f is a constant Boolean function, the number of such functions is given by 2^n. Therefore, the diagonal elements of the tables corresponding to any n are given by 2^n and the number of Boolean functions above the diagonal elements is 0 (as k can not be greater than n).

Table 1. The number of n-input n-output k-Simon functions for $1 \leq n, k \leq 5$.

n	k				
	1	2	3	4	5
1	2	0	0	0	0
2	36	4	0	0	0
3	11760	392	8	0	0
4	7783776000	1528800	3600	16	0
5	38986464×10^{16}	657351677×10^5	133771200	30752	32

Given a Boolean function $f : \mathbb{F}_2^n \to \mathbb{F}_2^n$ with an unknown shift space S, Simon's algorithm finds S using $O(n)$ many queries to the quantum oracle

70   S. Dutta et al.

U_f, provided the underlying quantum machine is error-free. In an ideal, non-erroneous quantum machine, it is expected to observe bit-patterns $y \in \mathbb{F}_2^n$ which satisfy $y \cdot s = 0$ for all $s \in S$, i.e., $y \in S^\perp$. However, since most of our present-day quantum machines are erroneous, upon measuring the query register from running Simon's algorithm, we often obtain $y \in \mathbb{F}_2^n$ such that $y \notin S^\perp$. Therefore, implementing Simon's algorithm in an erroneous quantum machine to recover the corresponding subspace takes more queries to the oracle, and the essential scenario for the class of 1-Simon functions is thoroughly analyzed in [5].

Assuming the access of noisy quantum devices only, we further extend the characterization for k-Simon functions for any k less than or equal to n and devise a strategy to determine a basis for the hidden subspace (subgroup) S with the number of queries to the oracle U_f as small as possible, followed by classical post-processing. In this regard, we propose an efficient implementation of quantum oracles U_f for any k-Simon function f, extending the Definition 1, as follows.

Definition 3. *Let $S_b = \{s_1, s_2, \ldots, s_k\} \subset \mathbb{F}_2^n \setminus \{0^n\}$ be a basis of the shift space S with $\dim(S) = k$ and let $l_1, l_2, \ldots, l_k \in [0, n-1]$ denote the position-index of the corresponding basis elements such that $(s_i)_{l_j} = 1$ if and only if $i = j$, and 0 otherwise. Then we define*

$$f_S : \mathbb{F}_2^n \to \mathbb{F}_2^n, \text{ such that } x \mapsto x \oplus \bigoplus_{i=1}^{k} x_{l_i} \cdot s_i.$$

This implementation reduces the circuit depth and the number of CNOT gates required to execute U_f, which subsequently helps in reducing the overall error while running the Simon's algorithm in the Noisy Intermediate-Scale Quantum (NISQ) era.

Remark 1. The conditions that the basis elements satisfying $(s_i)_{l_j} = 1$ if and only if $i = j$, and 0 otherwise implies that if a basis element has a '1' at any particular position, then no other basis element can have a '1' at the same position. However, note that this does not impose any additional restriction on the shift space S. Since, S_b is a basis of dimension k, all the elements of S_b combined must have 1 at least at k many positions, and even if two of them have 1s in the same position, the issue can be resolved by XOR-ing them, and S_b being a basis, makes sure that the XOR between them is never an existing element of S_b.

We now illustrate Definition 3 with the help of a continuing example.

Example 2. Let $f : \{0,1\}^4 \to \{0,1\}^4$ with $S = \{0000, 0101, 1011, 1110\}$ such that $S_b = \{0101, 1011\}$, i.e., $s_1 = 0101$ and $s_2 = 1011$. Considering, $l_1 = 2$ and $l_2 = 3$ we have $(s_1)_{l_1} = 1$, $(s_2)_{l_1} = 0$ and $(s_1)_{l_2} = 0$, $(s_2)_{l_2} = 1$. Thus, we construct the efficiently computable Boolean function $f_S : \{0,1\}^4 \to \{0,1\}^4$ as

$$\begin{aligned} f_S(x_3, x_2, x_1, x_0) &= x \oplus x_2 \cdot s_1 \oplus x_3 \cdot s_2 \\ &= (x_3, x_2, x_1, x_0) \oplus (0, x_2, 0, x_2) \oplus (x_3, 0, x_3, x_3) \\ &= 0, 0, (x_1 \oplus x_3), (x_0 \oplus x_2 \oplus x_3). \end{aligned}$$

The following theorem states that the Boolean function f_S defined as in Definition 3 is indeed a k-Simon function for $\dim(S) = k$. Moreover, every k-Simon functions belong to the same co-set of f_S.

Theorem 2. *Let $f_S(x) = x \oplus \bigoplus_{i=1}^{k} x_{l_i} \cdot s_i$ as in Definition 3, then the following holds.*

1. *f_S is a k-Simon function where the basis of the shift space S is given by $S_b = \{s_1, s_2, \ldots, s_k\}$, i.e., $f_S(x) = f_S(y)$ if and only if $(x \oplus y) \in S$.*
2. *Any k-Simon function can be written in the form $P \circ f_S$ where $P : \mathbb{F}_2^n \to \mathbb{F}_2^n$ denotes a bijective mapping.*

Proof. We proceed with the sketch of proofs as follows.

1. For all $x \in \mathbb{F}_2^n$ and for all possible XOR-combinations, $\bigoplus_j s_j \in S$, we have

$$f_S(x \oplus \bigoplus_j s_j) = (x \oplus \bigoplus_j s_j) \oplus \bigoplus_{i=1}^{k} (x \oplus \bigoplus_j s_j)_{l_i} \cdot s_i$$

$$= (x \oplus \bigoplus_j s_j) \oplus (\bigoplus_{i=1}^{k} x_{l_i} \cdot s_i) \oplus (\bigoplus_{i=1}^{k} (s_j)_{l_i} \cdot s_i).$$

Since, $(s_j)_{l_i} = 1$ if and only if $i = j$, and $(s_j)_{l_i} = 0$ otherwise, therefore, $\bigoplus_{i=1}^{k} (s_j)_{l_i} \cdot s_i = \bigoplus_j s_j$. Hence,

$$f_S(x \oplus \bigoplus_j s_j) = (x \oplus \bigoplus_j s_j) \oplus \bigoplus_{i=1}^{k} x_{l_i} \cdot s_i \oplus \bigoplus_j s_j = x \oplus \bigoplus_{i=1}^{k} x_{l_i} \cdot s_i = f_S(x)$$

proving that the Boolean function f_S is periodic with respect to the underlying k-dimensional shift space S. Next we show that $f_S(x) = f_S(y)$ if and only if $(x \oplus y) \in S$. In this regard, we have $f_S(x) = f_S(y) \Rightarrow (x \oplus \bigoplus_{i=1}^{k} x_{l_i} \cdot s_i) = (y \oplus \bigoplus_{i=1}^{k} y_{l_i} \cdot s_i)$. If $x_{l_i} = y_{l_i}$, for all $l_i : 1 \leq i \leq k$, then clearly $x = y$, whereas if $x_{l_i} \neq y_{l_i}$, for some l_i, then the above equation will turn out to be $x \oplus y = \left(\bigoplus_{i=1}^{k} x_{l_i} \cdot s_i\right) \oplus \left(\bigoplus_{i=1}^{k} y_{l_i} \cdot s_i\right) = \bigoplus_{i=1}^{k} (x_{l_i} \oplus y_{l_i}) \cdot s_i$. Suppose we denote the mismatching indexes by j. Even if there is a single j for which $x_j \neq y_j$, we can write $\bigoplus_{i=1}^{k} (x_{l_i} \oplus y_{l_i}) \cdot s_i = \bigoplus_j 1 \cdot s_j = \bigoplus_j s_j$. Therefore, in case if $x_{l_i} \neq y_{l_i}$, for some l_i, we have $x \oplus y = \bigoplus_j s_j \in S$.

2. Given $g : \mathbb{F}_2^n \to \mathbb{F}_2^n$ an arbitrary k-Simon function with the underlying shift space S. To write g in the form $g = P \circ f_S$, the following bijection, P suffices.

$$P : \mathbb{F}_2^n \to \mathbb{F}_2^n \text{ such that } x \mapsto g(x \oplus \bigoplus_{i=1}^{k} x_{l_i} \cdot s_i).$$

□

In [5], the authors defined a class of efficiently implementable 1-Simon function (Definition 1) with the minimum circuit depth that substantially reduced the error caused by the oracle, consequently reducing the overall circuit error. Here, we extend the definition of efficiently implementable quantum oracle for any k-Simon function (Definition 3), followed by different error mitigation techniques suggested in [5], such as minimization of gate counts for U_{f_S} by judiciously choosing the starting configuration and getting rid of redundant quantum gates, placing CNOT gates according to the CNOT map given for the respective quantum device, and different smoothing techniques, like permutations of qubits, Double-flip techniques, Hamming techniques, etc.

Example 3. Consider the 2-Simon function $f : \{0,1\}^4 \to \{0,1\}^4$ from Example 2 given by $f_S(x_3, x_2, x_1, x_0) = 0, 0, (x_1 \oplus x_3), (x_0 \oplus x_2 \oplus x_3)$. We run the Simon algorithm using the Qiskit backend "FakeMelbourne()" and present the result in Fig. 3.

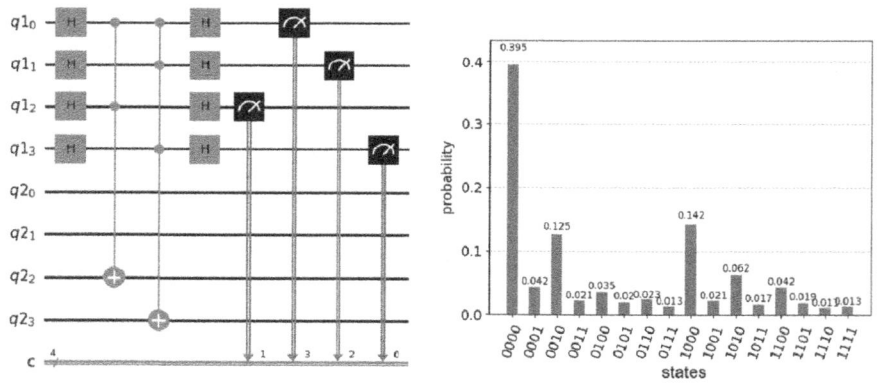

Fig. 3. Simon's algorithm on a 2-Simon function (Examples 3) using 'FakeMelbourne()' and the corresponding histogram.

Here, $S^\perp = \{0000, 1010, 0111, 1101\}$. However, only 0000 appears with high probability in the observed bit-patterns, and the rest are mixed with erroneous bit-patterns. However, using the strategies discussed in [5], one can recover the desired bit-patterns with time complexity comparable to the LWE problem.

In the following section, we explore another variety of k-Simon functions where the underlying Boolean function itself is erroneous. This situation might arise, when the implementation of a Boolean function may invite some noise in the circuit itself.

4 Determining the Unknown Shift Space for Near-Simon Functions

In our earlier sections, we discussed the Boolean functions that satisfy the promise of Simon's algorithm. However, in reality, we often deal with Boolean functions that fail to follow the required promise as in the Simon's algorithm. We call them the near-Simon function, defined as follows.

Definition 4. *A function $f : \mathbb{F}_2^n \to \mathbb{F}_2^n$ is defined as a t-near-k-Simon function if the output of f differs from a k-Simon function at t many points.*

A similar class of Boolean functions was also studied in [4] in terms of query complexity. In our present analysis, we includes Boolean functions having excess collisions exactly at t many points, i.e., when $f(x) = f(y)$ but $x \oplus y \notin S$, as well as the Boolean functions in which $x \oplus y \in S$ does not imply $f(x) = f(y)$, exactly for t many points. We proceed with the necessary theoretical analysis as follows.

Let $f : \mathbb{F}_2^n \to \mathbb{F}_2^n$ be a near-Simon Boolean function. From Definition 4, the output of f differs from a k-Simon function at t many points. Suppose the output set of f is partitioned as $A \sqcup A'$ such that the elements from A have exactly 2^k many pre-images and the elements from A' have less than 2^k many pre-images. From Eq. 1, the probability of observing a bit-string $y \in \mathbb{F}_2^n$ from running the Simon's algorithm is given by

$$\mathcal{P}(|y\rangle) = \|\frac{1}{2^n} \sum_{x \in \{0,1\}^n} (-1)^{x \cdot y} |f(x)\rangle\|^2$$

$$= \frac{1}{2^{2n}} \| \sum_{x \in \{0,1\}^n : z \in A} (-1)^{x \cdot y} |z\rangle + \sum_{x \in \{0,1\}^n : z \in A'} (-1)^{x \cdot y} |z\rangle \|^2$$

$$= \frac{1}{2^{2n}} \| \sum_{z \in A} (-1)^{x \cdot y} \left[1 + (-1)^{s_i \cdot y} + \ldots\right] |z\rangle + \sum_{z \in A'} (-1)^{x \cdot y} \left[1 + (-1)^{s_i \cdot y} + \ldots\right] |z\rangle \|^2.$$

Given $y \in \mathbb{F}_2^n$, satisfying $s_i \cdot y \neq 0$ for some $s_i \in S$, the first part of the above expression will always be equal to 0, as the series $+1$ and -1 will always cancel each other. However, in the second part of the equation, since the complete set of $s_i \in S$ is not present, exactly t many terms with $+1$ and exactly t many terms with -1 remain, which could not cancel each other. After taking the norm, each will contribute $+1$. Therefore,

$$\mathcal{P}(|y\rangle)|_{s_i \cdot y \neq 0} = 2t/2^{2n},$$

known as the error probability. When $t = 0$, i.e., for an exact k-Simon function, the probability of observing such bit-patterns is 0. However, in t-near-k-Simon function we have $t \geq 1$. Hence, the probability of observing such a bit-string is positive and increases with t. Further, since the sum of all the probabilities equals 1, the probability of observing bit-patterns $y \in \mathbb{F}_2^n$ with $s_i \cdot y = 0$ for all $s_i \in S$, is now reduced to

$$\mathcal{P}(|y\rangle)|_{s_i \cdot y = 0} = \frac{1}{2^{n-k}} - \frac{1}{2^{n-k}} (2^n - 2^{n-k}) \frac{2t}{2^{2n}} = \frac{1}{2^{n-k}} - (2^k - 1) \frac{2t}{2^{2n}}.$$

Therefore, upon running the Simon's algorithm on a t-near-k-Simon function f, we observe the desired bit-patterns $y \in \mathbb{F}_2^n$ satisfying $s_i \cdot y = 0$ with higher probabilities and the bit-patterns $y \in \mathbb{F}_2^n$ satisfying $s_i \cdot y \neq 0$, with smaller probabilities. Consequently, one can apply all the error mitigation techniques here as in [5] to find the desired shift space S.

We illustrate the functioning of Simon's algorithm for a t-near k-Simon function with the help of an example using the 'qasm_simulator' provided by Qiskit, as follows.

Example 4. Let $f(x_1, x_2, x_3) = x_2, (1 \oplus x_1 x_2 x_3), 0$ be a 1-near-2-Simon function, varies at the input 111 from its nearest 2-Simon function $f'(x_1, x_2, x_3) = x_2, 1, 0$. The corresponding quantum circuit and the observed histogram from the IBMQ simulator are as follows (Fig. 4).

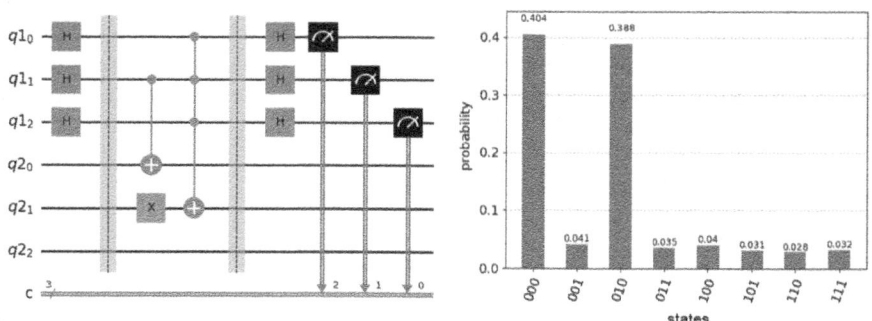

Fig. 4. Simon's algorithm on a 1-near-2-Simon function f using 'qasm_simulator' and the corresponding histogram.

Notice that the theoretical probabilities of bit-patterns $y \notin S^\perp$ is equal to $2t/2^6 = 1/32 = 0.03125$ and the probabilities of the bit-patterns $y \in S^\perp$ is equal to $(0.5 - (2^2 - 1) \times 0.03125) = 0.40625$, according to the values observed in the histogram (Fig. 3).

In Example 4, we considered f differing from a k-Simon function only at a single point, i.e., $t = 1$. However, we can further extend for $t \geq 1$, and consequently, the error probability increases with t. Hence, distinguishing $s_i \in S$ from an erroneous n-bit string becomes more challenging and requires more number of queries.

Example 5. Further, to implement the scenario where a near-Simon function is being implemented in a noisy quantum device, we run the same 1-near-2-Simon function $f(x_1, x_2, x_3) = x_2, (1 \oplus x_1 x_2 x_3), 0$ using the noisy quantum device 'FakeMelbourne()', and present the observed histogram as follows (Fig. 5).

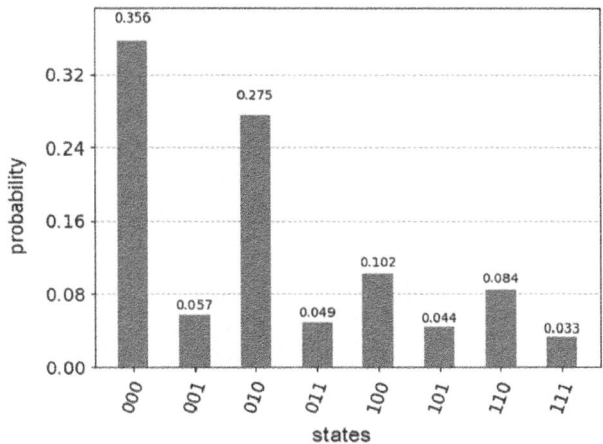

Fig. 5. Histogram obtained from running Simon's algorithm on 1-near-2-Simon function f using 'FakeMelbourne()'.

As in 'qasm_simulator' (behaving like an ideal quantum device), in this histogram, the desired bit-patterns 000 and 010 appear with a high probability. However, the erroneous states now appear more frequently compared to the earlier scenario.

5 Conclusion

This paper revisited Simon's algorithm for a Boolean function with more than one (2^k) shift and characterized the observed bit-patterns in a noisy quantum set-up. Given oracle access of an exact k-Simon function and the opportunity to use an ideal quantum device, the process of determining the hidden shift space S is thoroughly discussed in Sect. 2, and we also provided an exact count of such Boolean functions in Theorem 1. Next, given oracle access to an exact k-Simon function and Simon's algorithm is executed in a noisy quantum device, the process of determining the hidden shift space is thoroughly covered in Sect. 3. This contribution extends the idea presented in [5]. Moreover, we also provided the mathematical formulation for the efficient oracle implementation of any k-Simon function, which helps reduce the overall error while running Simon's algorithm.

After that, we studied the scenario where the given Boolean function differs from an exact k-Simon function at a few points and analyzed the erroneous bit-patterns $y \in \mathbb{F}_2^n$ obtained from running the Simon's algorithm in a noise-free quantum machine 'qasm_simulator' provided by Qiskit. However, due to the unavailability of the original 'ibmq_16_melbourne' device mentioned in [5], we employed the 'FakeMelbourne()' simulator as a substitute, which accurately simulates the behaviour of the 'ibmq_16_melbourne' device.

Acknowledgments. The third author acknowledges the support of MeitY, Government of India, related to the initiative "Cluster - Cryptography, Information Security Education and Awareness (ISEA) Project Phase - III". The second and the fourth authors contributed in this paper during their visits at Indian Statistical Institute, Kolkata in 2024. All the authors like to acknowledge the anonymous reviewers for their detailed comments that improved the technical as well as editorial quality of this paper.

Disclosure of Interests. The authors have no competing interests to declare that are relevant to the content of this article.

References

1. Bonnetain, X.: Tight bounds for Simon's algorithm. In: Longa, P., Ràfols, C. (eds.) LATINCRYPT 2021. LNCS, vol. 12912, pp. 3–23. Springer, Cham (2021). https://doi.org/10.1007/978-3-030-88238-9_1
2. Deutsch, D., Jozsa, R.: Rapid solution of problems by quantum computation. In: Proceedings of Royal Society London, vol. 439, no. 1907, pp. 553–558 (1992). https://doi.org/10.1098/rspa.1992.0167
3. Grover, L. K.: A fast quantum mechanical algorithm for database search. In: Proceedings of the 28-th ACM Symposium on Theory of Computing (STOC'96), pp. 212–219 (1996). https://doi.org/10.1145/237814.237866
4. Kaplan, M., Leurent, G., Leverrier, A., Naya-Plasencia, M.: Breaking symmetric cryptosystems using quantum period finding. In: Robshaw, M., Katz, J. (eds.) CRYPTO 2016. LNCS, vol. 9815, pp. 207–237. Springer, Heidelberg (2016). https://doi.org/10.1007/978-3-662-53008-5_8
5. May, A., Schlieper, L., Schwinger, J.: Noisy Simon period finding. In: Paterson, K.G. (ed.) CT-RSA 2021. LNCS, vol. 12704, pp. 75–99. Springer, Cham (2021). https://doi.org/10.1007/978-3-030-75539-3_4
6. Shor, P.W.: Polynomial-time algorithms for prime factorization and discrete logarithms on a quantum computer. SIAM J. Comput. **26**(5), 1484–1509 (1997). https://doi.org/10.1137/S0097539795293172
7. Simon, D.R.: On the power of quantum computation. SIAM J. Comput. **26**(5), 1474–1483 (1997). https://doi.org/10.1137/S0097539796298637
8. Strang, G.: The fundamental theorem of linear algebra. Am. Math. Mon. **100**(9), 848–855 (1993). https://doi.org/10.2307/2324660

Authentication and Authorization, Cyber-physical Systems Security, Privacy-preserving Technologies

Generation of Believable Fake Integral Equations for Cyber Deception

Nilin Prabhaker[1](✉), Rahul Maurya[2], Ghanshyam S. Bopche[1], and Michael Arock[1]

[1] National Institute of Technology, Tiruchirappalli, Tiruchirappalli 620015, India
nilinprabhaker@gmail.com
[2] Sardar Vallabhbhai National Institute of Technology (SVNIT), Surat 395007, India

Abstract. Due to the increased sophistication of cyber attacks over the last few decades, there has been an exponential rise in data exfiltration incidents worldwide. Cyber attackers often remain undetected in enterprise networks for a significant amount of time (312 days for a zero-day attack), sufficient to compromise sensitive, business-critical, or mission-critical data such as customer data, scientific documents, trade secrets, proprietary research, etc. Protecting such information is paramount, necessitating techniques to secure it even after theft. Recent research suggests the automatic generation of fake documents to increase burden on the attacker, who needs to correctly identify the correct document from a set of legitimate and counterfeit documents. Numerous works have been proposed in the literature for automatically generating fake documents by manipulating text, equations, images, tables, circuit diagrams, etc. Among all types of equations present in the document, Integral equations are one of the core components of novel innovation and play a crucial role in a diverse set of domains such as risk management, stock market prediction, weather forecast, or even the prediction of natural disasters, etc. In this work, we introduce the Fake Integral Equation Generation Engine (FIEGE) to produce many plausible decoy documents by manipulating the integral equations present in the scientific document. The generated fake document can confuse and mislead the potential attackers if stolen, slow them down, waste their time and resources in identifying the original document, and thereby increase the overall cost of attack. The system employs algorithms for efficient and practical fake integral equation generation, while human evaluation studies demonstrate its effectiveness in deceiving experts. Future research directions are discussed to enhance the performance and resilience of the FIEGE system, making it a promising tool for improving cybersecurity in organizations.

Keywords: Intellectual Property · Data Exfiltration · Dwell Time · Integral Equation · Cyber Deception · Digital Decoys

1 Introduction

Intellectual property (IP) documents are crucial for businesses or government organizations since they contain ideas for research and innovation. These documents are building blocks for many organizations and help them expand globally. Similarly, IP documents are essential for governments' economic growth as they help protect industries and make fair trade deals with other countries. Hence, the protection of IP is of paramount importance for both organizations and government entities. Due to technological advancements and attacks' sophistication, it is impossible to obtain foolproof security. According to Symantec's report [3], the average dwell time for a typical zero-day attack is 312 days (about ten and a half months). Here, the dwell time refers to the amount of time that an attacker remains undetected within a network after gaining unauthorized access. As long as the adversary remains undetected in the network, they will attempt lateral movements to seek out valuable data, exfiltrate increasing amounts of business or mission critical data, install backdoors, and potentially launch more advanced attacks or engage in other malicious activities. Therefore, organizations must minimize dwell time to mitigate the impact of a successful cyberattack. So, businesses and governments need to focus on security controls that can protect stolen IP documents even after a successful Cyber breach by affecting the adversary's decision-making capability.

A scientific document contains a diverse set of components such as text, equations, tables, graphs, circuit diagrams, flowcharts, etc. Mathematical equations are essential in technical and scientific documents for several reasons. At first, they provide a precise and concise way to represent complex relationships and phenomena. They allow researchers and engineers to communicate ideas and findings with clarity and accuracy, reducing the risk of misinterpretation. Moreover, they serve as a universal language, making it easier for scientists and experts from different backgrounds to understand and build upon each other's work. The equation present in documents may be polynomial, transcendental, differential, Boolean, or integral. Integral equations are powerful tools with significant applications across domains, such as signal processing, fluid dynamics, quantum mechanics, electromagnetic, etc. They are fundamental in solving real-life problems involving wave propagation, scattering, boundary value problems, risk management, stock market prediction, weather forecast, calculation of satellite momentum, their thrust, or even the prediction of natural disasters. In various scientific documents, integral equations are essential for advancing defense, aerospace, and security research. These documents often involve sensitive information, and keeping the specifics of these equations secret is crucial to maintaining national security and technological advantages. These documents can be research work, projects, or anything vital for an organization or individual. Losing these documents could harm the organization in several ways. Adversaries can use the equation present in the exfiltrated scientific document to extract the exact meaning of it, sell it to the business competitors, particularly in the darknet for monetary gain, collude with the enemy state in case of defense-related documents, or use it for any other malicious purpose to achieve their objectives. The net effect of such data exfiltration or data leakage for the victim organizations is financial loss, reputation damage, or even a national security failure in case of defense secrets. Therefore, organizations must protect such business-critical or mission-critical data.

Recent work suggests the use of data-level Cyber deception techniques [4,19,20,23] used to mislead the adversary during real-time network intrusion and even after data exfiltration. This can be done by deploying fake, believable digital artifacts throughout the enterprise network. Such decoy artifacts distract attackers from the target resource, confuse them, change their beliefs, affect their decision-making process, and waste their resources and time, thereby slowing them down. The data-level cyber deception techniques work as a last line of defense to protect the data if configured and deployed correctly. Essentially, the recent research in cyber deception primarily concentrates on creating fake documents by manipulating various elements such as text [5,12,15], tables [6], graphs [11] and equations (including polynomial, transcendental, and differential equations) [22] within scientific and technical documents. However, no existing work addresses the creation of convincing fake versions of documents by manipulation in integral equations. This paper addresses that gap by generating decoy documents with believable "K" fake versions of the integral equation. The generated equation should be sufficiently similar to convince the attacker it is genuine yet different enough to prevent them from producing the correct output.

We have proposed a Fake Integral Equation Generation Engine (FIEGE) to generate fake integral equations that look very similar to the real ones, making it hard for attackers to tell them apart. By doing this, we can protect the documents and keep sensitive information safe from potential adversaries. We have used the Trapezoidal rule to the original integral equation and the generated fake equations to obtain their respective approximated values. Essentially, the Trapezoidal rule is used to evaluate the accuracy of our approximation to choose one fake Integral equation over the other. In addition to the description of the equation, it is essential to maintain the relation among different integral equations in the same document, which we will explore in future work.

The rest of the paper is organized as follows: Sect. 2 presents a quick overview of related work on generating believable fake artifacts in documents. The overall FBIGE architecture, along with a definition of terms and algorithms, are presented in Sect. 3. Section 4 presents the experimental results for the sample Integral equation followed by discussion in Sect. 5. Finally, Sect. 6 concludes the paper with future work.

2 Related Work

Cyber deception [1,14] refers to an approach used to deceive or mislead adversaries from real entities in the enterprise network. It involves strategies and tactics to trick or confuse malicious actors by creating and deploying believable fake digital artifacts. Deception has been used in warfare for centuries [8,17]. In cybersecurity, attackers primarily use deception to carry out social engineering-based attacks such as phishing [7], smishing [13], vishing [10], etc., which aim to deceive victims into downloading benign-looking malicious attachments or clicking genuinely looking malicious URLs. However, the defensive use of cyber-deception [14] is a more recent development. Creation of decoy documents [21, 23] and canary files [19] are the deceptive approaches to protect the technical documents. Essentially, the decoy files are placed to mislead the attacker, whereas the canary files are used to generate alerts to the administrator besides misleading the adversaries. Yuill et al. [23] proposed honeyfiles, which trigger an alarm when fake documents are accessed. Since a document consists of diverse constituent parts such as text, tables, graphs, equations, and flowcharts, the generation of decoy technical documents is challenging. Chakrabarty et al. [5] proposed the Fake Online Repository Generation Engine (FORGE) system. The authors tried to generate fake documents by replacing the semantically similar concepts using ontology. However, the authors have yet to focus on the believability of the generated documents. To solve this problem, Karuna et al. [15] used word transposition and substitution to generate the fake text using parts of speech tagging and pre-collected n-grams. The subsequent approach of authors [16] involves increasing the comprehension burden of documents for attackers by shuffling, deleting, and adding sentences having important concepts. Moreover, the authors proposed the metric (Connectivity, Sequentiality, and Dispersion) to measure the cognitive effort of the attacker required to understand the fake document. Chen et al. [6] proposed the synthesis of fake tables consisting of large volumes of data using Generative Adversarial Networks. However, to date, only a few works in the literature focus on automatic fake equation generation. Xiong et al. [22] primarily focuses on generating fake equations for polynomial, transcendental, and differential equations. However, technical documents and patents often contain various other equations, such as integral and Boolean equations. In our previous work, we focused on the generation of fake documents by manipulating the Boolean logic circuit present in the documents [18]. Investigating the generation of fake integral equations would enhance the diversity and applicability of deception techniques in the real world. In the following section, we will explain the architecture for generating believable fake version of the scientific document by manipulating the integral equation.

3 Fake Integral Equation Generation Engine (FIEGE) Architecture

The architecture of the FIEGE framework is depicted in Fig. 1. It demonstrates the process for the generation of a believable "K" number of fake documents from the original document by manipulating the integral equation present in the original document. The original document containing real integral equations is passed as input to the system, and the goal is to generate several fake documents, each with a fake version of the original equation. There are numerous works [2,9] present in literature that focus on the extraction of mathematical equations present in the documents. Therefore, we have not focused on the extraction of integral equations. The extracted integral equation will be passed through the parser to find syntactical errors. Furthermore, the equation is tokenized into variables and operators to create a list of edit operators that contains information about the index and their types. The obtained list will be used to generate the integral equations within the specified budget. Here, the budget is the maximum feasible cost of edit operation. To increase the believability of the generated equation, we applied various constraints that optimize the result of the integral equation using FIEGE-FAST (Algorithm 2). The obtained optimal cost(Opt_{cost}) and optimal edit sequence ($OptEdit_{seq}$) will be used to check the overall cost($Cost_{sofar}$) of the modification if the cost of the edit sequence is less than the predefined budget (*Budget*). The equation generated using that sequence will be the best option to replace the equation present in the document. Similarly, the process will iterate until the length of the number of generated equations reaches "K". Finally, the generated integral equation will be used to create fake documents. Detailed explanations of terms, context-free grammar(CFG), and algorithms will be discussed in subsequent subsections.

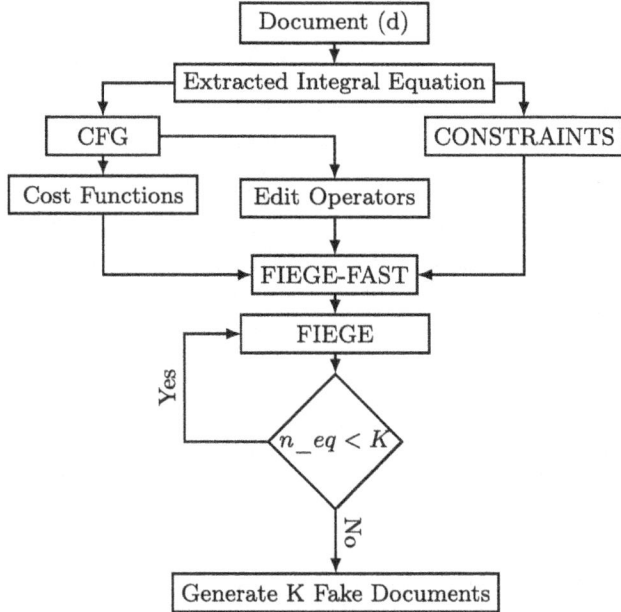

Fig. 1. Proposed architecture of Fake Integral Equation Generation Engine (FIEGE)

3.1 Context Free Grammar for Integral Equations

Essentially, the integral equation combines the integrand, the respective variable, and the limit of integration as represented in Eq. 1. The integrand may be a linear, polynomial, transcendental, exponential, logarithmic, differential equation, or even a combination of different equations. Each equation is recognized by different context-free grammar (CFG). The best example is the FEE framework [22], which contains a group of context-free grammars (CFGs) that try to understand the equation. These CFGs are designed for different equations, such as linear, transcendental, and differential equations. To parse the integral equation, we have modified the parser present in the existing FEE [22] framework. The approach for finding edit operators and constraints is the same. To find the optimal edit sequence within the budget, we have used the FIEGE-FAST algorithm, and the obtained edit sequence and operational cost for each modification will be passed to the FIEGE algorithm, which iteratively applies the edit sequence and generates the fake version of the original equation.

$$< IE > \rightarrow \int_{<l\_lim>}^{<u\_lim>} < integrand > d < variable > \tag{1}$$

3.2 Definitions and Example

- **Edit Operators**: Edit operators (σ) consist of three parameters $\sigma(t_i, r, t_r)$, where t_i is any token present in the equation, r is the position of token t_i, and t_r is the new token for the replacement of token t_i. If t_i is a variable, then t_r must be a variable or their negation; if t_i is a binary and unary operator, then t_r must be a binary or unary operator, respectively.
- **Edit Sequence**: An edit sequence consists of a set of edit operators wherein no two operators would try to modify the token at same position in an equation E. Formally, an edit sequence can be defined as a sequence of edit operators $\sigma_1, \ldots, \sigma_n$ and represented as $\sigma_n(\sigma_{n-1}(\ldots(\sigma_1(E))\ldots))$ such that all edit operators $\sigma_1, \ldots, \sigma_n$ are disjoint to each other in terms of their token position. If two edit operators try to modify the same token position of an equation($\sigma(3.2, 4, 4.2)$ and $\sigma(4.2, 4, 3.2)$), they will produce the same result later. Hence first of the two edit operators will not impact the final result. We are eliminating such edit operator from the edit sequence.
- **Cost Function**: Each alteration to the original equation changes its resulting value, and the change is quantified using a *cost* function. This function maps edit operations to the set $\mathbb{R}^+$ of positive real numbers. Cost functions can be applied to sequences of changes by assigning a cost to each individual modification in the equation. Specifically, the cost of a sequence of edits $(e_1, \ldots, e_m)$ is given by $\text{cost}(e_1, \ldots, e_m) = \sum_{i=1}^{m} \text{cost}(e_i)$.
- **Constraints**: Essentially, the generated equation must closely resemble the original integral to create confusion in the adversary's decision-making. However, it must not produce the same outcome as the original integral equation. To optimize the results of the proposed system, we incorporated constraints used in [22]. Specifically, the coefficients and exponents in the original equation are replaced with values within a defined range. At the same time, we substitute unary and binary operators with operators having similar properties.

Example

Let an equation $y = x^{2.15} + 3.2 * x + 1.4$ as a polynomial inside the integral equation. The edit operator $\sigma(+, 3, -)$ represent the modification in original equation by replacing + operator at location 3 with − operator. Here, we assumed that the cost of each edit operator is 1. Therefore the cost of the edit sequence $e_s = \langle r_{3.2;4;4.2}(s), r_{+;7;-}(s) \rangle$ i.e., $\text{cost}(e_s) = 2$ and the resulting fake equation is $y = x^{2.15} + 4.2 * x - 1.4$. Here, the constant(3.2) at location 4 and '+' sign at location 7 in original equation ($x^{2.15} + 3.2 * x + 1.4$) got replaced with 4.2 and '−' operator, respectively.

3.3 Generation of Believable Fake Integral Equations

The generation of believable fake integral equations starts with validating the extracted equation, which involves three main checks: syntax check, evaluation check, and mathematical rules check. Additionally, domain knowledge checks can be added to validate the integration equations further. The first step is to check the syntax of the integrand of the given equation. We use the Python `ast` module to parse the integrand and to find the syntactical errors. The obtained syntactically correct equation will be passed for evaluation. In the next phase, we evaluated the integral of the integrand symbolically using the `sympy` library. The integral variable is first defined as a symbolic variable using `sympy.Symbol()`. Then, the integral value of the integrand with respect to the integral variable is calculated. If any evaluation-related errors occur (e.g., `NameError`, `TypeError`, `ValueError`, `ZeroDivisionError`, or `sympy.SympifyError`), the equation is considered invalid. Further, the valid equation will be passed for a mathematical rule check, verifying the specific rules an integral equation must have. For example, the equation must contain the integral symbol ($\int$) and the integral variable (e.g., 'dx,' 'dt,' etc.). We check for the presence of these essential elements in the equation, and if either is missing, the equation is considered invalid. We pass the integral equation as a string to the function, and it will return a tuple containing the validation result (True for valid and False for invalid) and abstract syntax tree (AST) of the integrand.

$$P_{actual} = \int (x^{2.15} + 3.2x + 1.4) dx \qquad (2)$$

The validation function will store the validation result, and AST of the integrand in a human-readable format. The integral equation validation process helps to ensure the correctness and accuracy of the provided integration equations before further processing or analysis. Algorithms used to generate the believable fake equation will be discussed in the upcoming subsection.

FIEGE: To generate the K believable fake integral equation from the original equation EQ, within the predefined budget $Budget$. We have designed an iterative Algorithm 1. The algorithm uses sets, $Edit_{seq} and Fake_{EQ}$ to store the edit sequences and corresponding generated fake equations, respectively. It iterates until it has found the desired number ($K > 0$) of fake equations. In each iteration, the FEIGE call the FIEGE-FAST for optimal edit sequence along with cost which is used to calculate budget of overall manipulation. Each solution has a cost that fits within the overall budget ($Budget$), it is added to the set of fake equations $Fake_{EQ}$, and the corresponding edit sequence is added to $Edit_{seq}$. The algorithm repeats the process until K fake equations are generated. The run-time of the algorithm is $O(K \cdot T)$, where K is the desired number of fake equations and T is the time required to solve FIEGE-FAST, which has the complexity of $O(n^2)$. In the rest of the section, we will focus on the formulation of the optimization problem FIEGE-FAST, which is at the core of the FIEGE.

Algorithm 1: FIEGE

    Data: $EQ, K, Budget$
    Result: $Fake_{EQ}$
1   $Edit_{seq} \leftarrow \{\}$;
2   $Fake_{EQ} \leftarrow \{\}$;
3   $Edit_{op} \leftarrow tokenize(EQ)$;
4   **while** $|Fake_{EQ}| < K$ **do**
5       $Edit_{seqt}, CostEdit_{seqt} \leftarrow$ Solve FIEGE-FAST;
6   **if** $CostEdit_{seqt} \leq Budget$ **then**
7          $Edit_{seq} \leftarrow Edit_{seq} \cup \{Edit_{seqt}\}$;
8          $Fake_{EQ} \leftarrow Fake_{EQ} \cup \{Edit_{seqt}(EQ)\}$;
9   **end**
10   **else**
11   Print " Insufficient Budget to generate k fake Integral equations!";
12   break;
13   **end**
14 **end**

FIEGE-FAST: The algorithm takes the original equation(EQ), edit operators ($Edit_{op}$), and constraints ($CONSTR$) as input and returns the optimum cost of edit operation along with the optimal edit sequence ($OptEdit_{seq}$). The algorithm initializes an empty set for optimal edit sequence ($OptEdit_{seq}$) and a significant value of optimal cost. Then iterates through each value of the number within a range $(0, NUM)$, where NUM is a large number selected by the user according to the requirement (the value of NUM will be large if the user needs more fake equations). The algorithm iterates for each token present at a particular index in the original equation. It randomly selects the edit operator and tries to edit the original equation with the cost of value 1 for change in variable and operator and the absolute difference between coefficient if the value of the coefficient got changed. The edit sequence which has the minimum value of cost and satisfies the constraints is considered the optimal edit sequence. Finally, the algorithm returns the optimal edit sequence ($OptEdit_{seq}$) and the optimal cost (Opt_{cost}) to the FIEGE algorithm, which is being used to generate the fake equations.

Algorithm 2: FIEGE-FAST

Data: $EQ, Edit_{op}, CONSTR$
Result: $Opt_{cost}, OptEdit_{seq}$

1 $OptEdit_{seq} \leftarrow \{\}$;
2 $Opt_{cost} \leftarrow MAX$;
3 **for** *each i in range(0, NUM)* **do**
4     $Curr_{cost} \leftarrow 0$;
5     $Curr_{editseq} \leftarrow \{\}$;
6   **for** *each $token_{index}$ in EQ* **do**
7   Random select *eop* from $Edit_{op}$;
8        $Curr_{editseq} \leftarrow Curr_{editseq} \cup eop$;
9        $Curr_{cost} \leftarrow Cost(eop)$;
10   **if** ($Curr_{cost} < Opt_{cost}$ and $Curr_{editseq}$ not in $Edit_{seq}$ and satisfies $CONSTR$) **then**
11           $OptEdit_{seq} \leftarrow Curr_{editseq}$
12   **end**
13   **end**
14 **end**
15 **if** $OptEdit_{seq} = \phi$ **then**
16   Print "No eligible edit sequence exists!";
17 **end**

Result: $Opt_{cost}, OptEdit_{seq}$

4 Experiments and Result

A diverse set of equation had been considered in the experiment to generate the set of fake equations. The proposed algorithm tried to modify the equation in terms of coefficient, exponent, and operator present in the integral equation. The obtained results for Eq. 2 discussed in the previous section are depicted in Table 1. Furthermore, to evaluate the accuracy of our approximation, we first applied the Trapezoidal rule to the real integral equation. The result obtained by applying the Trapezoidal rule within the range 0 to 2 for the real integral is 12.02. Then, we applied the same Trapezoidal rule to generate a set of 10 fake integral equations and calculated the approximate value, operation cost, and absolute difference in the value of the integral. We sorted the equation in increasing order of the difference in the value of the integral and then the cost of operation involved in modification. Moreover, we applied Simpson's 1/3rd rule for further evaluation of the results. It is evident that the value of fake integrals (as depicted in Table 1) after applying Simpson's 1/3rd rule is almost similar to the value obtained through the Trapezoidal rule. We have generated the curve for the value of the original and fake equation at different values of x between 0 to 2. Figure 2 represents the similarity between original and fake equations (1 to 10) in polynomial form. Similarly, Fig. 3 represents the value of the equation after integration in the same range for different values of x. The curve in both figures follows a similar pattern for original and fake equations with small variations in magnitude. It is evident from the plots depicted in Fig. 2 and 3 that there is a consistency between the curve for each equation in the original form and after integration. Moreover, we have tested the proposed framework for the diverse set of equations and obtained similar results.

Table 1. Comparison of Fake Integral Equations with Real Integral Equation, where $x: 0 \leq x \leq 2$

Original Equation: $\int (x^{2.15} + 3.2x + 1.4)dx$				
Value of Integral: 12.02				
Sr. No.	Fake Equations	Value	Cost	Difference	Simpsons's 1/3rd
1	$\int (x^{1.84} + 3.56 * x + 0.89)\,dx$	11.42	1.18	0.60	11.42
2	$\int (x^{2.19} + 3.7 * x + 1.28)\,dx$	12.82	0.66	0.80	12.82
3	$\int (x^{1.99} + 3.73 * x + 0.38)\,dx$	10.88	1.71	1.13	10.87
4	$\int (x^{2.76} + 3.43 * x + 1.37)\,dx$	13.20	0.87	1.17	13.20
5	$\int (x^{2.5} + 3.16 * x + 1.92)\,dx$	13.39	0.91	1.37	13.39
6	$\int (x^{1.88} + 4.14 * x + 1.36)\,dx$	13.56	1.25	1.54	13.55
7	$\int (x^{3.11} + 3.37 * x + 2.23)\,dx$	15.40	1.96	3.38	15.40
8	$\int (x^{2.01} + 4.14 * x + 2.56)\,dx$	16.08	2.24	4.05	16.07
9	$\int (x^{1.83} + 3.25 * x - 1.18)\,dx$	6.65	1.59	5.36	6.65
10	$\int (x^{2.55} + 2.71 * x - 1.28)\,dx$	6.16	2.01	5.85	6.15

In order to assess the accuracy and believability of the generated fake integral equations, a human evaluation study was conducted. The actual and generated fake equations are mixed and shared with a team of five members for evaluation using questionnaires. It is evident from the result that none of the evaluators were able to tell the difference between the real and fake equations visually. Moreover, five human evaluators were asked to assess the accuracy of each fake equation in comparison to the original integral equation on a scale of 1 to 5, with 1 being "Inaccurate" and 5 being "Very Accurate." Additionally, they were asked to rate the believability of each fake equation on the same scale, with 1 being "Not Believable" and 5 being "Believable". The obtained result is depicted in Fig. 4.

Generated integral equations using FIEGE can be used to generate believable fake document provided the description of the equation should be modified. However, the modification in the description of equation is beyond the scope of this paper that can be addressed separately as a part of future work.

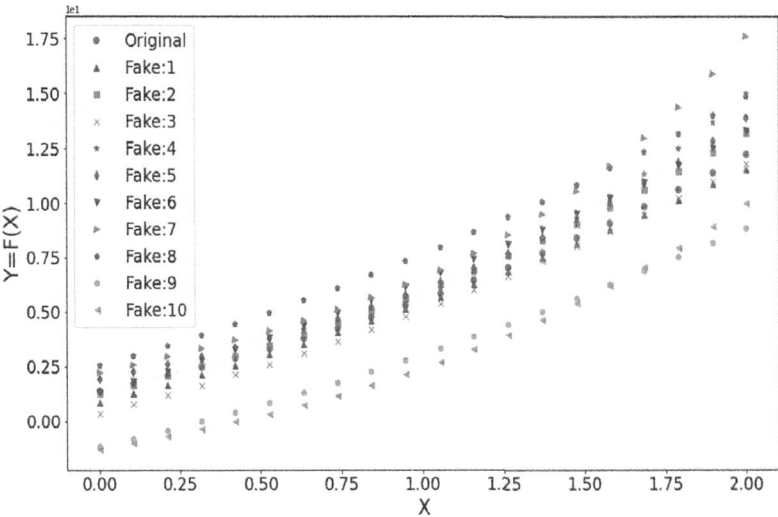

Fig. 2. Value of Polynomial Equations/Integrand (Original and Fake) (log transformed) at different value of x, where $0 \leq x \leq 2$

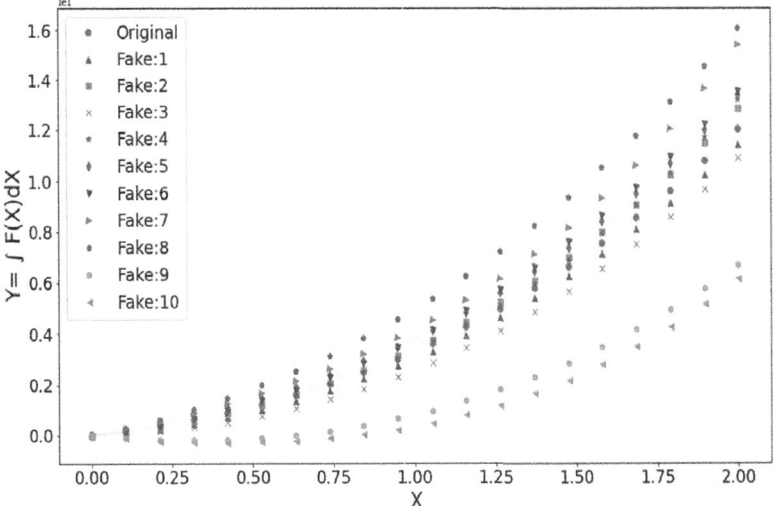

Fig. 3. Value of Integral Equations (Original and Fake) (log transformed) at different value of x, where $0 \leq x < 2$

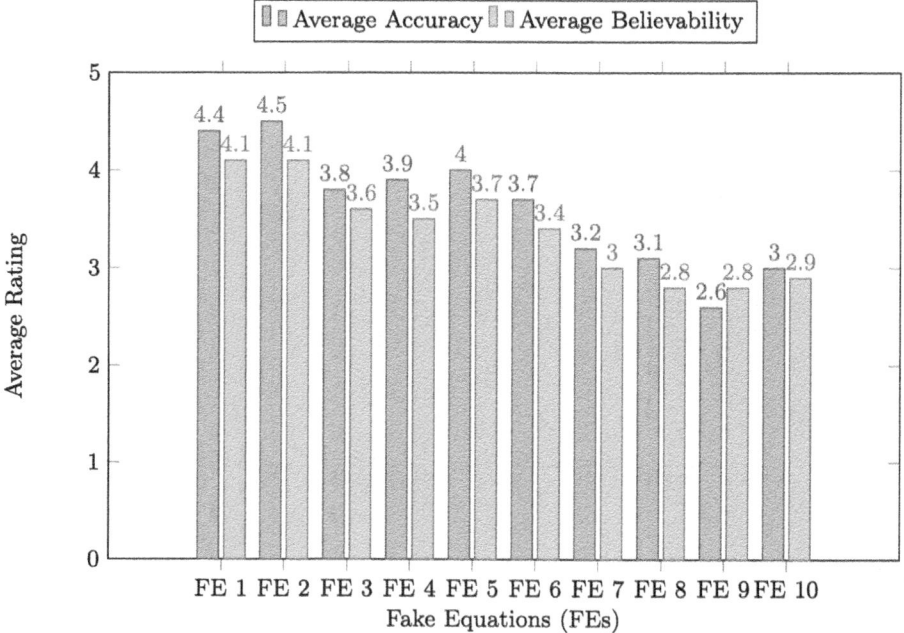

Fig. 4. Human Evaluation Metrics for Fake Integral Equations

5 Discussion

This research addresses the problem of intellectual property theft by developing the FIEGE framework, which focuses on generation of multiple fake document by modifying the integral equations present in the document. The generated fake version of document imposes a comprehensive burden on the adversaries which misleads and alter the decision-making capabilities. The adversaries will have to find the original document among the all exfiltrated documents. They have to make use of domain expert.

Essentially, the proposed system uses manual work for constraints extraction before inputting them into the FIEGE framework which indicates possibility for further improvement and automation to streamline the process to enhance the usability of the framework. Moreover, we need to create a pipeline for entire process to be automatic like starting from different forms of documents, extraction and detection of the type of equation, the generation of believable fake and finally the generation of fake documents. Overall, the contributions of this research lie in the development of the FIEGE framework for generating fake integral equations present in technical documents. It improves the security of sensitive information, imposes costs on attackers, and adds an additional layer of protection against intellectual property theft.

5.1 Challenges and Limitations

Till now, we have discussed the method of generation of fake integral equations for cyber deception. However, we have not yet discussed the challenges and limitations the proposed framework may face at the time of deployment in a real environment.

- **Generalization**: A scientific document consists of a diverse set of components such as text, equations, tables, images, circuit diagrams, etc., interrelated with each other. A simple change in one component may require a change in other components of the document, which is a challenging task and affects the believability of the generated fake. As far as the differential equation is concerned, it is already covered by Xiong et al. [22], and the generation of a fake circuit diagram is covered in our previous work [18]. However, there is still a need for a generalized framework for the generation of fake documents for cyber deception. Which we want to explore in our future work.
- **Scalability**: There is a possibility of variation in the representation of the integral equation in real-world examples of integral equations. We may encounter double or triple integrals in the documents that we have not considered in our experiment. However, a change in the context-free grammar (CFG) may provide a solution for these integral equations, which we will explore in our future work.
- **Security Analysis**: As far as the vulnerability of the proposed system is concerned, If an attacker(s) read the document carefully, they may get confused with the explanation, which may give a hint to attackers to distinguish real and fake. Hence, it is required to change the explanation of the equation present in the document with each change in the integral equation, which we have not covered yet. Moreover, We are keeping the original document among generated its K-fake version, so there may be a possibility that the attacker will get the real document at the very first instance, but the possibility of getting real at the first instance is $1/K+1$. If the value of K=10, the probability p=$1/11$, which is 0.09, increases the overall cost of the attacker.
- **Integration and Practical Deployment**: We also believe that the deployment of the proposed system in a real environment is necessary. Till now, we have only focused on the generation of fake integral equations; the integration and deployment of generated fake documents need proper strategies and planning, which will be covered in future work.
- **Legal and Ethical Consideration**: In general, the use of fake documents is both illegal and unethical, posing risks to individuals, organizations, and society. However, the key objective of the deception-driven approach for cyber defense is to understand and manipulate the attacker's perception of the system as well as to mislead the attacker's action in such a way that the defender can control and monitor the activities of the attacker. According to Zhu [24], there are a few important points that must be considered before using deception for cyber defense:
    - Defenders must engage with a genuine intent to protect the network and its users.

- It must be ensured that deception does not harm any legitimate users of the network.
- The rules and mechanism of defensive cyber deception must be transparent to all users such that they are aware of the use of deception in the network and can voluntarily consent to its use.
- The designed techniques must consider the perspective of all potential users.

6 Conclusion

This paper extends a system called the Fake Equation Engine (FEE) by generating fake integral equations for cyber deception. We used context-free grammar(CFG) and the iterative algorithm FIEGE to generate the fake integral equations. Essentially, the goal is to mislead potential attackers towards fake documents generated by replacing original equations with fake equations. To validate the generated equation, we have used the Trapezoidal Rule, which returns the approximate value of integral equations. The believability of the equation was done through a small human evaluation study. We found that the proposed system is effective in creating deceptive fake equations. Distinguishing the real equation from the fake is difficult for human beings. In this paper, our focus was on the manipulation of integrad present in the integral equations. However, we have not focused on the change in limit and variable present in the equation. In the future, we will explore it. Additionally, we will explore the manipulation of double and triple integral functions present in the document. In conclusion, the proposed system is a powerful tool for protecting sensitive documents from attackers by misleading towards deceptive documents. Improving the proposed algorithm for various uncovered equations may be the future research direction that ensures improved security and protection of intellectual property documents. Our framework complements the existing FEE framework in generating believable fake documents.

References

1. Almeshekah, M.H., Spafford, E.H.: Cyber security deception. In: Cyber Deception: Building the Scientific Foundation, pp. 23–50 (2016)
2. Alvaro, F., Sánchez, J.A., Benedí, J.M.: Recognition of on-line handwritten mathematical expressions using 2D stochastic context-free grammars and hidden Markov models. Pattern Recogn. Lett. **35**, 58–67 (2014)
3. Bilge, L., Dumitras, T.: Investigating zero-day attacks. Login **38**(4), 6–13 (2013)
4. Bowen, B.M., Hershkop, S., Keromytis, A.D., Stolfo, S.J.: Baiting inside attackers using decoy documents. In: International Conference on Security and Privacy in Communication Systems, pp. 51–70. Springer, Heidelberg (2009)
5. Chakraborty, T., Jajodia, S., Katz, J., Picariello, A., Sperli, G., Subrahmanian, V.S.: A fake online repository generation engine for cyber deception. IEEE Trans. Dependable Secure Comput. **18**(2), 518–533 (2021)

6. Chen, H., Jajodia, S., Liu, J., Park, N., Sokolov, V., Subrahmanian, V.: Faketables: using GANs to generate functional dependency preserving tables with bounded real data. In: IJCAI, pp. 2074–2080 (2019)
7. CISCO: The evolution of phishing. https://newsroom.cisco.com/c/r/newsroom/en/us/a/y2023/m02/security-history-the-evolution-of-phishing.html. Accessed 10 Nov 2023
8. Fowler, C.A., Nesbit, R.F.: Tactical deception in air-land warfare. J. Electron. Def. **18**(6), 37–45 (1995)
9. Garain, U., Chaudhuri, B.B.: Recognition of online handwritten mathematical expressions. IEEE Trans. Syst. Man Cybern. Part B (Cybern.) **34**(6), 2366–2376 (2004)
10. Griffin, S.E., Rackley, C.C.: Vishing. In: Proceedings of the 5th Annual Conference on Information Security Curriculum Development, pp. 33–35 (2008)
11. Han, Q., Molinaro, C., Picariello, A., Sperli, G., Subrahmanian, V.S., Xiong, Y.: Generating fake documents using probabilistic logic graphs. IEEE Trans. Dependable Secure Comput. **19**(4), 2428–2441 (2021)
12. Hu, Y., Lin, Y., Parolin, E.S., Khan, L., Hamlen, K.: Controllable fake document infilling for cyber deception. arXiv preprint arXiv:2210.09917 (2022)
13. IBM: What is smishing (SMS phishing)? https://www.ibm.com/topics/smishing. Accessed 10 Nov 2023
14. Jajodia, S., Subrahmanian, V., Swarup, V., Wang, C.: Cyber Deception. Springer, Cham (2016)
15. Karuna, P., Purohit, H., Ganesan, R., Jajodia, S.: Generating hard to comprehend fake documents for defensive cyber deception. IEEE Intell. Syst. **33**(5), 16–25 (2018)
16. Karuna, P., Purohit, H., Jajodia, S., Ganesan, R., Uzuner, O.: Fake document generation for cyber deception by manipulating text comprehensibility. IEEE Syst. J. **15**(1), 835–845 (2020)
17. Martin, C.L.: Military deception reconsidered. Ph.D. thesis, Monterey, California. Naval Postgraduate School (2008)
18. Prabhaker, N., Bopche, G.S., Mishra, A., Arock, M.: Generation of believable fake logic circuits for cyber deception. In: 2024 16th International Conference on Communication Systems & NETworkS (COMSNETS), pp. 13–18. IEEE (2024)
19. Whitham, B.: Automating the generation of fake documents to detect network intruders. Int. J. Cyber-Secur. Digit. Forensics **2**(1), 103 (2013)
20. Whitham, B.: Automating the generation of enticing text content for high-interaction honeyfiles (2017)
21. Whitham, B., Turner, T., Brown, L.: Automated processes for evaluating the realism of high-interaction honeyfiles. In: Proceedings of the 14th European Conference on Cyber Warfare and Security, p. 307 (2015)
22. Xiong, Y., Ramachandran, G.K., Ganesan, R., Jajodia, S., Subrahmanian, V.: Generating realistic fake equations in order to reduce intellectual property theft. IEEE Trans. Dependable Secure Comput. **19**(3), 1434–1445 (2020)
23. Yuill, J., Zappe, M., Denning, D., Feer, F.: Honeyfiles: deceptive files for intrusion detection. In: Proceedings from the Fifth Annual IEEE SMC Information Assurance Workshop, pp. 116–122. IEEE (2004)
24. Zhu, Q.: The doctrine of cyber effect: An ethics framework for defensive cyber deception. arXiv preprint arXiv:2302.13362 (2023)

A Security and Privacy Model for Automotive

Teodor-Cosmin Curcudel

Faculty of Computer Science, "Alexandru Ioan Cuza" University of Iași, Iași, Romania
teodor-cosmin.curcudel@info.uaic.ro

Abstract. With the rapid advancement of wireless technology in the automotive industry, vehicles have become increasingly interconnected. It is crucial that the communication and authentication protocols employed achieve a certain level of privacy. Very often, the privacy properties of these protocols are studied in an ad hoc or informal manner, leading to varying interpretations among different authors due to the absence of a unified model. In this paper, we address this gap by proposing a formal and unified approach to analyzing privacy in automotive communication systems. Drawing inspiration from the Hermans-Pashalidis-Vercauteren-Preneel (HPVP) model [2] and Vaudenay's model used in RFID technology, we introduce the first comprehensive privacy model specifically designed for the automotive sector. This model provides a structured basis for evaluating security and privacy properties, ensuring consistency and clarity across different studies. Additionally, we propose an automotive scheme similar to the PKE protocol that Vaudenay introduced in his work. We prove that our scheme achieves security and narrow-forward privacy within the context of the proposed model. Our work not only establishes a foundational step towards enhancing privacy standards in automotive wireless communications but also paves the way for future research to build upon this unified structure. By standardizing the analysis of privacy, we aim to improve security, reliability, and trust in the development of interconnected vehicular networks.

Keywords: Automotive · Security · Privacy · Indistinguishability

1 Introduction

The integration of wireless communication technologies into vehicles has revolutionized modern transportation systems, enabling enhanced connectivity and functionality. Vehicles now routinely exchange critical information with each other and roadside infrastructure, paving the way for improved traffic management, enhanced safety measures, and increased driver convenience. The data exchanged between vehicles includes information such as location, speed, driving patterns, and more.

This interconnectedness, however, brings forth significant security challenges. As vehicles become nodes in a larger network, the need to protect transmitted data from interception, tampering, and unauthorized access becomes paramount. Traditional cryptographic methods, while effective in conventional settings, may prove inadequate in vehicular environments characterized by high mobility and resource-constrained onboard units (OBUs).

To address these challenges, lightweight cryptographic algorithms have emerged as a crucial component of vehicular network security. These algorithms prioritize efficiency and minimal computational overhead, making them suitable for implementation on OBUs and sensors with limited processing capabilities. By ensuring real-time secure communication, these lightweight solutions safeguard the integrity, confidentiality, and authenticity of data exchanged within vehicular networks.

Security and privacy are not the same concept. Security entails ensuring protection against unauthorized access and threats to maintain the integrity and confidentiality of information while privacy means that certain elements are known, but certain actions are not known. The vehicle's identification information, ownership details and technical condition are considered known elements, accessible to authorities with specific responsibilities and mandates. Real-time location, travel history and driving habits are actions or behaviors that ideally should remain private or confidential to protect individuals' privacy.

For example, if a user drives a car from location A to location B, privacy could mean that an adversary knows the user has left location A but does not know their destination, location B. When an attacker tracks them using GPS, a significant portion of privacy is lost because they know exactly where the user is located. Security would mean protecting the integrity and confidentiality of the location data against unauthorized access or misuse. Currently, privacy in automotive contexts is also necessary.

As the proposed model is based on RFID technology, we will now discuss this topic briefly. RFID (Radio Frequency Identification) uses electromagnetic fields to identify and track tags attached to objects. The system comprises tags, which contain a microchip and an antenna, and readers, which emit radio waves and receive signals from the tags. Tags can be passive, powered by the reader's signal, or active, with their own battery. The reader sends a radio signal, the tag responds with its stored information, and the reader processes this information. RFID technology is widely used in inventory management, access control, supply chain tracking, and healthcare asset tracking due to its efficiency, speed, and ability to reduce human error while enhancing security and tracking capabilities.

Contribution. Many authors propose authentication protocols based on RFID for which the analysis of security and privacy properties is performed in an ad hoc or informal manner. It was found that these protocols often have vulnerabilities. This remark still holds for the automotive domain since automotive sensors, much like RFID tags, operate with limited storage capacity and computing power. Consequently, the analysis of communication protocols in the automotive context remains informal, leaving room for potential weaknesses. Building upon this observation, it becomes evident that addressing security concerns requires a more rigorous approach. Thus, in this paper, we will propose a model in which the privacy analysis is unified, helping the authors reach a consensus regarding the concept of privacy.

Paper Organization. In this paper, we structure our content as follows: the Sect. 2 introduces vehicular ad hoc networks, while the Sect. 3 discusses the proposed security and privacy model referred to as *TAutoPrivate* (or *AutoPrivate* for short, and occasionally simply as *model*). Section 4 analyzes an automotive scheme inspired by Vaudenay's PKE protocol given by the communication protocol between RSUs and cars. Finally, the Sect. 5 presents the conclusions of this paper.

2 Introduction to VANET

The integration of wireless technologies in the automotive industry has sparked significant interest in security research within vehicular ad hoc networks (VANETs) [3]. To achieve efficient and secure communication among vehicles in the future, intelligent transportation systems (ITS) are being developed. The primary goal of VANETs is to enhance both driver comfort and passenger safety by enabling efficient communication between vehicles.

The combination of wireless medium properties and an ad hoc approach defines the unique characteristics of VANETs. Due to this unique architecture and the associated challenges, the security requirements are much more complex than those for mobile or wireless networks. Here are some of these unique characteristics:

- Dynamic network topology: VANETs involve vehicles that enter and exit the network, vehicles that move at high speeds. This highly dynamic environment poses challenges in authenticating vehicles and establishing secure communication channels between them [3].
- Broadcast communication: The vehicles in VANETs extensively rely on broadcast communication to disseminate information such as traffic conditions, weather conditions, and potential hazards that may arise [6]. This broadcast communication involves sending messages to all nodes in the network, which increases the opportunities for an attacker to intervene or eavesdrop. Therefore, the network is more susceptible to eavesdropping and spoofing attacks.
- Constrained resources: Vehicles are constrained in terms of processing power and memory capacity. This imposes a challenge for implementing robust and efficient security mechanisms.
- Unbounded network density: Network density in VANETs is variable and primarily dependent on the number of vehicles, which can be high in congested urban areas and low in suburban and rural regions. The network has no limit to the number of vehicles that can join.

- Time critical data exchange: In VANETs, ensuring that information reaches legitimate nodes within a specific timeframe is essential for enabling swift responses based on decisions made by the nodes, with a crucial example being emergency vehicles.

The architecture of vehicle networks consists of two main wireless components: the On-Board Unit (OBU) and the Road Side Unit (RSU) [3]. These OBUs are integrated devices within vehicles, enabling communication with RSUs and other OBUs. RSUs are strategically positioned in critical locations, such as intersections or even integrated into infrastructure - concrete examples include intelligent traffic lights. Each terminal functions as a node capable of receiving and forwarding messages within a wireless network. These nodes can be thought of as routers that communicate with each other, as illustrated in Fig. 1.

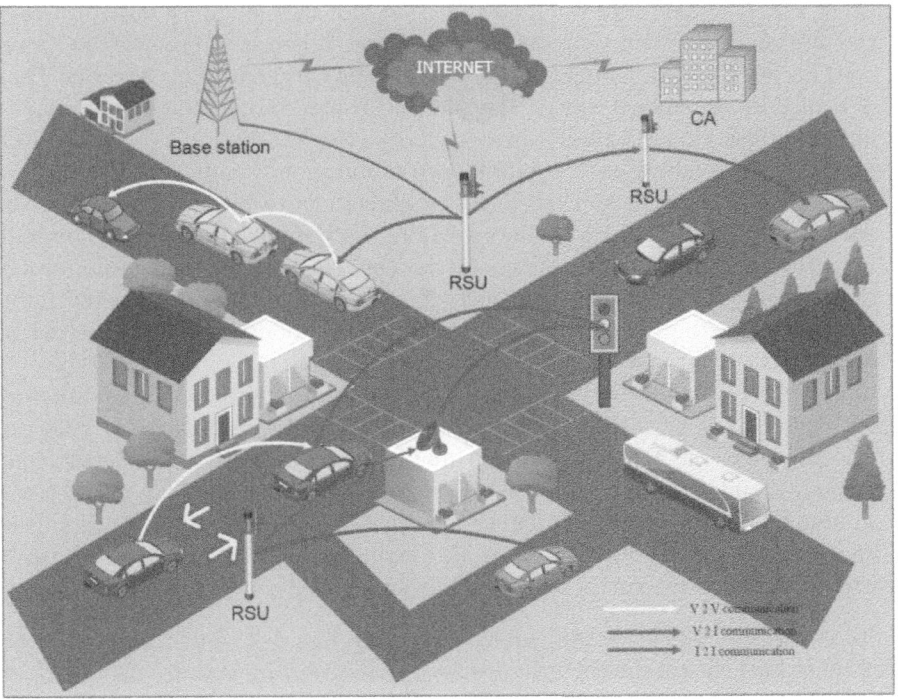

Fig. 1. Vehicular network architecture [3]

RSUs can be classified as fixed or mobile. Fixed RSUs are deployed on highways and major roads for traffic monitoring, incident detection, and automated toll collection, exemplified by the E-ZPass system in the USA. They can also be found in smart traffic lights at major intersections, which help manage traffic flow and prioritize emergency vehicles. Mobile RSUs, on the other hand, can be mounted on road maintenance vehicles to alert drivers about road closures or on drones and police vehicles for enhanced security and real-time data transmission during significant public events.

There are serveral types of communication in a vehicular network:

- Vehicle-to-Vehicle (V2V): This communication involves direct interaction between vehicles to transmit information such as speed, location, and direction. An example of this communication is the Semi-Autonomous Truck Platooning system developed by Volvo and Scania [1]. It involves a closely aligned convoy of trucks on highways, with the lead truck driven by a human driver and the following trucks operating semi-autonomously. The system aims to save time, fuel, and reduce emissions by utilizing the slipstream created by the lead truck.
- Vehicle-to-Infrastructure (V2I): This is the communication between vehicles and infrastructure to receive information related to traffic lights, road conditions, etc. Let's consider the following scenario: an ambulance needs to reach the site of an accident as quickly as possible. When it approaches an intersection, it can send a signal to the traffic lights to change their color. Then it transmits its current speed, the planned route, and a request for priority at the intersection via the Dedicated Short-Range Communications (DSRC) protocol. Depending on the ambulance's route, the traffic lights will turn green for its direction and red for other directions to block traffic. After the ambulance passes through the intersection, the traffic lights return to normal. In critical situations like this, this mechanism is essential. Other examples in this category of communication include managing traffic in congested intersections, collecting tolls, and providing warnings about other hazards such as construction zones or extreme weather conditions.
- Infrastructure-to-Infrastructure (I2I): In this communication, RSUs interact with each other or with base stations to relay received messages or synchronize information. Traffic lights can monitor traffic density on specific road segments and then transmit this data to a central server. The server can communicate with the traffic lights to adjust the duration of green signals at intersections during peak hours. Additionally, traffic lights can communicate with each other to synchronize and alleviate traffic congestion.

To ensure the efficiency and safety of the services described above, the network must authenticate every message sent or received by a node. An attack by an adversary or an error in message transmission can compromise public safety. For example, if an attacker sends false collision warnings, it can cause panic and unpredictable driving behavior, potentially leading to accidents. Manipulating traffic information can create hazardous situations by misdirecting drivers and causing traffic congestion. Below, we briefly present two fundamental requirements in V2V and V2I communication, assuming that I2I links are secure.

- Authentication and message integrity: Message authentication is a critical aspect of automotive security, as evident from the earlier discussion. The unique identifier ID and location, along with other information, must be

authenticated. Each received message should arrive unmodified, in the same state as when it was sent by the sender, ensuring its integrity. The recipient can verify whether the message has been altered during the time from sending to reception using integrity checks. By achieving authentication and integrity properties, we can ensure that a legitimate sender transmits trustworthy information.
- Privacy: An unauthorized node should not be able to access a driver's personal information, such as their name, frequently traveled routes, current location, or phone number. In vehicular networks, data is broadcasted to facilitate rapid and efficient message dissemination - a process crucial for accident prevention and traffic management. However, precisely because of this, there is a serious privacy threat. An adversary can collect and analyze messages sent by vehicles to discover patterns in driver behavior. For instance, if the adversary has access to the vehicle's location, they can intercept the first and last messages sent by a car within a specific time period. If these observations occur on a workday around 8 a.m., it is highly likely that the driver is commuting from home to work. Consequently, the driver's privacy has been compromised.

3 TAutoPrivate Privacy Model

To study the security and privacy properties of automotive systems, we must first introduce the formal concept of an automotive scheme/system. After this, we will present the adversary model against such a scheme as well as our understanding of security and privacy in an automotive system.

3.1 Automotive Scheme

An automotive scheme is a 4-tuple of probabilistic polynomial time algorithms as follows:

1. $SetupSystem()$ sets up the system state for the server, which all RSUs connect to, thereby allowing the vehicles to connect to the server through the RSUs. It generates a set of public parameters (pp) and secret parameters (sp), along with a database DB that is shared among all road units. This database stores information about vehicles, including a unique ID for each vehicle, the exact position of the vehicle, a history of communications with encountered units, traffic information, secret keys, and even potential fines.
2. $SetupCar(pk, ID, \lambda)$ initializes the state of the car identified by ID and, based on the security parameter λ, sets specific parameters for that particular vehicle. These parameters can be quite numerous and include secret keys for authentication, protection of communication, routing tables for managing data traffic, etc. Additionally, they may include parameters for communication with RSUs and for configuring driver assistance systems such as *Adaptive Cruise Control* (ACC), *Lane Keeping Assist* (LKA), and *Blind Spot Detection* (BSD).

For example, for ACC, the parameters that can be set include the distance between the current vehicle and the vehicle in front, the minimum and maximum speeds that can be adjusted by the system, the accuracy of sensors detecting other vehicles, the reaction time of the system, and many others. Due to this multitude of parameters that can be set in a vehicle, we will consider them all as being derived from a polynomial security parameter λ.

3. $SetupRSU(rsu\_id)$ initializes the state of an RSU with the ID rsu_id, imports the secret parameters sp from the system, and updates the database to indicate that this unit is active. An IP address is assigned for network communication, and specific applications for monitoring and managing traffic are installed. These applications include traffic incident detection systems, traffic management systems, etc. Additionally, methods for real-time data collection are established, such as road sensors, surveillance cameras, or even V2I systems. Lastly, algorithms for filtering and prioritizing messages are set up, ensuring that critical information is processed and transmitted promptly to other vehicles and to emergency or roadside assistance services.

4. $CommProtocol(RSU(DB, pk, sk); Car(ID_{car}, pk))$ is a communication protocol between RSU units and vehicles. This protocol is designed for unilateral authentication, where the car is authenticated by the RSU. It can be extended to achieve mutual authentication by using temporary variables.

An *automotive system* is an instantiation of the above scheme.

It should be noted that a vehicle communicates with only one unit at a time for practical reasons. Among these reasons are simplifying protocol design and optimizing the limited resources of the vehicle. We aim to avoid connecting to multiple RSUs simultaneously because protocol development is complex, requiring synchronization of messages and management of overlapping coverage areas of units. The limited resources of the vehicle include bandwidth, processing power, and memory. Using multiple simultaneous connections would excessively demand processing power and memory, potentially leading to performance degradation and data processing delays. By communicating with only one unit at a time, bandwidth is efficiently utilized, and this overloading of resources is avoided.

In the proposed model, we consider that information added by one unit to the database can be accessed by other units to ensure coherence and consistency of data throughout the entire system. This approach enables all units to have access to the same real-time updated data, which is essential for efficient communication, rapid response to traffic events, and scalability.

To justify this approach, we will consider the following real-life scenario: let's assume that a driver has exceeded the speed limit, and an RSU unit has detected this and automatically issued a fine, which will be recorded in the database. If the RSU cannot transmit the information about the fine to the database quickly enough, the driver may cross the border into another country without paying it. The causes of this delay can be varied: for example, an RSU unit located in an isolated region with weak wireless communication will certainly experience a delay between message transmission and database update. Another cause could be physical obstacles such as tall buildings and mountains, or even weather conditions. Consequently, other units will not have real-time information available.

Thus, several issues can arise, such as those related to road safety and emergency response where every second counts. Delays in transmitting information about collisions, obstacles, or adverse weather conditions can lead to delayed responses from vehicles, increasing the risk of accidents. Additionally, a route may be inefficiently planned if traffic information is not updated promptly.

In the *TAutoPrivate model*, we will assume that communication between units and the database is instantaneous, without any delay, to prevent the situations described above. This simplification of the model avoids the need to predict the extent of delays in different scenarios. By analyzing protocols under the assumption of instantaneous communication, we can achieve a clear and uncomplicated understanding of the level of privacy they offer in the proposed model. But in real life, we cannot achieve truly instant communication. However, with the development of technology and infrastructure, we will move closer to this ideal in the future.

3.2 The Adversary Model

To study privacy within the proposed model, we first need to determine the strength of an adversary attempting to attack a vehicle in the model. Given that vehicle sensors operate with very limited computing power, lightweight cryptography emerges as the most suitable option for this environment. In this context, lightweight cryptographic operations commonly involve XOR, circular permutations, and substitutions - fast computations that align with the constraints of low-powered vehicle sensors.

Considering all the aspects presented above and the unique characteristics of VANETs from the second section, we can infer that an adversary must execute a very swift and precisely targeted attack. In other words, knowing that the network is highly dynamic, if an attacker wants to uncover specific details about a node, thereby compromising privacy, they must act promptly. The respective vehicle could exit the communication range, the network might become congested, or physical or weather-related obstacles could disrupt communication and, consequently, the attack.

Therefore, we will consider an adversary with complexity at most $\mathcal{O}(\log n)$, meaning that the resources (time and space) required by the adversary to compromise a vehicle's privacy grow logarithmically with the input size. In the case of indistinguishability, the adversary needs to perform $\log n$ operations to differentiate between the two communicating vehicles.

Given that this adversary operates with such low complexity (indicating an efficient algorithm), we must design security mechanisms to protect user privacy within the proposed model. If we were to grant the adversary higher computational power, such as exponential complexity, it would not succeed in attacking vehicles due to the significant time required for operations, contradicting the highly dynamic nature of vehicular networks. Therefore, restricting the adversary to a complexity of at most $\mathcal{O}(\log n)$ is both reasonable and realistic within the context of dynamic topology and increased mobility in VANETs.

However, in an environment without constrained computational resources, where protocols do not rely on lightweight cryptography, we can treat the adversary as a probabilistic polynomial-time (PPT) algorithm. If we are dealing with equipment that has its own power source or can be constantly powered, then a much more robust cryptographic system can be implemented. For example, RSUs have more robust communication systems among themselves.

3.3 Oracles

We consider that the adversary can interact with the system by consulting a set of oracles. When we say that an adversary consults an oracle, we mean that the adversary interacts with the system according to the specific type of oracle. In the TAutoPrivate model, the adversary can consult the following oracles:

- *Launch(rsu_id)*: Launches a new communication protocol instance with the RSU identified by *rsu_id*, assigns a unique identifier π to it, and outputs π. Essentially, the attacker opens a new communication session with the RSU.
- *DrawCar(C_0, C_1)*: The attacker receives a fresh virtual reference that corresponds either to the car on the left C_0, or to the car on the right C_1, depending on the privacy game played by the challenger. This oracle can be generalized when the attacker is in the vicinity of a polynomial number of cars. In Vaudenay's model, it's as if they are drawing from a set of 2 elements with equal probabilities of $1/2$ for each element [7].
- *Free(vcar)*: This oracle deletes the reference *vcar*. Essentially, it moves the car referred to by the temporary identity *vcar* into a set of *free* cars, which can be drawn. This oracle does not return anything.
- *SendCar(m, vcar)*: Returns the response given by the vehicle when the message *m* is transmitted to the vehicle referenced by *vcar*.
- *SendRSU(RSU, m, π)*: The oracle returns the response of the *RSU* unit to the message *m* within session π.
- *Result(RSU, π, c)*: When the adversary consults this oracle, they want to determine whether the *RSU* has made a decision about the authenticity of car *c* in session π. The oracle returns $\perp$ if the *RSU* has not made a decision regarding the authenticity of car *c*, 1 if the RSU authenticated the car, and 0 if the car was not authenticated.
- *CorruptCar(car_id)*: The adversary corrupts a sensor of the car, making it unusable. The oracle returns the history of the sensor's internal state up to the moment of corruption.
- *CorruptCarAndModify(car_id)*: As with the *CorruptCar* oracle, the adversary corrupts a sensor of the car, but this time, they take control of the messages sent by the sensor. The attacker could replace parts of the messages sent by the car, such as the car's *ID* or its position. Essentially, the state of the sensor can be altered. The oracle provides the history of the sensor's internal state up to the moment of corruption.

- *CorruptRSU(rsu_id)*: The adversary corrupts the RSU unit with the ID *rsu_id*, gaining the RSU's private key, the ability to view the message history and send messages to cars in place of the unit. Essentially, the RSU unit is being impersonated.

These oracles are inspired by the HPVP and Vaudenay models developed for privacy in RFID, and they are adapted for privacy in the automotive domain [2,7].

3.4 Classification of Adversaries

Next, we will classify the adversaries based on the oracles they have access to.

(a) *Forward adversaries*: Once they access a corruption oracle (*CorruptCar* or *CorruptCarAndModify*), the only oracle they can continue to consult is that oracle;
(b) *Destructive adversaries*: They have access to the *CorruptCar* oracle through which they render the car's sensor unusable;
(c) *Strong adversaries*: They have access to the *CorruptCarAndModify* oracle;
(d) *Very strong adversaries*: They have access to the *CorruptRSU* oracle;
(e) *Narrow weak (narrow forward, narrow destructive, narrow strong)*: as above but the adversary has no access to the *Result* oracle.

If a forward adversary has managed to corrupt a car, they can no longer interact with the system. For example, the adversary corrupted the system and was detected by the intrusion detection systems. From that moment, they lose all communication capabilities, access to the system, and the ability to interact within it. However, cars that are already drawn or nearby can still be corrupted. The adversary can generate a random y and obtain a z as in Fig. 3 (the adversary takes control of the car), but they cannot forward these to the RSU unit because they are a forward-type adversary.

The adversary can analyze the system only using the information obtained up to that point, as they are no longer allowed to communicate. They have access to the *CorruptCar* and *CorruptCarAndModify* oracles because, even if they modify something, they cannot forward it. The case of corrupting an RSU is entirely different and is analyzed separately in Theorem 1.

3.5 Security of Automotive Schemes

By security, we mean that an adversary cannot impersonate a vehicle or a RSU without corrupting them, except with negligible probability. Specifically, one vehicle cannot impersonate another vehicle. The adversary has access to the corruption oracle because it is strong, but it wins if it manages to impersonate an uncorrupted vehicle. We will adapt Vaudenay's definition of privacy for the automotive domain [7]. Security means unilateral or mutual authentication. The car can authenticate itself to an RSU, and the RSU can authenticate itself to the car. If only one party authenticates, then the authentication is unilateral. When both parties authenticate, it is considered mutual authentication. This mutual authentication is necessary because the car needs to be precisely identified by an RSU unit, and vice versa, so the car knows that the unit authenticating it is legitimate. This authentication must be done in the face of a strong adversary. Even if the adversary is strong, the scheme ensures unilateral or mutual authentication against such an adversary.

3.6 Privacy

We have defined the adversary and now we will proceed to elaborate on what the advantage of an adversary signifies and what privacy involves. Regarding privacy, we further define the experiment $IND_{\mathcal{A},\Sigma}^{model\text{-}prv\text{-}b}(\lambda)$[1], where $b \in \{0,1\}$, $\mathcal{A}$ is an adversary and Σ is a security scheme for automotive applications, which we described in Subsect. 3.1.

$\underline{IND_{\mathcal{A},\Sigma}^{model\text{-}prv\text{-}b}(\lambda)}$

1. Challenger: $b \leftarrow \{0,1\}$;
2. $\mathcal{A}$ is given access to oracles. When $\mathcal{A}$ consults the *DrawCar* oracle, it receives a reference to the car b;
3. $\mathcal{A}$ outputs a bit b';
4. Return 1 if $b = b'$, or 0, otherwise;

For $b = 0$ ($b = 1$) this experiment will also be called the *left (right) privacy game*.

The advantage of $\mathcal{A}$ against scheme Σ is given by the formula:

$$Adv_{\mathcal{A},\Sigma}^{model\text{-}prv}(\lambda) = |P(IND_{\mathcal{A},\Sigma}^{model\text{-}prv\text{-}0}(\lambda) = 1) + P(IND_{\mathcal{A},\Sigma}^{model\text{-}prv\text{-}1}(\lambda) = 1) - 1| \tag{1}$$

We say that a scheme Σ is $\mathcal{C} - private$, where $\mathcal{C}$ is a class of adversaries, if the advantage of any adversary in class $\mathcal{C}$ attempting to attack scheme Σ is negligible.

We observe that the privacy experiment can be generalized to the case where there are n vehicles in the adversary's vicinity (within a radius of up to 1 km), provided that n is polynomial in the security parameter λ and the adversary tries to guess one vehicle out of n. Thus, the advantage of the adversary can also be generalized, resulting in the formula below. The number of vehicles must be polynomial because a sum of negligible quantities remains negligible. If n were exponential, this sum would no longer be negligible. However, we will not use this generalization for the subsequent discussions.

---

[1] The *model* represents *TAutoPrivate* (or *AutoPrivate* for short), the proposed model.

$$Adv_{\mathcal{A},\Sigma}^{\text{model-prv}}(\lambda) = \Big| \ P\left(\text{IND}_{\mathcal{A},\Sigma}^{\text{model-prv-0}}(\lambda) = 1\right)$$
$$+ P\left(\text{IND}_{\mathcal{A},\Sigma}^{\text{model-prv-1}}(\lambda) = 1\right)$$
$$+ \cdots \qquad\qquad\qquad\qquad\qquad\qquad (2)$$
$$+ P\left(\text{IND}_{\mathcal{A},\Sigma}^{\text{model-prv-(n-1)}}(\lambda) = 1\right)$$
$$-1\Big|$$

The classes of adversaries described above lead to a hierarchy of privacy properties in the proposed model, as observed in the diagram in Fig. 2. Each node corresponds to a level of privacy based on a specific type of adversary. We note that a very-strong adversary can successfully verify if a RSU authenticated a car using only the *CorruptRSU* oracle, so access to the *Result* oracle is not relevant. Therefore, we do not distinguish between *very strong adversaries* and *narrow-very strong adversaries*.

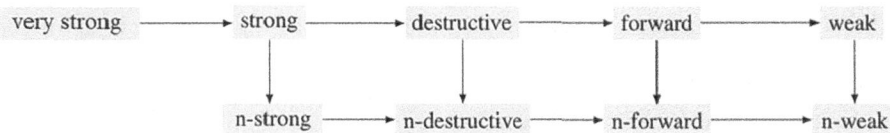

Fig. 2. Privacy levels in the TAutoPrivate model: "n-p" means "narrow p" and an arrow means "implication"

4 A PKE Based Automotive Scheme

In this section, we will present an automotive scheme inspired by Vaudenay's PKE protocol [4,5,7] that ensures unilateral security and narrow-forward privacy. This scheme is given by the communication protocol in Fig. 3, which aims to identify information sent by a vehicle in the database and authenticate this information. This information may include a vehicle identifier (ID_{car}) or a payment identifier for toll fees (ID, tax_code).

When handling a large volume of vehicles on the road, an RSU selects a vehicle randomly to identify it in the database. The RSU then sends a random x to the vehicle. The vehicle generates its own random y and encrypts x, y and its *ID* using the RSU's public key pk, resulting in z. The vehicle sends y and z back to the RSU. Upon receiving the message, the RSU decrypts it using its private key sk and searches the database for the *ID* obtained. If such an *ID* is found, it means the vehicle is a trusted user. Otherwise, communication with the vehicle is blocked, and $\perp$ is provided.

RSU $(DB, (pk, sk))$		**Car** (ID_{car}, pk)
1	$x \leftarrow \{0,1\}^\ell$ $\xrightarrow{x}$	
2	$\xleftarrow{y,z}$	$y \leftarrow \{0,1\}^m$ $z \leftarrow \{x, y, ID_{car}\}_{pk}$
3	$z \xrightarrow{sk} x, y, ID_{car}$ If $ID_{car} \in DB$ then, authenticate car else output $\perp$ (abort, stop communication)	

Fig. 3. The communication protocol of the PKE based automotive scheme

Let's assume that vehicles have paid a toll fee at the beginning of the road by passing through a toll booth. If verification of such a toll fee is needed, the vehicle will encrypt the tuple consisting of x, y, ID and tax_code. When the RSU receives the message, it decrypts it and checks the database to verify if the vehicle with the received ID has made a payment identified by tax_code.

The random values generated by the RSU and the vehicle have lengths of l and m, respectively. These parameters are polynomial in size relative to the security parameter λ of the automotive security scheme described previously.

This protocol ensures forward privacy, meaning that even if the current long-term encryption keys are compromised, the communication history or previously encrypted information with other keys cannot be decrypted. This property is ensured by generating the random values x and y each time the two entities (the vehicle and RSU) communicate.

It is easy to see that our scheme is correct in the sense that if the car is legitimate, it will always be verified by a legitimate RSU unit.

Theorem 1. *The PKE based scheme ensures security (unilateral authentication) in the TAutoPrivate privacy model, assuming that the public-key encryption scheme on which the protocol is built is IND-CCA and the adversary cannot corrupt RSU units.*

Proof. (Sketch) If we replace car by tag and RSU by reader, we get the RFID scheme from [7] which is secure (Theorem 19).

If there were only one RSU unit in the automotive system, and the adversary could not corrupt this unit, then our scheme could be likened to the PKE-based RFID scheme from [7]. Since this scheme is secure if public-key encryption is IND-CCA secure, our scheme would be secure in this case.

Assuming that in the scheme we have a single RSU unit, which the adversary can corrupt, then the adversary can obtain the unit's secret key and thus it can decrypt a message transmitted by a vehicle. As a result, it will be able to obtain the vehicle's identity and later impersonate this vehicle.

If we assume that the scheme generates multiple RSU units using the *SetupRSU* algorithm, with each RSU unit having its own specific private key, the security property can be restricted to the case of a single RSU unit. The probability of encountering the same secret key or being able to decrypt a message intended for another RSU unit is negligible.

The protection of the private keys of the RSU units can be achieved using PUFs.

For the privacy property, we cannot use the approach from [7] because the privacy model we use is based on indistinguishability between two vehicles, which is different from the approach in [7]. However, we can demonstrate the following.

Theorem 2. *The PKE based scheme is narrow-forward private in the TAuto-Private privacy model, assuming that the public-key encryption scheme on which the protocol is built is IND-CPA.*

Proof. (Sketch) We assume that the protocol is not narrow-forward private. The adversary uses the oracle *DrawCar* to obtain a reference *vcar* to a car based on the game played by the challenger[2]. The challenger (acting as an RSU) simulates the communication protocol with one of the two cars based on the game played, thereby obtaining z_0, x_0, y_0, ID_0 or z_1, x_1, y_1, ID_1. Then, the challenger sends either $\{z_0, x_0, y_0, ID_0\}_{pk}$ or $\{z_1, x_1, y_1, ID_1\}_{pk}$ to the adversary. From the initial assumption, it follows that an adversary knows how to distinguish between the two encrypted vectors, i.e., between the two cars. Thus, the adversary can distinguish between two encryptions with the key pk. Therefore, the encryption scheme is not IND-CPA, which contradicts the theorem's hypothesis. Hence, the theorem's statement holds.

Furthermore, if the encryption is IND-CCA, then the protocol is narrow-strong private [7]. We also observe that a protocol similar to Vaudenay's can be analyzed in any model, including the proposed model. We considered the narrow privacy level because the adversary does not receive the result of a communication session.

5 Conclusions

Communication between vehicles is becoming more prevalent, and new protocols are being developed to ensure privacy and security. Thus, I observed that there is a lack of a unified approach for studying the privacy of proposed protocols, with each author demonstrating this property ad-hoc or informally. This aspect raises the question of whether the notion of privacy, as defined and demonstrated by different authors, has the same meaning. In this paper, we developed a privacy model for automotive applications based on privacy models from RFID. Therefore, following an analysis, it can be stated that the protocols ensure the same level of privacy in the TAutoPrivate model.

---

[2] This game is set by the challenger and is not changed during the communication.

Technology in the automotive industry has developed tremendously in recent years. However, security for automotive applications is not yet well-defined, utilized, and implemented. Considering the fact that before this work there were no security and privacy models for automotive, this direction represents a future field with vast potential for discoveries and innovations, driven by the need to establish robust frameworks in a previously unexplored area.

Acknowledgements. I would like to express my sincere gratitude to Professor Dr. Țiplea Ferucio Laurențiu for their invaluable guidance, encouragement, and expertise throughout the research phase of my bachelor thesis, which forms the basis of this conference paper. He helped me through this challenging but beautiful journey offering insightful critiques that refined my research approach and encouraging me to explore innovative avenues.

References

1. Atasayar, H., Blass, P., Kaiser, S.: Truck Platooning Worldwide, pp. 13–19. Springer, Cham (2022)
2. Hermans, J., Pashalidis, A., Vercauteren, F., Preneel, B.: A new RFID privacy model. In: European Symposium on Research in Computer Security, pp. 568–587. Springer (2011)
3. Jadoon, A.K., Wang, L., Li, T., Zia, M.A.: Lightweight cryptographic techniques for automotive cybersecurity. Wirel. Commun. Mob. Comput. **2018**(1), 1640167 (2018)
4. Paise, R.I., Vaudenay, S.: Mutual authentication in RFID: security and privacy. In: Proceedings of the 2008 ACM Symposium on Information, Computer and Communications Security, pp. 292–299 (2008)
5. Țiplea, F.L., Hristea, C.: PUF protected variables: a solution to RFID security and privacy under corruption with temporary state disclosure. IEEE Trans. Inf. Forensics Secur. **16**, 999–1013 (2020)
6. Tran, P., Nguyen, D.C.: Advanced lightweight cryptography for automotive security: surveys, challenges and solutions. In: IoTBDS, pp. 304–311 (2022)
7. Vaudenay, S.: On privacy models for RFID. In: International Conference on the Theory and Application of Cryptology and Information Security, pp. 68–87. Springer (2007)

MAP-ECC: Mutual Authentication Protocol for e-Agriculture Using ECC

Manish Kumar Pandit, Sangram Ray[✉], and Priyanka Das

Department of Computer Science and Engineering, National Institute of Technology Sikkim, Ravangla 737139, Sikkim, India
b200060@nitsikkim.ac.in, sangram.ism@gmail.com

Abstract. The e-Agriculture plays a significant role in the evolving domain of the modern digital world. However, ensuring security and privacy in the e-Agricultural framework is a vital factor. From a rigorous literature review, we found that all the existing schemes are susceptible to various security and privacy-related issues or bear higher communication and computation overheads. Therefore, in this paper, we have introduced a novel mutual authentication protocol for e-Agriculture using ECC (MAP-ECC) which emphasizes to share a common session key among all the communicating entities for the secure exchange of crucial agricultural data. Further, the informal security analysis shows that our protocol is secure against all well-known security threats. On the other hand, the formal security validation of MAP-ECC using the AVISPA simulator ensures that our protocol is SAFE against both replay and man-in-the-middle (MITM) attack. Further, the performance evaluation of MAP-ECC in terms of computation and communication overheads is carried out and compared with the existing schemes. The comparative result shows that MAP-ECC incurs low computation and communication overheads than the existing schemes. Thus, the proposed MAP-ECC outperforms the existing schemes and ensures its feasibility for implementation in a real-world e-Agricultural sector.

Keywords: e-Agriculture · Security · Elliptic Curve Cryptography · Privacy · AVISPA

1 Introduction

Agriculture is the backbone of the economic growth of a country and the integration Internet of Things (IoT) into agriculture typically termed as "e-Agriculture" could play a significant role in maximizing the quality and quantity of crops with minimal human labor, thus revolutionizing the e-Agriculture sector [1]. This typical e-Agriculture framework consists of three key entities. They are - Agricultural User (AU), Gateway, and Sensor node [2]. In line with this, authentication in e-Agriculture framework ensures that only the authorized AU has access to the Sensor node's data via the Gateway. However, these entities communicate via an open channel and are vulnerable to eavesdropping attacks. Hence, ensuring security in the e-Agriculture framework is a matter of concern. To address this concern, it is a common practice to establish a mutual authentication scheme among communicating entities that assures both confidentiality and integrity in the e-Agriculture framework [3].

1.1 Security Requirements in e-Agriculture

As data of e-Agriculture framework are transmitted via public channel an adversary can easily forge, alter, and access this information, potentially compromise the framework. Therefore, to eradicate the security vulnerabilities it is significant to ensure that the below-mentioned vital security requirements are satisfied by the e-Agriculture framework:

- **Confidentiality:** Confidentiality aims to prevent adversary from accessing sensitive agricultural data such as - crop conditions, weather data, or farming strategies, etc.
- **Integrity:** Integrity in e-Agriculture framework ensures that the information collected from sensors is accurate and unaltered during transmission.
- **Availability:** In e-Agriculture framework, availability ensures that the agricultural data and resources are accessible to authorized entities whenever they need it.
- **Anonymity:** Anonymity in e-Agriculture framework ensures to protect the identity of Agricultural User (AU) or specific data sources.

1.2 Literature Review

A brief review of all the related literature [4–10] emphasizing their various pros and cons is demonstrated in this subsection.

In the year 2019, Wu et al. [4] proposed a secure blockchain-based intelligent agriculture network system which not only claimed to resist replay attack, impersonisation attack, etc., but also ensured to provide vital security requirements such as - preserve mutual authentication, perfect forward secrecy, etc. However, Vangala et al. [5] found out that the scheme [4] incurs higher computation and communication overheads. Further, Soe et al. [6] proposed another lightweight cyber-attack detection system for IoT environment which claimed to withstand replay attack, Man-in-the-Middle (MITM) attack, etc. But, Kumar et al. [7] identified that the scheme [6] is prone Denial-of-Service (DoS) attack, insider attack, etc. Similarly, Nasib et al. [8] proposed another lightweight authentication protocol for Wireless Sensor Network (WSN) which claimed to provide security against replay attack, insider attack, Man-in-the-Middle (MITM) attack, etc. However, Noor et al. [9] proved that the scheme [8] doesn't not provide user anonymity and is vulnerable to user, gateway and sensor impersonation attack. Later, Itoo et al. [10] introduced a novel mutual authentication scheme for smart agriculture framework which claimed not only to provide security against impersonation attack, replay attack, etc., but also ensured to incur minimal computation and communication overheads. However, we found out that the scheme [10] doesn't preserves user anonymity and is also prone to Man-in-the-Middle (MITM) attack.

Thus, all the related literature [4–10] are either susceptible to several security threats and/or incurs higher computation and/or communication overheads. Therefore, we are inspired to propose a novel **M**utual **A**uthentication **P**rotocol for e-Agriculture framework using **E**lliptic **C**urve **C**ryptography (*MAP-ECC*) that confirms to resist all the well-known security attacks.

1.3 Motivation and Contribution

As discussed in Subsect. 1.2 all of these existing protocols are either prone to several security limitations or bear high computation, communication, and storage overheads. Therefore, we are motivated to propose a novel **M**utual **A**uthentication **P**rotocol for e-Agriculture using **ECC** (***MAP-ECC***).
The significant contributions of our paper are:

- To mitigate the security threats, we have proposed a novel *MAP-ECC*.
- We have performed the informal security verification considering different security attack scenarios which proves that unlike other existing schemes [4–10], the *MAP-ECC* withstands all these security attacks.
- Further, we formally verified *MAP-ECC* using *AVISPA* simulator which shows that our protocol is **SAFE** against both replay and Man-in-the-Middle (*MITM*) attack.
- The comparative analysis of the *MAP-ECC* with existing schemes in terms computation and communication overheads show that our protocol incurs low computation and communication overheads than all the related literature.
- The proposed *MAP-ECC* outperforms all the existing schemes and maintains trade-off between security and efficiency which ensures its implement-ability in real-world e-Agriculture framework.

1.4 Organization

The rest of the paper is organized as follows - Sect. 2 gives a brief explanation of the different preliminaries which play a vital role in the proposed protocol whereas the working procedure of the proposed *MAP-ECC* is discussed in Sect. 3. Additionally, Sect. 4 presents both the informal and formal security verification of *MAP-ECC*. Further, the performance analysis of the proposed protocol is shown in Sect. 5. Finally, Sect. 6 concludes the paper.

2 Preliminaries

The elliptic curve E/F_q is defined as the set of all points $(x, y) \in F_q$ where F_q is the prime finite field and the curve equation is represented by the non-singular equation:

Table 1. Notations and their description used in the proposed *MAP-ECC*

Notation	Description
AU	Agricultural User
SN	Sensor Node
G	Gateway
ID_U, ID_G, ID_{SN}	Identity of user U, gateway G, and sensor node SN, respectively
PW_U, B_U	Password and Biometric of user U, respectively
E/D	Encryption and Decryption, respectively
h()	One-way secure hash function
||	Concatenation
F_q	Finite field
$E_q(a, b)$	An elliptic curve defined over on the finite field F_q with prime order n
P	A generator point on E/F_q with order n
K_x, K_y	K_x and K_y are the x and y coordinates of point K, respectively which is on the elliptic curve
(s_U, V_U)	Private-public key pair of user U based on ECC where $V_U = s_U.P$
(s_G, V_G)	Private-public key pair of gateway G based on ECC where $V_G = s_G.P$
(s_{SN}, V_{SN})	Private-public key pair of sensor node SN based on ECC where $V_{SN} = s_{SN}.P$
CA_U, CA_G and CA_{SN}	Public key certificate of user U, gateway G, and Sensor node, respectively based on ECC
R_U	Random point of the user U

$$y^2 \bmod q = (x^3 + ax + b) \bmod q \qquad (1)$$

Here, $(a, b) \in F_q$, the discriminant D = $(4a^3 + 27b^2) \bmod q \neq 0$ and $G_q = \{(x, y): x, y \in F_q\}$ and $\{(x, y) \in E/F_q\} \cup \{O\}$ defines elliptic curve additive group where O is known as point at infinity.

2.1 Group Operations

Scalar point multiplication: For elliptic curve,

$$n.P = P + P + ... + P(n\ times) = \sum_{1}^{n} P, where\ n \in \mathbb{Z}_q^*$$

Here, q and n are scalar numbers in the cyclic group G_q.

2.2 Threat Model

The e-Agriculture framework is dynamic in nature. Therefore, deployment of security mechanisms in this framework is an vital but critical task. Hence, considering this condition the broadly accepted "Dolev-Yao (DY) threat model" is used to analyze the proposed authentication mechanism. Additionally, some of the capabilities of an attacker that is used to prove the security of our protocol are mentioned as follows:

Assumption 1: An attacker can communicate only via the public communication channel. Additionally, both the communicating entities, Agricultural User (AU) and Sensor Node are not trusted entities whereas the Gateway is considered a semi-trusted authority.

Assumption 2: The messages that are exchanged via public channel among the trusted entities can be deleted, replayed, eavesdropped by an attacker. On the contrary, those messages that are transmitted over secured channel are not accessible to the attacker.

Assumption 3: The incorporation Elliptic Curve Diffie-Hellman (ECDH) algorithm ensures secure key exchange mechanisms without key transmission. Thus, the attacker cannot intercept and/or guess the secure keys.

3 Proposed Protocol

The working procedure of the proposed **M**utual **A**uthentication **P**rotocol for e-Agriculture using **ECC**: **MAP-ECC** is discussed in this section.

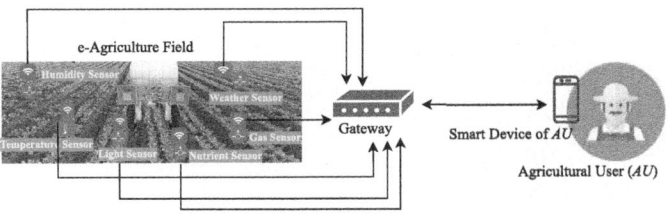

Fig. 1. Proposed e-Agricultural framework

3.1 Proposed Architecture

The proposed architecture consists of four primary entities: Sensor nodes, Agricultural user (AU), Gateway, and Registry Authority (RA). Each of these entities plays a crucial role in collecting, processing, and utilizing data efficiently. A brief description of each is as follows. Additionally, the proposed architecture is illustrated in Fig. 1.

Sensor Nodes: A sensor node is a small autonomous device that detects and measures the environmental or physical attributes of a target e-Agriculture framework. A few sensor nodes which play a significant role in the target e-Agricultural framework are as follows:

- **Soil Moisture Sensors:** Measure soil moisture levels.
- **Temperature Sensors:** Monitor environmental temperatures.
- **Humidity Sensors:** Measure atmospheric moisture levels.
- **Light Sensors:** Gauge light intensity for photosynthesis.
- **Weather Sensors:** Collect data on rainfall, wind speed, etc.
- **Nutrient Sensors:** Measure soil nutrient levels.
- **Gas Sensors:** Detect gases like CO_2 and methane.

Agricultural User (AU): Here, the farmer or the end-user who relies on the information gathered by the sensor nodes is defined as Agricultural User (AU).

Registration Authority (RA): The RA serves as the central authority responsible for managing and authenticating the identities of all the entities within the network.

Gateway: The gateway serves as a bridge between the sensor nodes in the target e-Agricultural framework and the AU.

3.2 Notation

The notations and their descriptions used in the proposed $MAP\text{-}ECC$ are tabulated in Table 1.

3.3 Working Procedure of MAP-ECC

The proposed $MAP\text{-}ECC$ consists of (i) System Setup Phase, (ii) Registration Phase, (iii) Login Phase, and (iv) Mutual authentication Phase. Each of these phases is discussed in detail below.

i. ***System Setup Phase:*** Initially, the Registration Authority (RA) assigns a public-private key pair for each sensor node and the gateway. Further, using their assigned public keys all the sensor nodes and the gateway receive their corresponding ECC-based digital certificates generated by the Certificate Authority (CA). Finally, all these intended sensor nodes and the gateway are deployed in the target e-Agricultural framework.

ii. ***Registration Phase:*** The registration phase consists of- (a) *Agricultural User (AU) registration phase*, (b) *Sensor node registration phase*. Both the AU and the Sensor node register to the Gateway via a secure channel (represented by $\rightarrow$). Additionally, each of these registration phases is explained in detail below.

MAP-ECC: Mutual Authentication Protocol for e-Agriculture Using ECC 115

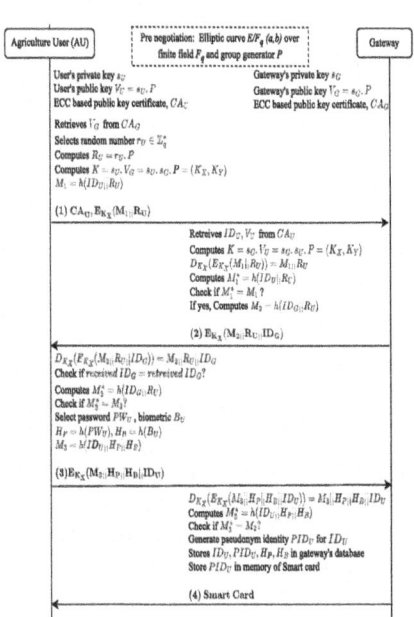

Fig. 2. Agricultural User (AU) registration phase

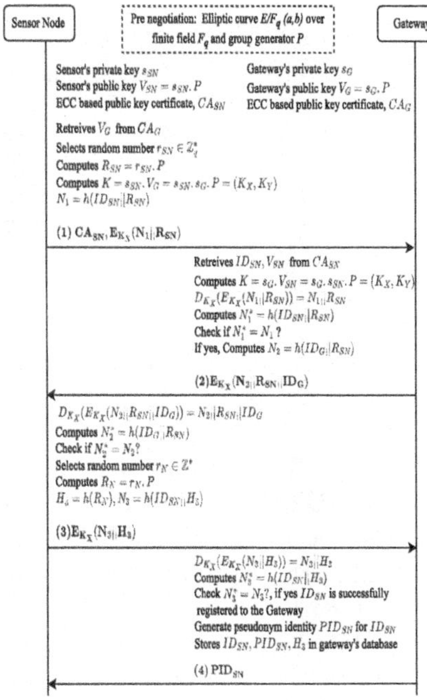

Fig. 3. Sensor Node registration phase

(a) *Agricultural User (AU) registration phase:* The working procedure AU registration phase is discussed below in step-wise format and is illustrated in Fig. 2.

Step 1. *Agricultural User (AU) $\rightarrow$ Gateway:* $\{CA_U, E_{K_X}(M_1 \| R_U)\}$

AU selects one random number r_U such that $r_U \in \mathbb{Z}_q^*$ and computes $R_U = r_U.P$ and then calculates Elliptic Curve Diffie-Hellman (ECDH)-based common session value K using her/his private key and the public key of the gateway as $K = s_U.V_G = (K_X, K_Y)$ where K_X is used as a symmetric session key for encryption/decryption. Now, the AU calculates $M_1 = h(ID_U \| R_U)$. Finally, s/he sends $\{CA_U, E_{K_X}(M_1 \| R_U)\}$ to gateway.

Step 2. *Gateway $\rightarrow$ Agricultural User (AU):* $\{E_{K_X}(M_2 \| R_U \| ID_G)\}$

After receiving $\{CA_U, E_{K_X}(M_1 \| R_U)\}$ from the AU, the gateway retrieves ID_U and V_U from the AU's certificate CA_U. Then, it computes the common session value $K = s_G \cdot V_U = (K_X, K_Y)$. Now, the gateway decrypts $E_{K_X}(M_1 \| R_U)$ and obtains M_1 and R_U and then calculates $M_1^* = h(ID_U \| R_U)$. Further, checks whether $M_1^* = M_1$. If yes, then the gateway computes $M_2 = h(ID_G \| R_U)$. Finally, it sends $\{E_{K_X}(M_2 \| R_U \| ID_G)\}$ to AU.

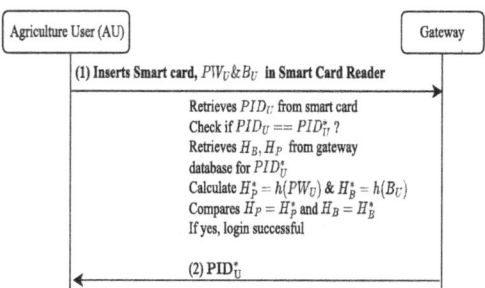

Fig. 4. Login of Agriculture User (AU) to Gateway

Step 3. *Agricultural User (AU) → Gateway:* $\{E_{K_X}(M_3\|H_P\|H_B\|ID_U)\}$
On receiving $\{E_{K_X}(M_2\|R_U\|ID_G)\}$ from the gateway, the AU decrypts $E_{K_X}(M_2\|R_U\|ID_G)$ and obtains M_2, R_U, and ID_G. Then, the AU checks if the received ID_G = retrieved ID_G. If yes, it computes $M_2^* = h(ID_G\|R_U)$ and verifies if $M_2^* = M_2$. If yes, then the AU selects a password PW_U and a biometric B_U. Further AU calculates the hash of both password and biometric $H_P = h(PW_U)$ and $H_B = h(B_U)$, respectively and then computes $M_3 = h(ID_U\|H_P\|H_B)$. Finally, the AU sends the message $\{E_{K_X}(M_3\|H_P\|H_B\|ID_U)\}$ to the gateway.

Step 4. *Gateway → Agricultural User (AU): Smart Card (SC)*
Now, the gateway decrypts $\{E_{K_X}(M_3\|H_P\|H_B\|ID_U)\}$ and obtains M_3, H_P, H_B, and ID_U. Further, it computes $M_3^* = h(ID_U\|H_P\|H_B)$ and verifies if $M_3^* = M_3$. If yes, the gateway generates pseudo-identity PID_U for the AU and stores ID_U, PID_U, H_P, and H_B in its database. Moreover, stores PID_U in the memory of the AU's Smart Card (SC). Finally, the gateway sends the SC to the AU.

(b) *Sensor registration phase:* The working procedure sensor node registration phase is discussed below in step-wise format and is illustrated in Fig. 3:

Step 1. *Sensor Node → Gateway* : $\{CA_{SN}, E_{K_X}(M_1\|R_{SN})\}$ Sensor node selects a random number r_{SN} such that $r_{SN} \in \mathbb{Z}_q^*$ and computes $R_{SN} = r_{SN}.P$. Then it calculates ECDH-based common session value $K = s_{SN}.V_G = (K_X, K_Y)$ where K_X will be used as a symmetric session key for encryption/decryption. Now, it calculates $N_1 = h(ID_{SN}\|R_{SN})$. Finally, it sends $\{CA_{SN}, E_{K_X}(N_1\|R_{SN})\}$ to gateway.

Step 2. *Gateway → Sensor Node:* $\{E_{K_X}(N_2\|R_{SN}\|ID_G)\}$
After receiving $\{CA_{SN}, E_{K_X}(N_1\|R_{SN})\}$ from the sensor node, gateway retrieves ID_{SN}, and V_{SN} from the public key certificate CA_{SN}. Now, the gateway calculates ECDH-based common session value $K = s_G.V_{SN} = (K_X, K_Y)$ where K_X will be used as a symmetric session key for encryption/decryption. Now, the gateway decrypts $E_{K_X}(N_1\|R_{SN})$ and gets N_1 and R_{SN} and then calculates $N_1^* = h(ID_{SN}\|R_{SN})$ and com-

pares it with the received N_1. If it matches, then the gateway computes $N_2 = h(ID_G || R_{SN})$. Finally, it sends $\{E_{K_X}(N_2 || R_G || ID_G)\}$ to sensor node.

Step 3. *Sensor Node* → *Gateway*: $\{E_{K_X}(N_3 || H_3)\}$

On receiving $\{E_{K_X}(N_2 || R_G || ID_G)\}$ from the gateway, sensor node decrypts $E_{K_X}(N_2 || R_{SN} || ID_G)$ and gets N_2, R_{SN}, and ID_G. Then the sensor node computes $N_2^* = h(\text{ID}_G || R_{SN})$ and verifies if $N_2^* = N_2$. If yes, the sensor node selects a random number $r_N \in \mathbb{Z}^*$ and computes $R_N = r_N \cdot P$, $H_3 = h(R_N)$ and $N_3 = h(\text{ID}_{SN} || H_3)$. Finally, the sensor node sends the message $\{E_{K_X}(N_3 || H_3)\}$ to the gateway.

Step 4. *Gateway* → *Sensor Node*: $\{PID_{SN}\}$

After receiving $\{E_{K_X}(N_3 || H_3)\}$ from sensor node, the gateway decrypts $E_{K_X}(N_3 || H_3)$ and obtains N_3 and H_3. Then, the gateway computes $N_3^* = h(\text{ID}_{SN} || H_3)$ and verifies if $N_3^* = N_3$. If yes, the gateway registers ID_{SN} successfully and generates pseudo-identity PID_{SN}. Finally, it stores $\text{ID}_{SN}, PID_{SN}, H_3$ in its database.

iii. ***Login Phase:*** The working procedure of the login phase is illustrated in Fig. 4 and discussed as follows.

Step 1: *Agricultural User (AU)* → *Gateway*: $\{PW_U, B_U\}$

Here, the *AU* enters her/his *SC* in the smart card reader and enters her/his password PW_U and biometric B_U for logging. Now, the gateway retrieves PID_U from the *SC* and checks $PID_U^* = PID_U$. If yes, then it further retrieves the H_P and H_B corresponding to PID_U^*. Now, computes $H_P^* = h(PW_U)$ and $H_B^* = h(B_U)$. Finally, it compares $H_P = H_P^*, H_B = H_B^*$. If yes, the login is successful and then the gateway sends PID_U^* to *AU*.

iv. ***Mutual Authentication Phase:*** Once the *AU* has registered and logged in to the system, s/he sends an authentication request to the gateway to generate a session key for communicating with any sensor node over an open/insecure channel (represented by --→). The working procedure of the mutual authentication phase is explained in a step-wise format below and depicted in Fig. 5.

Step 1. *Agricultural User (AU)* → *Gateway* : $\{PID_U, E_{K_{1X}}(ID_{SN} || R_U || H_1), T_1\}$

The *AU* selects a random number $r_U \in \mathbb{Z}^*$ and computes $R_U = r_U \cdot P$. Then, the *AU* computes a shared secret key $K_1 = s_U.V_G = s_U.s_G \cdot P = (K_{1X}, K_{1Y})$, and $H_1 = h(PID_U || R_U)$. Then, the *AU* records a timestamp T_1 and sends $\{PID_U, E_{K_{1X}}(ID_{SN}, R_U, H_1), T_1\}$ to the gateway.

Step 2. *Gateway* → *Sensor Node* : $\{E_{K_{2X}}(PID_U || ID_G || ID_{SN} || R_U || H_2), T_2\}$

The gateway records a timestamp T_2 for the current time and checks if the time difference $(T_2 - T_1)$ is less than a predefined threshold ΔT. If the time difference is acceptable, it checks if the received PID_U is in its database. If yes, it retrieves the corresponding ID_U. Then, it computes a shared secret key $K_1 = s_G.V_U = s_G.s_U \cdot P = (K_{1X}, K_{1Y})$. Then, it decrypts $E_{K_{1X}}(ID_{SN} || R_U || H_1)$ using the key K_{1X}. Now, the gateway computes H_1^*

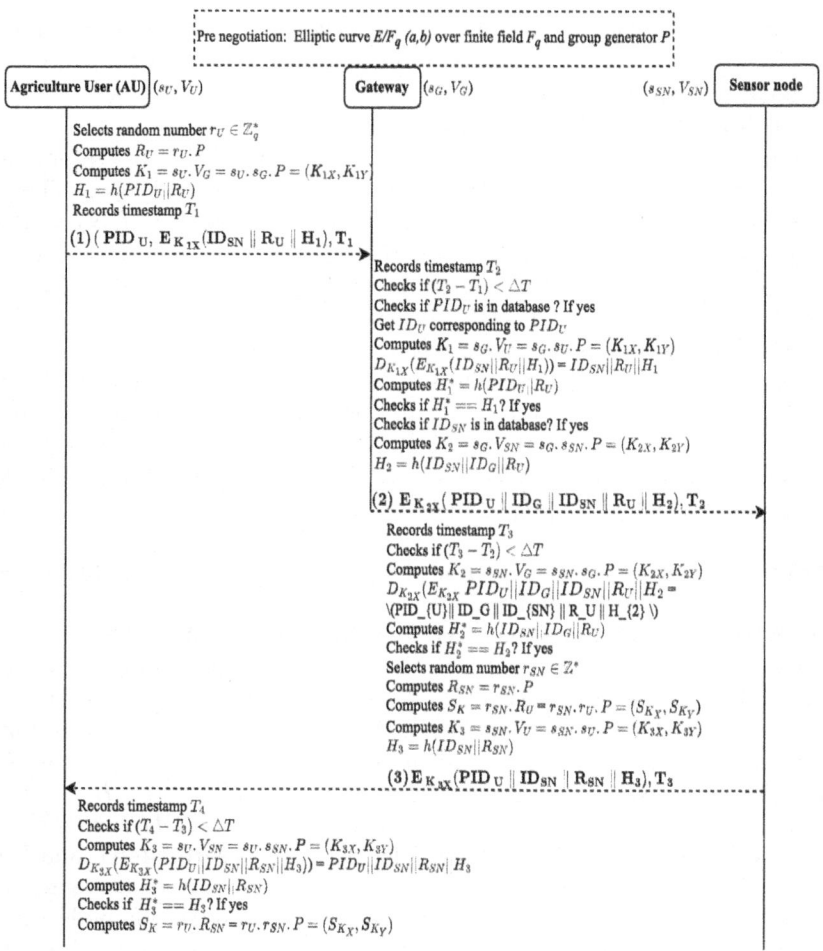

Fig. 5. Mutual authentication phase

$= h(PID_U \parallel R_U)$ and check if $H_1^* = H_1$. If yes, further checks if ID_{SN} is in its database. If yes, it computes $K_2 = s_G.V_{SN} = s_G.s_{SN} \cdot P = (K_{2X}, K_{2Y})$ and calculates $H_2 = h(ID_{SN} \parallel ID_G \parallel R_U)$. Finally, sends $\{E_{K_{2X}}(PID_U \parallel ID_G \parallel ID_{SN} \parallel R_U \parallel H_2), T_2\}$ to sensor node.

Step

3. Sensor Node $\rightarrow$ Agricultural User (AU): $\{\mathbf{E_{K_{3X}}(PID_U \parallel ID_{SN} \parallel R_{SN} \parallel H_3), T_3}\}$

The sensor node records a timestamp T_3 representing the current time and checks if the time difference $(T_3 - T_2)$ is less than a predefined threshold $\triangle T$. If the time difference is acceptable, then it computes a shared secret key $K_2 = s_SN.V_G = s_SN.s_G \cdot P = (K_{2X}, K_{2Y})$. Then, it decrypts $E_{K_{2X}}(PID_U \parallel ID_G \parallel ID_{SN} \parallel R_U \parallel H_2)$ using the key K_{2X}. After decryption, it computes $H_2^* = h(ID_{SN} \| ID_G \| R_U)$. Further, checks if $H_2^* = H_2$. If yes, then it selects a random number r_{SN} and computes a new point $R_{SN} = r_{SN} \cdot P$. Further, it computes the session key $S_K = r_{SN} \cdot R_U = r_{SN}.r_U.P = (S_{K_X}, S_{K_Y})$, $K_3 = s_{SN}.V_U = s_{SN}.s_U.P = (K_{3X}, K_{3Y})$, $H_3 = h(ID_{SN} \| R_{SN})$. Finally, the sensor node sends $\{E_{K_{3X}}(PID_U \| ID_{SN} \| R_{SN} \| H_3), T_3\}$ to gateway.

Step 4. *Agricultural User (AU) gets session key*

The AU records a timestamp T_4 representing the current time and checks if the time difference $(T_4 - T_3)$ is less than a predefined threshold $\triangle T$. If the time difference is acceptable, then it computes a shared secret key $K_3 = s_{SN}.V_U = s_{SN}.s_U.P = (K_{3X}, K_{3Y})$. Then, it decrypts $E_{K_{3X}}(PID_U \| ID_{SN} \| R_{SN} \| H_3)$ using the key K_{3X}. Further, it computes $H_3^* = h(ID_{SN} \| R_{SN})$. Now, the AU checks if $H_3^* = H_3$. If yes, finally it computes the session key $S_K = r_{SN} \cdot R_U = r_{SN}.r_U.P = (S_{K_X}, S_{K_Y})$. Thus, mutual authentication is established among all the communicating entities (AU, GW, SN) based on the session key S_K.

4 Security Verification of MAP-ECC

The informal and formal security verification of *MAP-ECC* is performed and presented as follows:

4.1 Informal Security Verification

We have taken various security attack scenarios to prove that *MAP-ECC* is secure and robust [11].

Theorem 1. *MAP-ECC resists Man-in-the-Middle (MITM) attack.*

Proof: For instance, an adversary ($[1pt]A\circ$) might try to intercept a transmitted message of our protocol. But, even if s/he gets the messages, s/he won't be able to decrypt them as all the messages of *MAP-ECC* are encrypted using a key K generated using the private keys of the sender and receiver. Hence, *MAP-ECC* resists the Man-in-the-Middle (*MITM*) attack.

Theorem 2. *MAP-ECC preserves perfect forward secrecy.*

Proof. Even if an adversary ($[1pt]A\circ$) gains access to one session key and decrypts the communication for that particular session, they cannot use that same session key to decrypt past or future sessions [12]. This is because each session key S_k is generated independently, typically using a combination of random values (r_u and r_{sn}). As a result, even if the session key of one session is compromised, the security of past and future sessions remains intact. Thus, *MAP-ECC* preserves perfect forward secrecy [13].

Theorem 3. *MAP-ECC resists impersonation attack.*

Proof: Let, us assume that the adversary ($[1pt]A\circ$) is impersonating a legitimate entity (Agricultural User, Gateway, Sensor node) to acquire information. However, in any of such cases, it won't be possible to gain information as they are encrypted using the public key of the receiver, and to decrypt this, s/he must know the corresponding private key. Additionally, it is computationally impossible to get the secret key from the public key due to the ECDLP property of ECC. Hence, *MAP-ECC* withstands impersonation attack.

Theorem 4. *MAP-ECC resists replay attack.*

Proof: If an adversary ($[1pt]A\circ$) captures data packets during communication and tries to spoof the system by maliciously retransmitting these data packets, it won't be possible because each message in our protocol is incorporated with a Timestamp (T_i), and each time a receiver gets a message, it checks how recent the message is by comparing the difference between the current time and the received timestamp with a set time limit. If the difference is more than the set time limit then the message is discarded. Thus, *MAP-ECC* resists replay attack.

Theorem 5. *MAP-ECC resists Denial-of-Service (DoS) attack.*

Proof: In the *MAP-ECC* protocol, we have restricted the number of login attempts to 3 for any user. If the user is not able to submit the right credentials within 3 attempts then s/he will be restricted from sending login request for an extended length of time. Hence, our protocol effectively resists DoS attack.

4.2 Formal Security Verification

MAP-ECC is formally verified using **A**utomated **V**erification **I**nternet **S**ecurity **P**rotocol and **A**nalysis (*AVISPA*) simulator in which there are three participating entities [14]. They are- AU, GW, and SN. Additionally, to define the role in the High-Level Protocol Specification Language (*HLPSL*), we have five different roles - AU, GW, SN, session, and environment.

Secrecy Goals
secrecy_of_sec_1: Ensures the symmetric key Kds between the SN and the GW remains confidential.
secrecy_of_sec_2: Ensures the temporary data Td generated during the SN registration phase remains confidential.
secrecy_of_sec_3: Ensures the symmetric key Kug between the AU and the GW remains confidential.
secrecy_of_sec_4: Ensures the AU's password $Pwdu$ remains confidential.
secrecy_of_sec_5: Ensures the temporary data Tu generated during the AU registration phase remains confidential.
secrecy_of_sec_6: Ensures the session key remains C confidential.

Authentication Goals
authentication_on_auth_Td: Ensures mutual authentication on the temporary data Td during the registration phase between the SN and the GW.

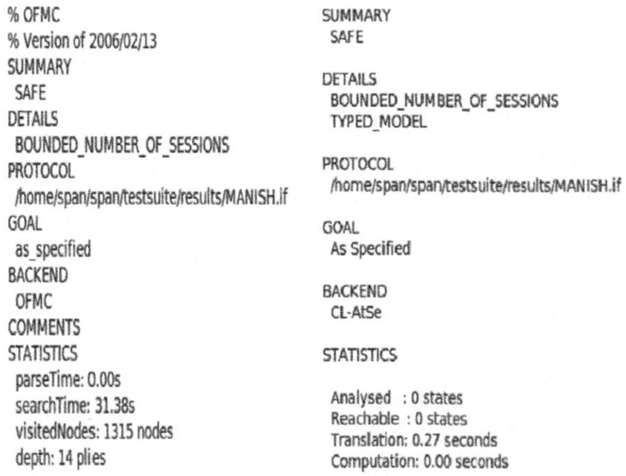

```
% OFMC                                    SUMMARY
% Version of 2006/02/13                     SAFE
 SUMMARY
   SAFE                                   DETAILS
 DETAILS                                    BOUNDED_NUMBER_OF_SESSIONS
   BOUNDED_NUMBER_OF_SESSIONS               TYPED_MODEL
 PROTOCOL
   /home/span/span/testsuite/results/MANISH.if   PROTOCOL
 GOAL                                       /home/span/span/testsuite/results/MANISH.if
   as_specified                           GOAL
 BACKEND                                    As Specified
   OFMC                                   BACKEND
 COMMENTS                                   CL-AtSe
 STATISTICS
   parseTime: 0.00s                       STATISTICS
   searchTime: 31.38s                       Analysed  : 0 states
   visitedNodes: 1315 nodes                 Reachable : 0 states
   depth: 14 plies                          Translation: 0.27 seconds
                                            Computation: 0.00 seconds
```

Fig. 6. OFMC and CL-AtSe backend result of the MAP-ECC

authentication_on auth_TS3: Ensures mutual authentication on the temporary data $TS3$ during the authentication phase between the SN and the GW.

Simulation Results. The simulation result considering *OFMC* and *CL-AtSe* back-ends of *AVISPA* simulator illustrated in Fig. 6 shows that *MAP-ECC* is **SAFE** against both replay and man-in-the-middle (*MITM*) attacks, respectively.

5 Performance Analysis

The performance analysis in terms of computation and communication overhead of the *MAP-ECC* is shown in this section.

5.1 Computation Overhead

The execution time required to run a cryptographic operation is termed as computation overhead [15]. In this line, the execution time of various cryptographic operations along with their notations are tabulated in Table 2.

The comparative analysis of the *MAP-ECC* in terms of computation overhead with the existing schemes is tabulated in Table 3 which shows that our protocol incurs comparatively low computation overhead than all existing schemes.

Table 2. Execution time and notation for various cryptographic operations [10]

Operation	Description	Computation Overhead (ms)
t_{mod}	Modular exponentiation operation	3.8500
t_{bp}	Bilinear pairing operation	05.811
t_{ecm}	ECC scalar point multiplication	02.226
$t_{s\text{-}enc/dec}$	Symmetric encryption/decryption	0.0046
t_h	One-way hash function (SHA-1 256)	0.0023
$t_{as\text{-}enc/dec}$	Public key encryption/decryption	3.8500
t_{eca}	ECC-based point addition	0.0288

Table 3. Comparison of computation overhead

Protocols	Operations	Computation Overhead (ms)
[17]	$12t_h + 14t_{ecm}$	≈ 31.1916
[18]	$7t_h + 2t_{ecm} + 4t_{bp}$	≈ 27.7121
[19]	$31t_h + 6t_{ecm} + 1t_{fe}$	≈ 15.6533
[20]	$12t_h + 2t_{bp} + 4t_{s\text{-}enc/dec} + 2t_{ecm} + 1t_{mod}$	≈ 19.9700
MAP-ECC	$8t_h + 6t_{ecm} + 6t_{s\text{-}enc/dec}$	≈ 13.4020

5.2 Communication Overhead

The total number of bits required to exchange the messages to establish mutual authentication among the involved entities is termed as communication overhead [16]. In line with this, the byte size of different attributes to compute the communication overhead is tabulated in Table 4.

The comparative analysis of the *MAP-ECC* in terms of communication overhead with the existing schemes is tabulated in Table 5 which exhibits that our protocol incurs comparatively low communication overhead than all existing schemes.

Table 4. Prerequisite for communication overhead [10]

Attribute	Size (Bytes)
User, Sensor & Gateway Identity, Timestamp	8
Password	4
Irreversible hash function	16
Symmetric Key encryption/decryption	20

Table 5. Comparison of communication overhead

Protocols	No. of Messages	Communication Overhead (bytes)
[17]	3	460
[18]	4	352
[19]	4	308
[20]	4	292
MAP-ECC	3	124

6 Conclusion

In this paper we have designed a novel mutual authentication protocol for e-Agriculture using *ECC* called *MAP-ECC* to eradicate the loopholes of existing literatures. Further, we have performed the informal and formal security verification of the *MAP-ECC* which proves that it achieves comparable higher security than the existing schemes. The performance analysis in terms of computation and communication overheads exhibits that *MAP-ECC* is feasible for implementation in the real-world e-Agricultural sector satisfying all the security requirements with conceivable computation and communication overheads.

Acknowledgment. This work is supported by Ministry of Education, Government of India.

References

1. Khan, M.N., Rahman, H.U., Hussain, T., Yang, B., Qaisar, S.M.: Enabling trust in automotive IoT: lightweight mutual authentication scheme for electronic connected devices in internet of things. IEEE Trans. Consum. Electron. (2024)
2. Nguyen-Tan, T., Dang-Ngoc, C., Le-Trung, Q.: A smart agriculture solution includes intelligent irrigation and security. In: International Conference on Industrial Networks and Intelligent Systems, pp. 3–18 (2023)
3. Yu, H.F., Mu, W.Z.: ABE-based postquantum cross-blockchain data exchange approach for smart agriculture. IEEE Trans. Ind. Inform. (2024)
4. Wu, T.H., Tsai, C.W.: An intelligent agriculture network security system based on private blockchains. J. Commun. Netw. **21**, 503–508 (2019)
5. Vangala, A., Das, A.K., Chamola, V., Korotaev, V., Rodrigues, J.J.: Security in IoT-enabled smart agriculture: architecture, security solutions and challenges. Clust. Comput. **26**, 879–902 (2023)
6. Soe, Y.N., Feng, Y., Santosa, P.I., Hartanto, R., Sakurai, K.: Towards a lightweight detection system for cyber attacks in the IoT environment using corresponding features. Electronics **9**(1), 144 (2020)
7. Kumar, R., Kumar, P., Tripathi, R., Gupta, G.P., Gadekallu, T.R., Srivastava, G.: SP2F: a secured privacy-preserving framework for smart agricultural unmanned aerial vehicles. Comput. Netw. **187**, 107819 (2021)

8. Li, Y., Tian, Y.: A lightweight and secure three-factor authentication protocol with adaptive privacy-preserving property for wireless sensor networks. IEEE Syst. J. **16**, 6197–6208 (2022)
9. Fatima, M.N., Obaidat, M.S., Mahmood, K., Shamshad, S., Saleem, M.A., Ayub, M.F.: Privacy-preserving three-factor authentication protocol for wireless sensor networks deployed in agricultural field. ACM Trans. Sensor Netw. (2023)
10. Itoo, S., Khan, A.A., Ahmad, M., Idrisi, M.J.: A secure and privacy-preserving lightweight authentication and key exchange algorithm for smart agriculture monitoring system. IEEE Access **11**, 56875–56890 (2023)
11. Ray, S., Biswas, G.P.: An ECC based public key infrastructure usable for mobile applications. In: Proceedings of the Second International Conference on Computational Science, Engineering and Information Technology, pp. 562–568 (2012)
12. Wan, T., Ge, J., Liao, W., Zhao, H.: A lightweight two-factor continuous authentication protocol for agricultural IoT devices. Wirel. Pers. Commun. 1–25 (2024)
13. Ray, S., Nandan, R., Biswas, G.P.: ECC based IKE protocol design for internet applications. Procedia Technol. **4**, 522–529 (2012)
14. Rangwani, D., Sadhukhan, D., Ray, S., Khan, M.K., Dasgupta, M.: A robust provable-secure privacy-preserving authentication protocol for industrial internet of things. Peer-to-Peer Netw. Appl. **14**(3), 1548–1571 (2021). https://doi.org/10.1007/s12083-020-01063-5
15. Chen, C.M., Wang, K.H., Fang, W., Wu, T.Y., Wang, E.K.: Reconsidering a lightweight anonymous authentication protocol. J. Chin. Inst. Eng. **421**, 9–14 (2019)
16. Chettri, I.B., Ray, S., Das, P.: SAK-SAE: a secure authentication and key-exchange scheme for smart agricultural environment using fuzzy extractor. In: 2023 OITS International Conference on Information Technology (OCIT), pp. 867–873 (2023)
17. Challa, S., et al.: An efficient ECC-based provably secure three-factor user authentication and key agreement protocol for wireless healthcare sensor networks. Comput. Electr. Eng. **69**, 534–554 (2018)
18. Liu, C.H., Chung, Y.F.: Secure user authentication scheme for wireless healthcare sensor networks. Comput. Electr. Eng. **59**, 250–261 (2017)
19. Soni, P., Pal, A.K., Islam, S.H.: An improved three-factor authentication scheme for patient monitoring using WSN in remote health-care system. Comput. Methods Programs Biomed. **182**, 105054 (2019)
20. Vinoth, R., Deborah, L.J.: An efficient key agreement and authentication protocol for secure communication in industrial IoT applications. J. Ambient. Intell. Humaniz. Comput. **14**, 1431–1443 (2023)

Blockchain and Cryptocurrency, IoT Security and Privacy, Database Security

Robust Image Steganography: A SLIC and QWT-Based Approach for Secure Data Embedding

Gatram Sravan Kumar[1], Kamalakanta Sethi[1(✉)], Piyush Joshi[1], and Padmalochan Bera[2]

[1] Indian Institute of Information Technology, Sricity, India
{sravankumar.g21,kamalakanta.s,piyush.j}@iiits.in
[2] Indian Institute of Technology, Bhubaneswar, Bhubaneswar, India
plb@iitbbs.ac.in

Abstract. Steganography is the art and science of hiding secret data within a carrier medium, such as digital images, without altering its perceptible quality. In this research, we introduce an advanced steganography technique that combines SLIC segmentation with Quaternion Wavelet Transform (QWT) to securely and robustly embed encrypted messages into images. Our steganography technique overcomes several drawbacks of traditional methods such as noticeable visual distortions, and susceptibility to various attacks. Initially, the image is segmented into foreground and background regions using SLIC, ensuring that the embedding process respects the perceptual importance of different areas within the image. We then apply QWT to decompose the image into approximation and detail coefficients. The secret message undergoes dual encryption using both substitution and transposition ciphers, significantly improving its confidentiality. This encrypted message is subsequently converted into binary form and embedded into the approximation coefficients of the wavelet-transformed image. To evaluate the efficiency of our method, we computed PSNR (Peak Signal-to-Noise Ratio), MSE (Mean Square Error), and SSIM (Structural Similarity Index) metrics, demonstrating superior performance compared to traditional techniques such as DCT (Discrete Cosine Transform), DWT (Discrete Wavelet Transform), and LSB (Least Significant Bit) methods. Additionally, we tested the robustness of our steganographic images against various attacks, including Gaussian noise, salt-and-pepper noise, rotation, translation, blurring, and compression, using Bit Correct Rate (BCR) as the evaluation metric. Our results show that the proposed method achieves BCR values exceeding 94%.

Keywords: Steganography · SLIC · QWT · PSNR · MSE · SSIM · BCR

1 Introduction

Steganography is the practice of concealing information within digital media, such as images, audio, or video files. This technique ensures that the existence of the hidden information is not directly visible to the observer, thereby providing a layer of security for sensitive data. Various methods have been developed for embedding secret messages into digital media, each with its own strengths and weaknesses in terms of security, imperceptibility, and capacity.

In this study, we focus on image steganography in which we hide confidential information inside images as shown in Fig. 1. This field has seen significant advancements due to the widespread use of digital images in various applications. Traditional techniques like Discrete Cosine Transform (DCT) [6], Discrete Wavelet Transform (DWT) [10], and Least Significant Bit (LSB) [1] substitution are widely used for embedding secret data into images. However, these methods often face challenges related to capacity, maintaining the quality of the steganographic image, and ensuring the robustness of the hidden data against various forms of image processing and attacks.

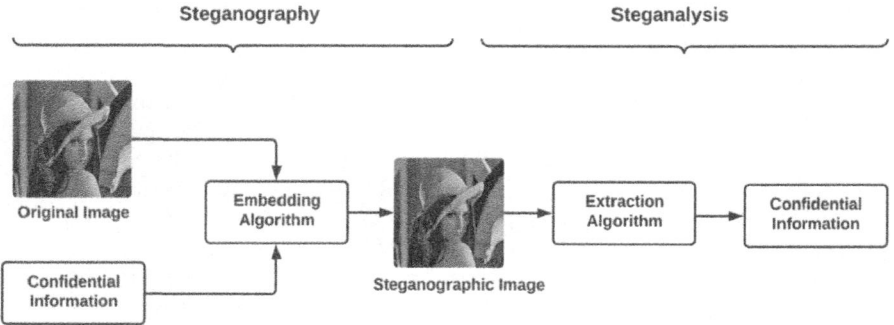

Fig. 1. General working process of steganography

To overcome the limitations of traditional techniques we proposed a novel approach that begins by segmenting the image into foreground and background regions using SLIC segmentation [18]. This step ensures that the embedding process is performed based on the perceptual importance of different areas within the image which helps to preserve the quality of the image. We then apply QWT [21] to decompose the image into approximation and detail coefficients, providing a robust foundation for data embedding. The secret message is encrypted using both substitution and transposition ciphers for added security. The encrypted text is converted into a binary format and embedded into the approximation coefficients. This dual encryption method enhances the confidentiality of the hidden data.

To evaluate the effectiveness of our proposed technique, we conducted extensive experiments using standard high-quality images in the field of steganography. The results are measured in terms of Peak Signal-to-Noise Ratio (PSNR),

Mean Squared Error (MSE), and Structural Similarity Index (SSIM). The results demonstrate that our method significantly outperforms traditional steganographic techniques. The high PSNR and low MSE values indicate minimal distortion, while the SSIM values confirm the preservation of structural information.

The remainder of the paper is structured as follows. In Sect. 2 we discussed the state-of-the-art steganographic approaches. Our proposed steganography approach is discussed in detail in Sect. 3. The security analysis of our proposed approach is presented in Sect. 4. The experimental results are shown in Sect. 5. We conclude the paper with future work in Sect. 6.

2 Related Work

In this section, we will discuss some of the existing works that use LSB, DCT, DWT, and hybrid techniques in image steganography.

Raja Rajeswari et al. [1] utilized LSB steganography to encode and decode text within images, leveraging Python Image Library and Tkinter for implementation. AI-based encryption methods are integrated to enhance data security and fortify information concealment within images. In [2] authors proposed a modified inverted LSB technique that uses a three-bit LSB pattern, improving image quality over the traditional two-bit method. Additionally, combining chaotic map-based message encryption with the inverted LSB method further boosts message security. Aimee D. Molato et al. [3] presented a novel steganography method combining Diffie-Hellman Key Exchange with a modified Collatz Conjecture, resulting in highly imperceptible stego-images. In [4] authors introduced a novel approach to image steganography using LSB algorithm with Hamming code, emphasizing minimal visual distortion and enhanced embedding capacity. Poornima Mohan et al. [5] This paper introduces an innovative Image Steganography technique focusing on embedding messages using the Block Truncation Coding and Least Significant Bit (LSB) approach. The LSB embedding technique is simple but susceptible to visual degradation and low embedding capacity, limiting its robustness in more complex scenarios. Researchers have explored DCT and DWT as alternatives in steganography, leveraging its ability to distribute hidden data across frequency domains for improved security and visual fidelity.

B. A. Dharani et al. [6] explored LSB and DCT methods in multimodal steganography, emphasizing data capacity versus robustness and quality. It recommends LSB for high capacity needs and DCT for robustness, proposing hybrid approaches for balanced security and capacity in practical applications. In paper [7], the authors investigated the influence of the Discrete Cosine Transform (DCT) phase on image hiding schemes, contrasting it with a traditional emphasis on DCT magnitude. Hassan Vakani et al. [8] introduced a novel DCT-in-DCT-Adaptive Scaling technique for steganography, enhancing payload imperceptibility while maintaining stego quality. In [9], authors explored image steganography methods, focusing on spatial (LSB) and transform domain (DCT) techniques, using ALASKA2 and BOSSBase datasets.

Su-Ho Chiu et al. [10], authors presented a novel coverless image steganography method leveraging SIFT and DWT sequence mapping to enhance sequence diversity and reduce reliance on numerous images. In [11] authors explored steganography by embedding secret text within images using Discrete Wavelet Transform (DWT) for encoding and decoding, alongside Convolutional Neural Network (CNN) for image preprocessing and training. In [12] The authors proposed steganography algorithm utilizes singular value decomposition (SVD) in the stationary wavelet domain to embed secret messages robustly in images, overcoming challenges posed by lossy compression and scaling in network platforms. In papers [13–17] authors presented hybrid techniques in image steganography by combining LSB, DCT and DWT techniques. These hybrid techniques improved the image quality and robustness as compared to previous state-of-the-art approaches.

In papers [18–20] the authors proposed a SLIC segmentation algorithm that significantly reduces computational complexity by clustering pixels in a 5-dimensional space combining color and spatial proximity. Additionally, SLIC enhances boundary adherence and overcomes the limitations of other algorithms in preserving object boundaries and detail. In papers [21, 22] authors presented QWT which outperforms traditional transforms like DCT and DWT by efficiently handling color images and capturing both spatial and spectral information simultaneously. It offers a superior representation of multi-dimensional data, resulting in better preservation of image details and improved robustness in steganography.

In conclusion, LSB-based steganography is simple but it has significant drawbacks such as lower security and reduced steganographic image quality as it directly alters the least significant bits of an image, making it vulnerable to steganalysis. DCT and DWT steganography techniques are more robust but often result in visible distortions. Our proposed approach combines SLIC segmentation and Quaternion Wavelet Transform (QWT), effectively addressing these challenges by embedding encrypted data in perceptually significant regions, thereby maintaining the quality of the steganographic image.

Although SLIC and QWT have several advantages over traditional techniques they are not yet explored in the field of steganography. Consequently, our objective is to develop a robust and efficient image steganography algorithm by combining the principles of SLIC and QWT which helps to enhance the steganographic image quality.

3 Proposed Stegnography Approach

In this section, we delve into the methodology employed for our image steganography approach. The workflow of our proposed method is depicted in Fig. 2 highlighting the sequential steps involved. As illustrated, our steganography algorithm comprises several distinct stages, each crucial to the overall process. We will now provide a detailed discussion of each step.

3.1 Step-1: SLIC Segmentation

In this step, an original image is taken as input to the SLIC algorithm. SLIC segmentation is used to segment the image into foreground and background regions based on color similarity. It starts by initializing cluster centers evenly spaced throughout the image. Each pixel in the image gets assigned to the nearest cluster center based on its color similarity. SLIC calculates color similarity using the Euclidean distance metric in the LAB color space. LAB color space is a color-opponent space with three components: L represents the lightness of the color, A represents the position of the color on the green-red axis, and B represents the position of the color on the blue-yellow axis. This color space is designed to approximate human vision and perceptual uniformity. In LAB color space, L ranges from 0 to 100, while both A and B range from -128 to 127. The distance metric used for the calculation of color similarity is given below.

$$D = \sqrt{(L_p - L_q)^2 + (a_p - a_q)^2 + (b_p - b_q)^2 + \left(\frac{S_{\max}}{S_p - S_q}\right)^2} \quad (1)$$

Here, L_p, a_p, b_p are the LAB color components of pixel **p**. L_q, a_q, b_q are the LAB color components of pixel **q**. S_p, S_q are the spatial coordinates of pixels **p** and **q**. $S_{\max}$ is the maximum spatial distance in the image.

After all the pixels are assigned to a particular cluster center, the cluster centers move to the average position of all the pixels in their group. This procedure is iteratively done until the cluster centers stop moving. After this complete process, we end up with groups of pixels (clusters) that have similar colors. A cluster of darker pixels are considered as foreground and relatively lighter pixels are considered as background regions. SLIC algorithm labels each pixel as 0 or 1 where 0 indicates a background pixel and 1 indicates a foreground pixel. Higher embedding strength is used in foreground regions as distortions in foreground regions are less compared to background regions. The segmentation of the image helps to maintain image quality and also increases the embedding strength.

3.2 Step-2: Substitution and Transposition Encryption

Encryption adds an extra layer of security by ensuring that even if the hidden information is detected, it remains inaccessible without the encryption key. This ensures that even if steganography is compromised, the encrypted data remains protected. This dual strategy enhances the protection of the hidden message making it more resilient to common steganalysis techniques. In this step, the user gives a secret text message which he wants to embed into the image. The confidential message is encrypted using both substitution and transposition encryption techniques. In substitution encryption, the secret message undergoes encryption using a substitution cipher. In this cipher, each character in the message is replaced by another character based on a fixed shift value. After substitution encryption, the resulting encrypted text undergoes another encryption process using a transposition cipher. This cipher rearranges the characters of the text based on a fixed pattern defined by a key value.

3.3 Step-3: Embedding the Encrypted Data Using QWT

Before embedding the encrypted text is converted into 8-digit binary code to make it more suitable for embedding. The binary code is embedded into the image using QWT. QWT transforms the original image into its wavelet domain representation, which facilitates the embedding of encrypted text while preserving image quality. During the QWT process, the image is decomposed into several sub-bands, including approximation coefficients (cA) and detail coefficients (cH, cV, cD). The approximation coefficients (cA) represent the low-intensity components of the image, capturing its overall structure and essential details.

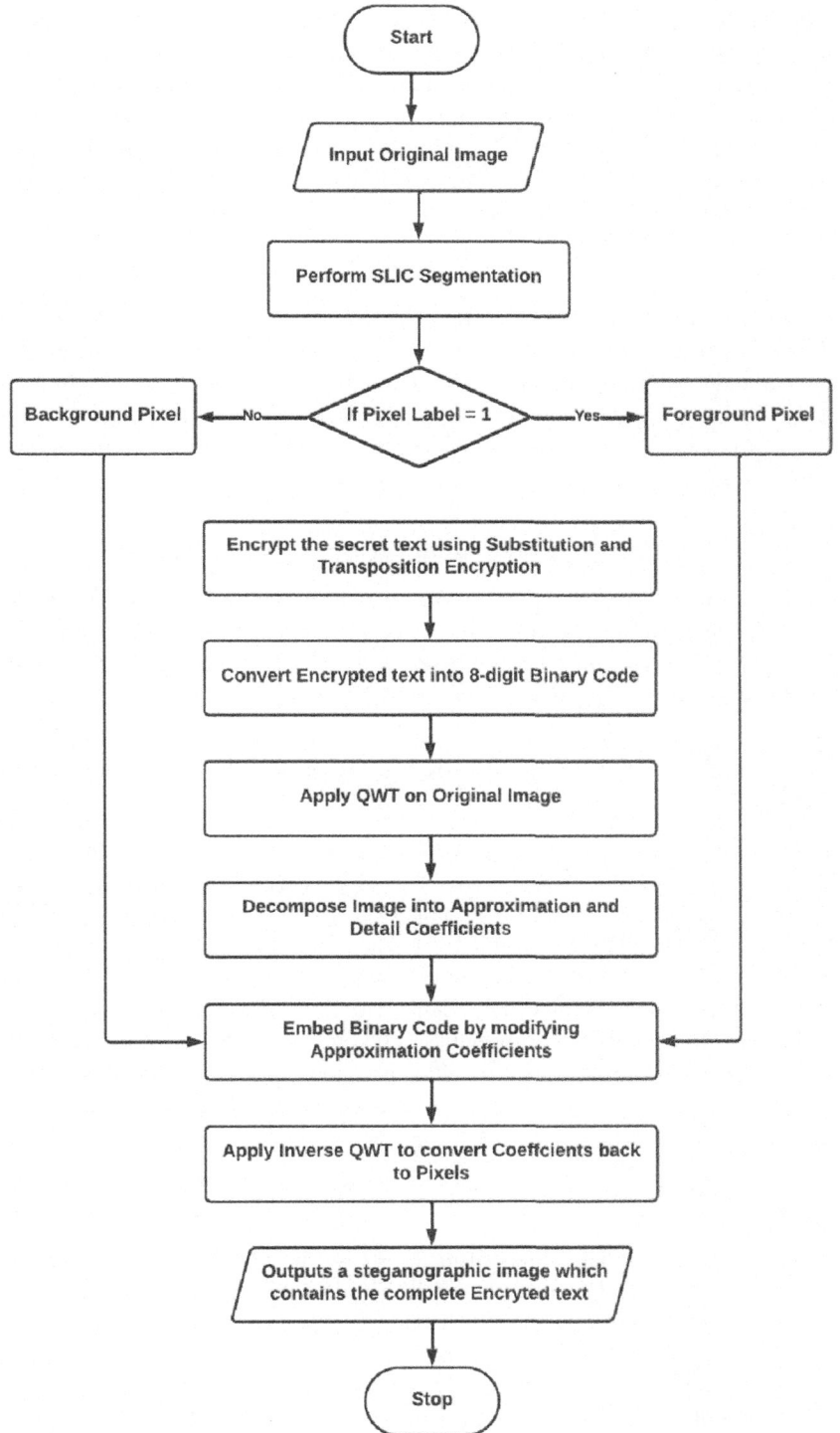

Fig. 2. Work flow of our steganography method

On the other hand, the detail coefficients (cH, cV, cD) contain high-intensity highlighting fine details and edges within the image. We embed the binary code by modifying the cA intensity coefficients. We Iterate through each pixel in the image and check its corresponding label in the SLIC labels. If the label of the pixel is 1, the foreground embedding strength value is used else the background embedding strength value is used. We modify the pixel intensity for embedding the binary code into the pixels based on the equation below.

$$U = O + (\text{Binary Code Bit} \times E) \qquad (2)$$

where U represents the Updated Intensity, O represents the Original Intensity, and E represents the embedding strength. This equation represents modifying the cA coefficients (Intensities) of a pixel in the image during the embedding process. This embedding process is done for each color channel (R, G, B) of a pixel in an image. This completes the process of embedding an encrypted secret text into the image.

3.4 Step-4: Applying Inverse Quantarion Wavelet Transform

Finally, we applied the Inverse QWT to the updated cA frequency coefficients to convert intensities back into pixels. The output of inverse QWT is a steganographic image that contains the embedded secret information. This concludes the workflow of the proposed steganography approach.

3.5 Step-5: Recovery of Embedded Data from the Steganographic Image

In the SLIC and QWT-based approach recovering the hidden data from the steganographic image involves several steps. First, the steganographic image is segmented using the same SLIC segmentation method used during embedding, which separates the foreground and background regions. This ensures that the data recovery focuses on the specific regions where the secret message was embedded. Next, the Quaternion Wavelet Transform (QWT) is applied to decompose the image into its frequency components. The encrypted binary data, which was embedded into the approximation coefficients (low-frequency components) during the embedding process is extracted from the modified intensity values of the pixels as shown in Eq. 3.

$$\text{Binary Code Bit} = \frac{U - O}{E} \qquad (3)$$

where U represents the Updated Intensity, O represents the Original Intensity, and E represents the embedding strength. Finally, the binary data is decrypted using the reverse process of the encryption methods (substitution and transposition ciphers) to recover the original secret message. This method ensures high accuracy in data recovery due to the robustness of QWT and the selective embedding enabled by SLIC segmentation. This concludes the recovery process of our approach.

4 Security Analysis of Proposed Steganographic Technique

The security of the proposed steganography approach integrating SLIC segmentation with Quantized Wavelet Transform (QWT) embedding lies in its ability to distribute the hidden message across both foreground and background segments of the image, enhancing the resistance to detection. By embedding data in the wavelet coefficients rather than directly altering the pixel domain, the method minimizes vulnerability to statistical attacks like chi-square or histogram-based analysis. SLIC segmentation enables selective embedding, reducing the likelihood of concentrated distortions in any particular region. To further improve security, the hidden message is encrypted using a combination of substitution and transposition ciphers before embedding. It adds an extra layer of protection by making the message unreadable even if detected. This layered strategy, which combines encryption with both spatial and frequency domain techniques, significantly enhances robustness against steganalysis tools while preserving the image's visual quality.

5 Results and Discussions

5.1 Implementation Results

We implemented the proposed steganography approach in Python using Jupyter Notebook and evaluated its efficiency through extensive experiments. To assess the quality of the steganographic images, we employed three widely recognized metrics in the field of steganography which are PSNR (Peak Signal-to-Noise Ratio), MSE (Mean Square Error), and SSIM (Structural Similarity Index).

MSE is a metric that quantifies the average squared difference between the original and the steganographic image pixels. Lower MSE values indicate less error and thus higher quality, meaning the embedded data causes minimal distortion to the image. This is important for ensuring that the hidden data does not significantly alter the visual perception of the image.

$$\text{MSE} = \frac{1}{N} \sum_{i=1}^{N} (\text{original}_i - \text{modified}_i)^2 \quad (4)$$

In Eq. (3) $original_i$ and $modified_i$ are the pixel values at position i in the original and modified images, respectively and N is the total number of pixels.

PSNR is a metric that quantifies the difference between an original image and a modified one. It measures the ratio between the maximum possible signal value and the power of the noise that distorts the image. A higher PSNR value indicates that the image has less noise and is closer in quality to the original.

$$\text{PSNR} = 20 \cdot \log_{10}\left(\frac{255}{\sqrt{\text{MSE}}}\right) \quad (5)$$

In Eq. (2) $original_i$ and $modified_i$ are the pixel values at position i in the original and modified images, respectively and N is the total number of pixels.

SSIM evaluates the structural similarity between the original and steganographic images. It considers changes in structural information, luminance, and contrast. An SSIM value close to 1 indicates high similarity, ensuring that the essential perceptual quality of the image remains intact after embedding the message.

$$\text{SSIM}(x, y) = \frac{(2\mu_x\mu_y + C_1)(2\sigma_{xy} + C_2)}{(\mu_x^2 + \mu_y^2 + C_1)(\sigma_x^2 + \sigma_y^2 + C_2)} \tag{6}$$

In Eq. (5) μ_x and μ_y are the means of the cover and steganographic images, respectively. σ_x^2 and σ_y^2 are the variances of the cover and steganographic images, respectively. σ_{xy} is the covariance between the cover and steganographic images. The C_1 and C_2 are small constants to stabilize the division with a weak denominator.

These evaluation metrics collectively provide a comprehensive assessment of our steganography method's effectiveness in preserving image quality while embedding secret data.

Fig. 3. Original Image

Fig. 4. Stegnographic Image

Figure 3 depicts the original pepper image which is vastly used in the field of steganography. Figure 4 showcases the steganographic image obtained after embedding the confidential information using our proposed technique. The accompanying Table 1 provides a comprehensive comparison of PSNR, MSE, and SSIM values across various steganographic methods, including traditional techniques like LSB, DCT, DWT, hybrid techniques, and our proposed method. This comparative analysis highlights the effectiveness and robustness of our approach in maintaining the image quality with high PSNR, low MSE, and high SSIM values of the steganographic image w.r.t state-of-the-art approaches.

Table 1. Comparison of PSNR, MSE and SSIM values w.r.t Figs. 3 and 4

Sl. No.	Method	PSNR(db)	MSE	SSIM
1	DCT	57.51	0.21	0.953
2	DWT	54.89	0.36	0.936
3	LSB	56.12	0.27	0.948
4	Hybrid Techniques	61.23	0.14	0.966
5	Proposed Approach (SLIC + QWT)	**72.16**	**0.08**	**0.981**

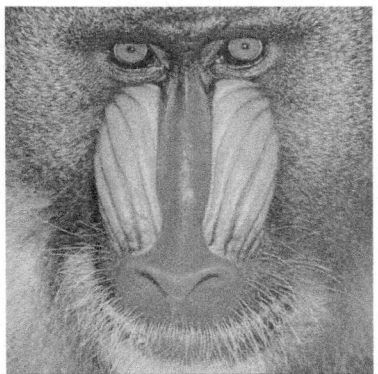
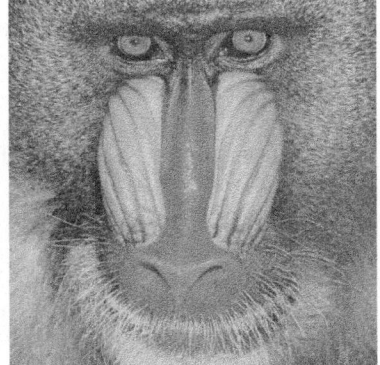

Fig. 5. Original Image **Fig. 6.** Stegnographic Image

Figure 5 depicts the original baboon image which is vastly used in the field of steganography. Figure 6 showcases the steganographic image obtained after embedding the confidential information using our proposed technique. The accompanying Table 2 provides a comprehensive comparison of PSNR, MSE, and SSIM values across various steganographic methods, including traditional techniques like LSB, DCT, DWT, hybrid techniques, and our proposed method. This comparative analysis highlights the effectiveness and robustness of our approach in maintaining the image quality with high PSNR, low MSE, and high SSIM values of the steganographic image w.r.t state-of-the-art approaches.

Table 2. Comparison of PSNR, MSE and SSIM values w.r.t Figs. 5 and 6

Sl. No.	Method	PSNR(db)	MSE	SSIM
1	DCT	58.12	0.23	0.958
2	DWT	55.37	0.32	0.941
3	LSB	56.89	0.29	0.953
4	Hybrid Techniques	63.17	0.14	0.963
5	Proposed Approach (SLIC + QWT)	**74.32**	**0.05**	**0.989**

Table 3 represents the average PSNR, MSE, and SSIM values calculated on 50 different high-quality images generally used in the field of steganography and their respective steganographic images. Table 3 depicts that our proposed steganographic procedure gives high PSNR, low MSE and high SSIM values in comparison to the traditional techniques.

Table 3. Comparision of average PSNR, MSE, and SSIM values on 50 images.

Sl. No.	Method	PSNR(db)	MSE	SSIM
1	DCT	57.39	0.25	0.961
2	DWT	55.42	0.37	0.945
3	LSB	56.87	0.26	0.957
4	Hybrid Techniques	61.73	0.18	0.973
5	Proposed Approach (SLIC + QWT)	**73.89**	**0.07**	**0.984**

Table 4. Bit Correct Rate (BCR) for Different Image Attacks

Attacks	BCR (in %)
Gaussian Noise (0.002)	99.93
Salt & Pepper Noise (0.002)	99.87
Rotation (30°)	94.32
Translation (5,5)	96.89
Blurring	98.12
JPEG Compression (50)	98.48

We evaluated the robustness of our proposed method against a variety of attacks, including noise (Gaussian, Salt, and Pepper), rotation, translation, blurring, and compression. Bit Correct Ratio (BCR) is used as the evaluation metric to evaluate the quality of the image against different image attacks. The results summarized in Table 4 demonstrate that our steganography technique consistently achieves BCR values exceeding 94% across all types of attacks. These results highlight the superior robustness and resilience of our method on various image attacks.

5.2 Time Complexity Analysis

The time complexities of the traditional approaches and the proposed approach are explained subsequently. The time complexity of LSB embedding is $O(n)$ because it processes each pixel linearly by embedding the message in the least significant bits of the color channels. In contrast, DCT embedding has a time complexity of $O(n \log n)$ due to the computational overhead of applying the Discrete Cosine Transform which involves a logarithmic factor from the Fourier transform process. DWT embedding operates in $O(n)$ since it performs a wavelet transform that scales linearly with the number of pixels similar to LSB. Our proposed embedding approach, which integrates SLIC segmentation with Quaternion Wavelet Transforms, also maintains a time complexity of $O(n)$. This is due to the fact that both the segmentation and subsequent embedding processes operate on fixed-size segments and require linear scans through the data.

6 Conclusion and Future Work

In this paper, we presented a novel steganography approach that combines SLIC segmentation, Quaternary Wavelet Transform (QWT), and dual encryption using substitution and transposition ciphers. Our method effectively embeds secret messages into images while maintaining high visual quality and robustness against various attacks. Experimental results demonstrate that our proposed technique outperforms traditional methods in terms of PSNR, MSE, and SSIM metrics. Additionally, the robustness evaluation indicates that our method maintains high BCR values under different types of attacks, further validating its effectiveness. For future work, we plan to explore the integration of advanced cryptographic techniques with our steganography method to enhance security further. Additionally, we aim to investigate the application of deep learning techniques to optimize the embedding and extraction processes, potentially improving the efficiency and resilience of the system. By leveraging the strengths of cryptography, steganography, and deep learning, we hope to develop a more secure and robust data-hiding solution.

References

1. Raja Rajeswari, N., Meenadshi, M.: AI-enhanced LSB steganography interface: concealed data embedding framework. In: 2023 9th International Conference on Smart Structures and Systems (ICSSS), Chennai, India, pp. 1–4 (2023). https://doi.org/10.1109/ICSSS58085.2023.10407062
2. Rafrastara, F.A., Prahasiwi, R., Rachmawanto, E.H., Sari, C.A.: Image steganography using inverted LSB based on 2nd, 3rd and 4th LSB pattern. In: 2019 International Conference on Information and Communications Technology (ICOIACT), Yogyakarta, Indonesia, pp. 179–184 (2019). https://doi.org/10.1109/ICOIACT46704.2019.8938503
3. Molato, A.D., Calanda, F.B., Sison, A.M., Medina, R.P.: LSB-based random embedding image steganography technique using modified collatz conjecture. In: 2022 7th International Conference on Signal and Image Processing (ICSIP), Suzhou, China, pp. 367–371 (2022). https://doi.org/10.1109/ICSIP55141.2022.9886754

4. Ramapriya, B., Kalpana, Y.: A framework for medical image steganography with modified LSB and hamming code. In: 2024 Fourth International Conference on Advances in Electrical, Computing, Communication and Sustainable Technologies (ICAECT), Bhilai, India, pp. 1–7 (2024). https://doi.org/10.1109/ICAECT60202.2024.10468898
5. Mohan, P., Menon, P.B., Rahul, P.K., Sidharth, K.S.: Image steganography-a new approach using block truncation coding and LSB embedding. In: 2022 6th International Conference on Trends in Electronics and Informatics (ICOEI), Tirunelveli, India, pp. 1527–1530 (2022). https://doi.org/10.1109/ICOEI53556.2022.9776874
6. Dharani, B.A., Yashaswini, B., Shyashyankha Reddy, G.R., Rajagopal, S.M.: Multimodal steganography: a comparative analysis of LSB and DCT methods for image and audio data concealment. In: 2024 IEEE 9th International Conference for Convergence in Technology (I2CT), Pune, India, pp. 1–5 (2024). https://doi.org/10.1109/I2CT61223.2024.10543932
7. Baziyad, M., Obaidat, M.S.: On the importance of the DCT phase for image steganography schemes. In: 2020 IEEE 5th International Conference on Computing Communication and Automation (ICCCA), Greater Noida, India, pp. 791–795 (2020). https://doi.org/10.1109/ICCCA49541.2020.9250849
8. Vakani, H., Abdallah, S., Kamel, I., Rabie, T., Baziyad, M.: DCT-in-DCT: a novel steganography scheme for enhanced payload extraction quality. In: 2021 IEEE International Conference on Industry 4.0, Artificial Intelligence, and Communications Technology (IAICT), Bandung, Indonesia, pp. 201–206 (2021). https://doi.org/10.1109/IAICT52856.2021.9532553
9. Shehada, D., Bouridane, A.: A comparative analysis of image steganography techniques in spatial and transform domains. In: 2023 IEEE International Conference on Dependable, Autonomic and Secure Computing, International Conference on Pervasive Intelligence and Computing, International Conference on Cloud and Big Data Computing, International Conference on Cyber Science and Technology Congress (DASC/PiCom/CBDCom/CyberSciTech), Abu Dhabi, United Arab Emirates, pp. 0155–0160 (2023). https://doi.org/10.1109/DASC/PiCom/CBDCom/Cy59711.2023.10361384
10. Chiu, S.-H., Lin, C.-Y.: Robust coverless image steganography based on SIFT and DWT sequence mapping. In: 2024 4th Asia Conference on Information Engineering (ACIE), Singapore, Singapore, pp. 41–45 (2024). https://doi.org/10.1109/ACIE61839.2024.00014
11. Gurumurthy, S.B., Danti, A.: Image steganography using discrete wavelet transform and convolutional NeuralNetwork. In: 2022 International Interdisciplinary Humanitarian Conference for Sustainability (IIHC), Bengaluru, India, pp. 862–868 (2022). https://doi.org/10.1109/IIHC55949.2022.10060110
12. Liu, J., Song, X., Li, G., Han, K.: Robust JPEG image steganography using wavelet domain SVD and adaptive QIM. In: 2023 8th International Conference on Signal and Image Processing (ICSIP), Wuxi, China, pp. 434–438 (2023). https://doi.org/10.1109/ICSIP57908.2023.10270839
13. vyas, A.O., Dudul, S.V.: Hybrid DWT- DCT image steganography for encrypted secret image. In: 2019 International Conference on Recent Advances in Energy-Efficient Computing and Communication (ICRAECC), Nagercoil, India, pp. 1–7 (2019). https://doi.org/10.1109/ICRAECC43874.2019.8995111
14. Nururrahmah, A.T., Ahmad, T.: Analysis of image steganography using wavelet and cosine transforms. In: 2021 13th International Conference on Information and

Communication Technology and System (ICTS), Surabaya, Indonesia, pp. 40–45 (2021). https://doi.org/10.1109/ICTS52701.2021.9609062
15. Sheidaee, A., Farzinvash, L.: A novel image steganography method based on DCT and LSB. In: 2017 9th International Conference on Information and Knowledge Technology (IKT), Tehran, Iran, pp. 116–123 (2017). https://doi.org/10.1109/IKT.2017.8258628
16. Yadahalli, S.S., Rege, S., Sonkusare, R.: Implementation and analysis of image steganography using least significant bit and discrete wavelet transform techniques. In: 2020 5th International Conference on Communication and Electronics Systems (ICCES), Coimbatore, India, pp. 1325–1330 (2020). https://doi.org/10.1109/ICCES48766.2020.9137887
17. Ardiansyah, G., Sari, C.A., Setiadi, D.R.I.M., Rachmawanto, E.H.: Hybrid method using 3-DES, DWT and LSB for secure image steganography algorithm. In: 2017 2nd International conferences on Information Technology, Information Systems and Electrical Engineering (ICITISEE), Yogyakarta, Indonesia, pp. 249–254 (2017). https://doi.org/10.1109/ICITISEE.2017.8285505
18. Cheng, X., Liu, X., Dong, X., Zhao, M., Yin, C.: Image segmentation based on improved SLIC and spectral clustering. In: 2020 Chinese Automation Congress (CAC), Shanghai, China, pp. 3058–3062 (2020). https://doi.org/10.1109/CAC51589.2020.9326495
19. Chen, Z., Zhong, Z., Pan, X., Xi, X.: A novel improved SLIC superpixel segmentation algorithm. In: 2022 IEEE 4th International Conference on Civil Aviation Safety and Information Technology (ICCASIT), Dali, China, pp. 1202–1206 (2022). https://doi.org/10.1109/ICCASIT55263.2022.9987217
20. Yang, T., Li, B., Zhang, Y., Fan, D., Wei, A.: Bright-dark channel defogging algorithm based on SLIC super-pixel segmentation. In: 2023 IEEE 3rd International Conference on Information Technology, Big Data and Artificial Intelligence (ICIBA), Chongqing, China, pp. 1165–1169 (2023). https://doi.org/10.1109/ICIBA56860.2023.10165279
21. Cheng, W., Qiao, Y.: Quaternion graph wavelet transform for color texture classification. In: 2022 7th International Conference on Signal and Image Processing (ICSIP), Suzhou, China, pp. 521–526 (2022). https://doi.org/10.1109/ICSIP55141.2022.9886681
22. Wang, J., Li, T., Luo, X., Shi, Y.-Q., Jha, S.K.: Identifying computer generated images based on quaternion central moments in color quaternion wavelet domain. IEEE Trans. Circuits Syst. Video Technol. **29**(9), 2775–2785 (2019). https://doi.org/10.1109/TCSVT.2018.2867786

A Secure and Decentralized EHR System Using Blockchain and IPFS

Narendra Kumar Ch[ID], Dinesh Kumar[✉][ID], and Amit Prakash[ID]

National Institute of Technology Jamshedpur, Jamshedpur 831014, Jharkhand, India
{2021rsec006,dineshkumar.cse,amitprakash.ece}@nitjsr.ac.in

Abstract. The healthcare sector produces enormous data, including the patient's medical history, treatment, test reports, etc. The same is being shared within the healthcare system among the stakeholders. This data must be kept accurate and secure. Also, it should be kept accessible only to the authorized individuals. The traditional management of healthcare records, being a centralized system, is prone to risks of security concerns. This study addresses the issue of secure storage of healthcare data. It proposes a blockchain based Electronic Health Record (EHR) system for storage and data sharing among the participants while achieving security. In the proposed system, an InterPlanetary File System (IPFS) is used to store the data in a decentralized way while ensuring security. The system considers patients, doctors, and insurers as stakeholders in handling and sharing data.

Keywords: Blockchain · EHR · IPFS · Ethereum

1 Introduction

Today, enormous amounts of data from various industries are being produced around the globe. One such industry that produces data throughout the year is the healthcare industry. Hospitals constitute patients, doctors, and labs that conduct medical tests. Additionally, insurance companies provide policies to individuals based on their requirements. All the above stakeholders generate information related to the patient's health. This healthcare data is enormous in amount and is of great importance to hospitals, doctors, patients and other associated stakeholders in the healthcare system.

In conventional healthcare systems, patient data is shared manually with other parties, such as hospitals or research institutes. This may be inconvenient, particularly if patients relocate without prior intimation. Generally, private hospitals and organizations can share the data among their branches. However, data transfer across institutions is difficult and time-consuming. Concerns over privacy and security breaches are also becoming more prevalent.

Security or privacy breaches in the healthcare sector severely impact patients' treatment and general health conditions. A large number of healthcare data breaches have taken place over the years [1]. The OCR breach portal showed 133 million individuals had their protected health information exposed or stolen in 2023 [2]. A comprehensive evaluation of the literature on cyber risk in the healthcare industry, as reported in [3], finds few research contributions to address cyber risk management issues in the healthcare sector. Different cyber-attack types that affect the healthcare system were listed and explained [4]. The security and privacy issues were reviewed [5]. Ensuring data quality, security, and accessibility while securely maintaining electronic health records (EHR) presents substantial issues for the healthcare business. Conventional centralised systems are susceptible to fraud and privacy violations due to data breaches, tampering, and unauthorised access. The creation of a reliable electronic health record system utilising blockchain technology is recommended by researchers using blockchain technology [6], to address these problems. Blockchain's decentralized architecture has the potential to improve current centralized healthcare systems.

Because of its immutable and decentralized nature, blockchain technology enhances security. Blockchain distributes the data among a network of nodes, in contrast to the traditional systems that manage and control data through a central authority. Because of this decentralization, it is very difficult for a single entity to change or manipulate data without the network's approval. The blockchain creates an impenetrable chain of records by cryptographically connecting every block to another.

Additionally, by utilising cryptographic techniques, blockchain improves security. A distinct digital signature is used to authenticate and document every transaction, guaranteeing that only authorized individuals can approve it. High degrees of data integrity are ensured; once a transaction is confirmed, it cannot be changed. Smart contracts, self-executing contracts with predetermined rules, increase security by autonomously enforcing agreements' terms without the need for middlemen. This reduces the risk of fraud or human error.

The first utilization of blockchain was done in 2008 by Satoshi Nakamoto when Bitcoin [7], a cryptocurrency, was introduced. Widespread usage of this blockchain technology is seen today in various applications like banking, supply-chain management, security, healthcare, etc. Peer-to-peer (p2p) technology is used by a blockchain, a decentralized network, to track every transaction. It is devoid of a single point of contact or centralised authority. Instead, a collection of nodes maintains the system's functionality. The network's nodes ensure the highest level of security for every transaction. An extra layer of security is added to the network with encryption. Every system node has a duplicate copy of the digital record. Every node needs to confirm a transaction's legitimacy before adding it into the block. A digital ledger is made up of several blocks. Every block provides a thorough summary of every transaction. Being a distributed and decentralized technology, it benefits the health sector in many ways. The native coin of Ethereum, ETH, powers the Ethereum blockchain. A peer-to-peer network is established by Ethereum, a decentralized blockchain platform, to execute and validate smart contract code safely. It enables programmers to write smart contracts and communicate with the network using Decentralized Applications (dApps).

A blockchain-based healthcare data storage solution is proposed in this study. The goal is to create a blockchain-based system that facilitates patient data storage, management, and security. This system creates a decentralized, safe and accessible healthcare ecosystem using smart contracts and Ethereum. Using blockchain technology, this system will store and manage electronic health records in a secure, unchangeable repository. Smart contracts will automate data-sharing agreements, enforce access control restrictions, and promote interoperability between healthcare providers. InterPlanetary File System (IPFS) was used to store medical records in a decentralized way. Health records will be encrypted and stored on the Ethereum blockchain, whereby only authorised stakeholders can access/alter the data. The system allows users to share medical records only with the authorised physicians, insurers, and laboratories.

The system is developed as follows. First, a personal blockchain using Ganache was constructed on the Ethereum network. The project was launched with Truffle, a frontend was developed using Web3.js to connect to the local blockchain, and smart contracts were written in solidity language. Then these contracts were compiled and deployed to the Ganache blockchain.

The structure of the remaining paper is as follows: The related study on the role of blockchain in storing medical data is discussed in Sect. 2. In Sect. 3, the model for the storage of medical records is proposed. Section 4 presents the implementation details and analysis of the results, followed by the conclusion in Sect. 5.

2 Related Study

An efficient patient data accessibility model is proposed using blockchain technology in [6]. The patient would first register, and the doctor would have access to add or append the patient's data and retrieve it. A peer (healthcare provider) registration through consortium blockchain is proposed in [8]. Doctors would use the web interface to upload the COVID-19 patient's reports, where miners validate them and create a block on the chain. In contrast, the reports are stored off-chain in the IPFS by generating a hash of the content address stored in the blockchain. A similar off-chain storage method using IPFS is proposed in [9]. A block-based access control scheme to maintain the Electronic Medical Record (EMR) is proposed in [10]. It eliminates the agent layer while the authorization, encryption and decryption are done using the Public Key Interface. The patient-centric agent proposed in [11], uses blockchain technology to maintain data confidentiality and privacy during end-to-end communication in a remote patient monitoring system.

A blockchain-based network called Medrec, proposed in [12], allows healthcare organisations to share data securely. It tackles patient participation, better data sharing, interoperability, and fragmented data availability. A registry contract, a summary contract, and a patient's provider contract are the three forms of smart contracts that Medrec employs. MedChain, a Blockchain-based electronic medical system, was proposed for interoperability, security, and quick data access while protecting patient privacy. The authors used the proxy re-encryption service for transferring encrypted health records and the smart contract for permission revocation [13]. MediChain, proposed in [14], utilized the Hyperledger to manage medical data assets, which consist of a user interface, off-chain data storage, and an access control module. The hash is stored on the Blockchain, and the data is kept on cloud servers in an encrypted format, but the system does not consider interoperability.

Authors in [15] developed a prototype to maintain the integrity of medical data using public blockchain and integrate it with a cloud-based EHR system using a blockchain handshaking method. A Blockchain-based structure proposed in [16] developed an EHR system to share and manage Electronic Medical records of cancer patients among healthcare providers and research institutions. A blockchain-based architecture is proposed [17], consisting of a decentralized storage layer, a Blockchain layer, and a User Layer. While the Blockchain layer manages ownership and metadata and offers permission management services for data sharing, the decentralized storage layer holds encrypted data. External users communicate with the blockchain network using dApps.

In [18], a blockchain model with federated learning is designed to detect the patterns of COVID-19 from the lung CT scans collected from different sources. A blockchain technology-based, HonestChain [19] is used to secure healthcare records. It also provides intensives for accessing and providing health records and uses a chatbot interface and a consortium blockchain method to ensure data requesters abide by norms and maintain reputations. For efficient access control and retrieval of encrypted personal healthcare records from the cloud server, a Blockchain-based Hierarchical Data Sharing Framework (BHDSF) [20] is presented. A private blockchain for enhanced security and AI for efficient big data analytics is used for home monitoring in the IoMT-enabled COVID-19 [21] environment that stores the data in a cloud server. A comparative analysis is done in the Table 1 to understand the different technologies in different applications.

Unlike traditional techniques, which rely on centralized databases and less secure data management, blockchain-based EHR systems offer improved security, data integrity, interoperability, patient control, transparency, and trust. Traditional systems store medical data in a database, which lacks strict rules for access control and is very vulnerable to hacking or tampering by unauthorized users, resulting in reliability issues. On the other hand, blockchain-based EHR systems store medical data on the blockchain, in which smart contracts enforce access control, and each change is securely recorded, preventing tampering as only the authorized user has access.

Storing data on blockchain is expensive. So, it is stored on IPFS in a decentralized format. IPFS has nodes like blockchain. These nodes store the data or files. Access the IPFS from the servers that provide them. The file is encrypted to hash using algorithms like SHA 256, RSA, etc. Upon uploading a file on IPFS, a unique hash, known as the content identifier (CID), is generated. These files are stored in an IPFS object. The object can store 256kb of data. The file is

Table 1. Comparitive Analysis of Different Technologies in Different Applications

Authors	Objective	Blockchain	Off-Chain	Remarks
Ramani et al., 2018 [6]	A secure healthcare system for doctors and patients to access data	Ethereum Blockchain	Medical server	The address of the medical server is stored in the blockchain
Alrubei et al., 2020 [8]	To process and share the patient data securely	Customized	No	No off-chain data
Daraghmi et al., 2019 [13]	An effective healthcare system to maintain and access data	Ethereum Blockchain (MedChain)	Medical record link	The hash value of the link is stored
Zhang et al., 2022 [19]	A data-sharing framework that shares hierarchically	EthereumBlockchain	Cloud	Cloud servers can be compromised
Bera et al., 2023 [21]	A home monitoring IoMT-enabled COVID-19 environment	PrivateBlockchain	Cloud	Cloud servers can be compromised
Purohit et al., 2021 [20]	A system to share real-time healthcare data	Hyperledger Fabric	IPFS	Encryption algorithms are not discussed
Proposed system	Decentralized medical data management using blockchain-based EHR	Ethereum Blockchain	IPFS	Encrypted data is stored in IPFS

split into multiple IPFS objects of 256kb to store a large file, and then an empty IPFS object is created that links to all the other files.

When a file is uploaded, it cannot be altered. A new hash (CID) is generated when a file is updated and re-uploaded. The updated file will be linked to the previous file. This makes sure that the files stored cannot be modified. To access the file stored on IPFS, a query is made on the IPFS node. Then, the node queries its peers for the file, and when the query reaches the node that stores the file, the hash is decrypted, and the file is accessed. This is called content addressing, which differs from the traditional locating address.

The system's front end was designed with React.js, Hypertext Markup Language (HTML), and Cascading Style Sheets (CSS). With Node.js and the Solidity programming language, the website's server and back end are managed. To construct the system, two tools are employed to generate local Ethereum blockchains: Truffle and Ganache. The blockchain is established, and the system is accessed or used through the Ethereum virtual interface, MetaMask (as a wallet), Truffle (as an IDE), npm (command-line interface), Ganache (account creation), and Local Web3 (web interface).

3 The Proposed Framework

In this paper, a decentralized electronic health record platform that is secure, easily accessible, and transparent has been created for the healthcare industry using blockchain technology. The system will prioritise data security and integrity by encrypting health records and storing them on the Ethereum blockchain, ensuring that only allowed parties may access and update the data.

An Ethereum based EHR system is developed through which the user can upload, provide access, and manage medical records to the authorized. Figure 1 demonstrates the architecture of the proposed Blockchain-based EHR application. The suggested framework consists of the subsequent steps.

1. Uploading the healthcare data by the registered users (Patients).
2. The healthcare data is stored using IPFS.

3. The data entered is encrypted using the RSA algorithm.
4. The encrypted hash is stored in the blockchain.

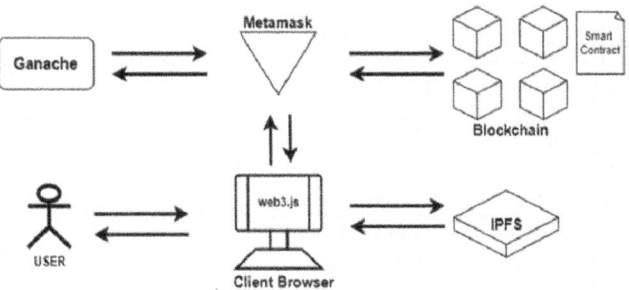

Fig. 1. The architecture of the proposed Blockchain-based application

The hash from the blockchain is decrypted and accessed to obtain the files. The system's frontend user interface gives users a graphical interface to interact with the EHR platform. Users can upload, view, and manage their medical records via the user interface. Healthcare data is stored in a distributed and decentralized manner using the IPFS. IPFS allows data to be stored over a node-based network, guaranteeing accessibility and redundancy while upholding security and integrity. Data is encrypted and decrypted using the RSA algorithm before being uploaded to the IPFS for storage. This ensures the confidentiality and security of sensitive medical data during transmission and storage.

The exchanges and transactions within the EHR system are managed by smart contracts, which are implemented on the Ethereum blockchain. These contracts enable transparent and unchangeable user authentication, access control, and data management features. The EHR system offers a robust architecture for safely handling healthcare data by integrating these elements, guaranteeing privacy, integrity, and accessibility for all parties.

Only the users who have registered with the network can view the list of transactions. A hospital or physician can only join the blockchain network after completing the user registration procedure. A user's registration and verification process is listed in Algorithm 1.

User registration and verification
After registration and verification, an authorized user can upload, download, and edit a patient's records based on the permissions granted. The same rules apply when accessing patient records from the database. An authorised registered user can only access a patient's medical data using the patient's registered address provided during the patient registration process. Only the authorized user can access the patient data, as listed in Algorithm 2.

Algorithm 1 Algorithm for adding agents

Input: `Name, Age, Designation, Hash`
Output: Agent registration with verification
1: `addr = msg.sender;`   // initializing mapping address //
2: `if designation == 0 then`
3:     //designation 0 is for patients //
4:     create a patient struct and append it to the patient list
5: `else if designation == 1 then`
6:     //designation 1 is for doctors //
7:     create doctor struct and append to doctor list
8: `else if designation == 2 then`
9:     //designation 2 is for insurers //
10:    create insurer struct and append to insurer list
11: `else if designation == 3 then`
12:    //designation 3 is for laboratories //
13:    create laboratory struct and append to laboratory list
14: `else`
15:    `revert;`
16: `end if`

Accessing the patient information from the database

Algorithm 2 : Algorithm to get patient information from the database

1: **Input:** `addr`
2: // address of the patient for whom the information is required //
3: **Output:** Returns the patient's information.
4: // checks the authorization and returns the patient's details //
5: **Check** if `msg.sender` is authorized to access the patient's data
6: `if addr == patientInfo[addr] then`
7:    // Maps address to patient struct. //
8:    Assign patient to `patientInfo[addr]`
9: `else`
10:   `return false;`
11: `end if`

Key Features of the Proposed System

- *Registration and authentication:* The individuals can create an account through the site and use the safe digital wallet MetaMask to confirm their identity. This protects sensitive medical data by ensuring only authorised users can access the system.
- *Safe Handling of Medical Records:* Patients can safely upload and control their medical records on the Ethereum Blockchain. This lowers the possibility of illegal access or data tampering because their health information

is kept in a decentralized, tamper-proof manner. Patients are in complete control of who can access their records, and they can give authorization to physicians, labs, and insurance companies as needed.

- **Patient-Doctor Communication:** Patients' Medical records are accessible to doctors with the proper authorization. This enables them to engage with patients safely via the platform, add new records, and review previous diagnoses-improved patient-physician collaboration results in improved healthcare outcomes.
- **Processing Insurance:** Patients can safely share their medical records for claims and coverage with insurers. Using blockchain technology, insurers can confirm the legitimacy of medical records, expediting the claims procedure and lowering the risk of fraud. By doing this, patients can be guaranteed prompt and accurate insurance coverage for their medical costs.
- **Laboratory Integration:** To upload the test results and reports onto the blockchain, laboratories are granted access to patient's medical records. This guarantees the accuracy and transparency of medical data.

4 Results and Discussion

Results: Two user-friendly frameworks, Truffle and Ganache, were used for building local Ethereum blockchains are used for constructing this system. The Solidity programming language and Node.js have been used to control the system's server and back end.

The Ethereum virtual interface, MetaMask (as a wallet), Truffle (as an IDE), NPM (command-line interface), Ganache (account creation), and Local Web3 (web interface) are used to construct a blockchain and access the system.

Log-in/Register Page: If the user is already registered, click the "Login" button, as shown in Fig. 2, and this will connect to the user's MetaMask account, allowing the user to obtain their data.

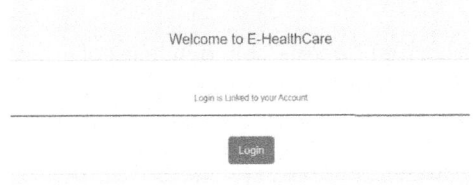

Fig. 2. Log-in page

Registering as a new user is simple and quick, as shown in Fig. 3. Users must enter their information and select if they want to be patients, physicians, insurers, or laboratory managers.

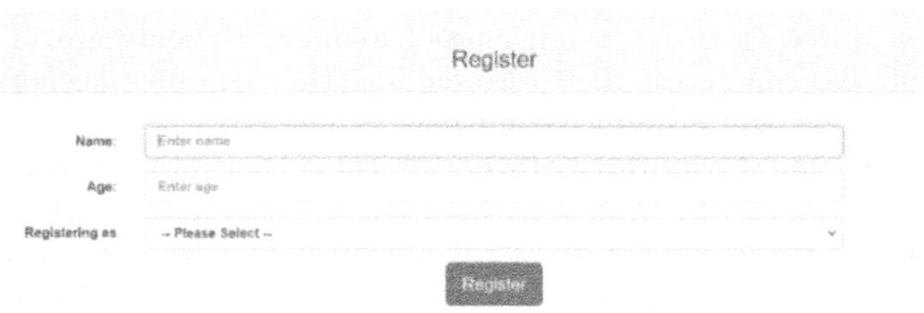

Fig. 3. Registration page

Patient Page. The user registered as a patient can easily access their medical reports, as shown in Fig. 4a. The user can authorize certain healthcare providers and insurance companies for claims or labs for tests listed in the user's file, as shown in Fig. 4b.

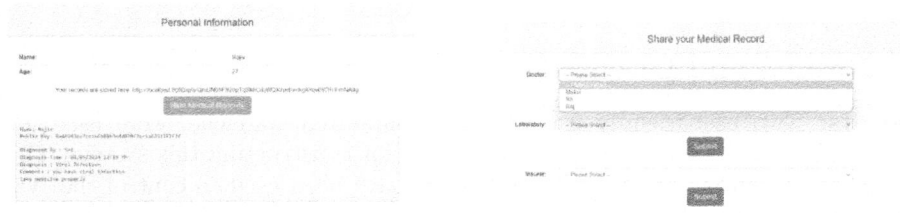

(a) Patient information and medical records

(b) Patient's page for sharing medical data

Fig. 4. Side-by-side figures of patient information and sharing medical data.

The user also has the option to remove access from anyone who was previously authorised to view the user's medical records, as shown in Fig. 5. This degree of control guarantees the protection of the user's privacy and makes it easier for the user to work seamlessly with their healthcare team when needed.

Doctor's Page: Authorized doctors can view patients' medical records, giving them permission on the doctor's page, as shown in Fig. 6. After reviewing these documents, medical professionals treat the patient as needed and update the patient's medical history with the results of those visits. To protect patient privacy and control, authorization to view the records is immediately withdrawn after treatment. If a patient wants to continue receiving care from the physician, they must reauthorize access.

Insurer's Page: Patients can give insurers access to their medical records through the insurer's page, allowing insurers to confirm claim costs. The medical tests specified in the records are accessible to laboratories in the interim.

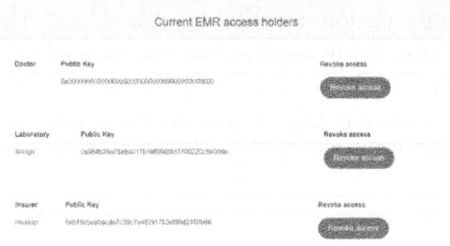

Fig. 5. User permission for medical report

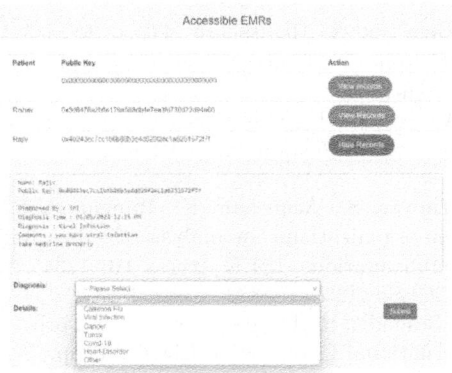

Fig. 6. Doctor's dashboard

To ensure complete and current medical information, laboratories upload test results to the patient's file after performing tests.

Discussion: Blockchain technology in healthcare systems enhances data security, privacy, and transparency. It uses decentralization and encryption to protect patient data, while its immutable ledger promotes accountability and reduces fraud. Once the patient data is entered, it cannot be changed or removed. It can only be appended. However, a modified patient data report can again be stored in IPFS with a new transaction, and the hash generated is stored in a new block. This improves interoperability, allowing seamless medical information sharing and editing across authorized providers. Patients gain control over their health records, ensuring transparency. Blockchain can lower costs by automating administrative processes and ensuring data integrity. Overall, blockchain creates a secure, efficient, and patient-centered healthcare ecosystem.

5 Conclusion

Compared to conventional approaches, the blockchain-based Electronic Health Record (EHR) system provides a more secure and decentralized way to manage medical data. Information is reliably stored and unchangeable because of blockchain technology. Additionally, this technology facilitates data sharing across various healthcare systems and gives patients authority over who can view their records. The security, dependability, and patient control are improved in the EHR system, indicating improved prospects for healthcare data management.

References

1. Murray-Watson, D.R.: Healthcare data breach statistics. HIPAA J. (2024). Accessed 24 June 2024. https://www.hipaajournal.com/healthcare-data-breach-statistics/
2. Alder, S.: December 2023 Healthcare Data Breach Report. HIPAA J. (2024). Accessed 24 June 2024. https://www.hipaajournal.com/december-2023-healthcare-data-breach-report/
3. Sardi, A., Rizzi, A., Sorano, E., Guerrieri, A.: Cyber risk in health facilities: a systematic literature review. Sustainability **12**(17), 17 (2020). https://doi.org/10.3390/su12177002
4. Kandasamy, K., Srinivas, S., Achuthan, K., Rangan, V.P.: Digital healthcare - cyberattacks in asian organizations: an analysis of vulnerabilities, risks, NIST perspectives, and recommendations. IEEE Access **10**, 12345–12364 (2022). https://doi.org/10.1109/ACCESS.2022.3145372
5. Kupwade Patil, H., Seshadri, R.: Big data security and privacy issues in healthcare. In: 2014 IEEE International Congress on Big Data, pp. 762–765 (2014). https://doi.org/10.1109/BigData.Congress.2014.112
6. Ramani, V., Kumar, T., Bracken, A., Liyanage, M., Ylianttila, M.: Secure and efficient data accessibility in blockchain based healthcare systems. In: 2018 IEEE Global Communications Conference (GLOBECOM), pp. 206–212 (2018). https://doi.org/10.1109/GLOCOM.2018.8647221
7. Nakamoto, S.: Bitcoin: a peer-to-peer electronic cash system. Cryptography Mailing list (2009). https://metzdowd.com
8. Alrubei, S., Ball, E., Rigelsford, J.: A secure distributed blockchain platform for use in AI-enabled IoT applications. In: Presented at the 2020 IEEE Cloud Summit, pp. 85–90. IEEE Computer Society (2020). https://doi.org/10.1109/IEEECloudSummit48914.2020.00019
9. Kumar, R., Marchang, N., Tripathi, R.: Distributed off-chain storage of patient diagnostic reports in healthcare system using IPFS and blockchain. In: 2020 International Conference on COMmunication Systems & NETworkS (COMSNETS), pp. 1–5 (2020). https://doi.org/10.1109/COMSNETS48256.2020.9027313
10. Zhang, X., Poslad, S., Ma, Z.: Block-based access control for blockchain-based electronic medical records (EMRs) query in eHealth. In: 2018 IEEE Global Communications Conference (GLOBECOM), pp. 1–7 (2018). https://doi.org/10.1109/GLOCOM.2018.8647433
11. Uddin, M.A., Stranieri, A., Gondal, I., Balasubramanian, V.: Continuous patient monitoring with a patient centric agent: a block architecture. IEEE Access **6**, 32700–32726 (2018). https://doi.org/10.1109/ACCESS.2018.2846779
12. Azaria, A., Ekblaw, A., Vieira, T., Lippman, A.: MedRec: using blockchain for medical data access and permission management. In: 2016 2nd International Conference on Open and Big Data (OBD), pp. 25–30 (2016). https://doi.org/10.1109/OBD.2016.11

13. Daraghmi, E.-Y., Daraghmi, Y.-A., Yuan, S.-M.: MedChain: a design of blockchain-based system for medical records access and permissions management. IEEE Access **7**, 164595–164613 (2019). https://doi.org/10.1109/ACCESS.2019.2952942
14. Rouhani, S., Butterworth, L., Simmons, A.D., Humphery, D.G., Deters, R.: MediChain^{TM}: a secure decentralized medical data asset management system. In: 2018 IEEE International Conference on Internet of Things (iThings) and IEEE Green Computing and Communications (GreenCom) and IEEE Cyber, Physical and Social Computing (CPSCom) and IEEE Smart Data (SmartData), pp. 1533–1538 (2018). https://doi.org/10.1109/Cybermatics_2018.2018.00258
15. Rahman, M.S., Khalil, I., Mahawaga Arachchige, P.C., Bouras, A., Yi, X.: A novel architecture for tamper proof electronic health record management system using blockchain wrapper. In: Proceedings of the 2019 ACM International Symposium on Blockchain and Secure Critical Infrastructure, BSCI '19, pp. 97–105. Association for Computing Machinery, New York (2019). https://doi.org/10.1145/3327960.3332392
16. Dubovitskaya, A., Xu, Z., Ryu, S., Schumacher, M., Wang, F.: Secure and trustable electronic medical records sharing using blockchain. In: AMIA Annual Symposium Proceedings 2017, pp. 650–659 (2018)
17. Shuaib, K., Abdella, J., Sallabi, F., Serhani, M.A.: Secure decentralized electronic health records sharing system based on blockchains. J. King Saud Univ. Comput. Inf. Sci. **34**(8), 5045–5058 (2022). https://doi.org/10.1016/j.jksuci.2021.05.002
18. Kumar, R., et al.: Blockchain-federated-learning and deep learning models for COVID-19 detection using CT imaging. IEEE Sens. J. **21**(14), 16301–16314 (2021). https://doi.org/10.1109/JSEN.2021.3076767
19. Purohit, S., Calyam, P., Alarcon, M.L., Bhamidipati, N.R., Mosa, A., Salah, K.: HonestChain: consortium blockchain for protected data sharing in health information systems. Peer-to-Peer Network. Appl. **14**(5), 3012–3028 (2021). https://doi.org/10.1007/s12083-021-01153-y
20. Zhang, J., Yang, Y., Liu, X., Ma, J.: An efficient blockchain-based hierarchical data sharing for healthcare internet of things. IEEE Trans. Ind. Inf. **18**(10), 7139–7150 (2022). https://doi.org/10.1109/TII.2022.3145851
21. Bera, B., Mitra, A., Das, A.K., Puthal, D., Park, Y.: Private blockchain-based AI-envisioned home monitoring framework in IoMT-enabled COVID-19 environment. IEEE Consum. Electron. Maga. **12**(3), 62–71 (2023). https://doi.org/10.1109/MCE.2021.3137104

SQL Injection Detection Using Recurrent Neural Networks (RNN)

V. Valli Kumari[1(✉)] and Y. Prasanna Kumar[2]

[1] Department of Computer Science and Systems Engineering,
Andhra University College of Engineering, Visakhapatnam, India
[2] Department of Information Technology and Computer Applications,
Andhra University College of Engineering, Visakhapatnam, India

Abstract. Web applications are still at risk from SQL injection (SQLi), which calls for strong detection systems that can recognize nefarious SQL queries. This study investigates the use of two recurrent neural network (RNN) variants-Long Short-Term Memory (LSTM) and Gated Recurrent Unit (GRU) models-for SQL injection attack detection. In contrast to conventional techniques, LSTM and GRU models are good at identifying long-term patterns and sequential dependencies, which makes them good options for improving SQL injection detection's efficacy and accuracy. A comprehensive dataset with a variety of legal queries and SQL injection attack cases is used to assess the performance of the LSTM and GRU designs. The results show high levels of sensitivity, specificity, and accuracy, successfully reducing false positives while correctly recognizing possible threats.

Keywords: Granted recurrent unit (GRU) · Long short-term model (LSTM) · SQL injection

1 Introduction

Web applications are always vulnerable to security breaches, and one of the most common and dangerous vulnerabilities is SQL injection (SQLi). This research investigates the use of deep learning methods, particularly Long Short-Term Memory (LSTM) and Gated Recurrent Unit (GRU) models, for the automated detection of SQL injection attacks.

2 Literature Survey

S. S. Hasan and R. U. Shahnaz (2020). The review looks at many ways to find and stop SQL injection, with a particular emphasis on static and dynamic code analysis approaches. It evaluates how well these methods work to find weaknesses and stop exploitation while pointing out the trade-offs between various strategies [1]. B. K. Singh and A. Sharma (2020). A comprehensive summary of supervised and unsupervised learning techniques for SQL injection detection is given in this review of machine learning models [2]. Gupta and Sharma, N. C. (2020). The research mostly focuses on GRU models and how to use them to identify SQL injection threats. It talks about how GRUs are better than other models, especially when it comes to handling sequence data and computational efficiency [3]. V. J. Patel and S. D. Kumar (2020). The use of feature engineering in neural network applications for SQL injection detection is the main topic of this paper. It talks about how various attributes can be taken out and used to train neural network models more efficiently in order to detect fraudulent SQL queries [4]. J. K. Roberts and R. L. Moore (2020). In order to identify SQL injection in real time, the study investigates methods for implementing deep learning models. It talks about the difficulties of processing data in real time and how deep learning models might be modified to offer real-time danger detection [5]. Hybrid detection techniques, which integrate many approaches to identify SQL injection threats, are investigated by T. Sharma and K. Patel (2020). In order to improve detection accuracy, the study examines strategies that combine machine learning with conventional heuristic and rule-based techniques [6]. A thorough evaluation of SQL injection prevention methods, including runtime monitoring and static code analysis, is given by S. Kim and J. Park (2020) [7]. K. Moore and C (2020). Thompson discuss the particular difficulties associated with detecting SQL injection in cloud computing settings. In addition to discussing solutions designed specifically for these contexts, the paper addresses specific problems associated with cloud-based architectures, such as multi-tenancy and dynamic resource allocation [8]. N. Patel and A. Sharma (2020). Investigate the particular difficulties and remedies for preventing and detecting SQL injection in mobile applications. The survey examines methods such as secure coding practices, runtime protection mechanisms, and mobile-specific detection algorithms that are specifically designed to meet the specific limitations and dangers that are connected with mobile platforms [9]. An overview of integrating SQL injection detection strategies with more comprehensive intrusion detection systems (IDS) is given by L. Carter and M. Johnson (2020). The article explains how augmenting IDS with SQL injection detection can improve overall security by offering a more complete picture of possible threats [10]. H. Davis and J. Smith (2020). Investigate methods of behavioural analysis for detecting SQL injection. The survey examines techniques that examine user and application behaviour to spot questionable SQL injection-related activity [11]. M. M. A. El-Attar and O. S. Alasmary (2021). SQL injection attacks and the countermeasures used to prevent them are both covered in this paper. It examines several protective tactics, such as prepared statements, anomaly detection systems, and code sanitization [12]. R. K. Gupta and N. S. Aslam (2021). This survey explores SQL injection detection using machine learning techniques. It examines several methods and assesses how well they detect fraudulent SQL queries, including decision trees, support vector machines, and neural networks [13]. S. K. Park and J. Lee (2021). The use of Long Short-Term Memory (LSTM) networks for SQL injection detection is examined in this article. It examines how well LSTMs handle sequential data and how well they can recognize patterns in SQL queries to find possible injection points [14]. E. D. Miller and L. T. Johnson (2021). The efficacy of LSTM and GRU models in detecting SQL injection is compared in this study. It discusses whether model is more appropriate for detecting and forecasting SQL injection patterns and offers an analysis of their performance indicators [15]. K. R. Davis and J. M. Lee (2021). The usage of ensemble approaches, which incorporate several machine learning models to enhance SQL injection detection, is covered in the survey. It illustrates how these techniques might improve detection performance by utilizing the advantages of different individual models [16]. A. T. Sharma and P. S. Patel (2021). Case examples on the realworld implementation of machine learning models for SQL injection detection are presented in this study. It talks about the difficulties encountered and the solutions used to incorporate these models into the security systems that are currently in place [17]. L. R. Zhang and C. M. Davis (2021). This paper examines several case studies of machine learning techniques applied to web application SQL injection detection. It demonstrates how well various models and approaches detect injections in a range of application scenarios [18]. R. C. Harris and A. P. Thompson (2021). From a machine learning standpoint, the article offers insights into new trends and potential directions in SQL injection detection. It talks about cutting-edge methods and tools that could influence SQL injection defense and detection in the future [19]. The focus of M. Johnson and T. Lee (2021). is on behaviourally based detection techniques that look at application behaviour to find SQL injection vulnerabilities. The survey examines different methods for keeping an eye on user behaviour and query trends in order to spot irregularities that could be signs of SQL injection attempts [20]. The use of natural language processing (NLP) approaches for SQL injection detection is examined by P. Williams and L. Davis (2021). In the study, it is discussed how to utilize natural language processing (NLP) to analyze and comprehend the structure of SQL queries and identify potentially harmful trends using syntactic and semantic analysis [21]. A comparison of machine learning and conventional methods for SQL injection detection is presented by H. Zhang and F. Liu (2021). The survey assesses the effectiveness of a range of detection techniques, such as machine learning, pattern-matching, and heuristic-based methods [22]. The application of data mining techniques to SQL injection detection is examined by J. Clark and E. Harris (2021). The effectiveness of several data mining techniques, including association rule mining, clustering, and classification, in spotting trends and abnormalities linked to SQL injection assaults is reviewed in this research [23]. A. K. Gupta and R. Patel (2021). Investigate the use of anomaly detection methods to spot SQL injection threats. The survey examines several machine learning and statistical techniques for anomaly identification, which find variations from typical query patterns [24]. Ensemble learning techniques for SQL injection detection are the focus of N. Rao and P. Singh (2021). The survey looks at how detection performance might be increased by integrating many machine learning models into an ensemble [25]. S. Kumar and R. Sharma (2021). Talk about hybrid approaches for SQL injection detection that include machine learning and static code analysis methods. The study examines how merging these techniques might capitalize on the advantages of each, including enhancing detection precision and decreasing false positives, and offers instances of effective applications. The difficulties of identifying SQL injection attacks in distributed systems are examined in [26]. A thorough analysis of dynamic approaches for SQL injection detection is given by T. Lee and K. Kumar (2021). The study covers techniques for in-the-moment SQL query analysis, such as dynamic query profiling, runtime monitoring, and dynamic taint analysis [27]. SQL injection detection in Internet of Things (IoT) context is the focus of N. Wilson and S. Patel's work (2021). The paper examines particular issues and methods for protecting IoT systems and devices from SQL injection attacks [28]. T. J. A. Rose and R. J. C. Paul (2022). This review offers an in-depth examination of several techniques for identifying SQL injection threats. It covers pattern-matching methods that look for known attack signatures in SQL statements as well as heuristicbased methods that analyze dangerous queries using established patterns [29]. V. A. Nair and P. S. Kumar (2022). A thorough analysis of machine learning methods specifically used in SQL injection detection is presented in this research. It covers a range of models and assesses how well they differentiate between benign and malicious queries, including ensemble approaches and neural networks [30]. R. R. Mehta and K. S. Patel (2022). The application of deep learning models for SQL injection detection, such as recurrent neural networks (RNNs) and convolutional neural networks (CNNs), is the main topic of this survey. It talks about how deep learning approaches can help identify intricate patterns and sequences in SQL queries that conventional approaches would overlook [31]. M. L. Singh and A. B. Rao (2022). In order to detect SQL injection, this research contrasts the Gated Recurrent Unit (GRU) and LSTM models. It evaluates the effectiveness of both models, stressing the benefits and drawbacks of each in terms of capturing sequential dependencies in SQL queries [32]. A. K. Singh and R. C. Patel (2022). In order to improve SQL injection detection, this work investigates hybrid models that include machine learning techniques with alternative approaches. It examines a range of hybrid strategies, such as those that combine machine learning with statistical analysis for improved detection precision [33]. M. F. Chen and T. E (2022). White The difficulties of using machine learning approaches for SQL injection detection are covered in this study. These obstacles include problems with data quality, interpretability of models, and flexibility in response to changing attack patterns [34]. R. Smith and D. Brown (2022). Investigate SQL injection detection using network traffic analysis. The paper examines approaches such as flow analysis and packet inspection that examine network traffic patterns in order to detect fraudulent SQL queries [35]. A. Patel and M. Brown (2022). Data consistency, distributed query processing, and inter-node communication are among the topics covered in this work [36]. The detection strategies for SQL injection attacks that particularly target web services are examined by P. Brown and L. White (2022). The survey examines a number of approaches, such as web service monitoring, request validation techniques, and examination of service-oriented architecture (SOA) [37]. Wilson, T. N. and

Smith, J. M (2023). An overview of the use of deep learning techniques for SQL injection detection is given in the study. It examines several deep learning architectures and their uses, pointing out that these models can provide enhanced precision and resilience when identifying complex injection assaults [38]. Deep reinforcement learning (DRL) is applied to SQL injection detection by A. Gupta and N. Patel (2023). The study explores how DRL might interact with an environment to learn and enhance detection tactics in an adaptive manner, enabling the model to perform better over time [39].

3 Methodology

This project's goal is to create and assess machine learning models for identifying SQL injection attacks in online applications, with a focus on Long Short-Term Memory (LSTM) and Gated Recurrent Unit (GRU) networks. The aim is to improve detection capabilities by utilizing sophisticated sequence modeling approaches, with SQL injection being a key security risk. To train and test these models, the project will gather, preprocess, and analyze SQL query datasets. Afterward, the performance of the models will be compared to ascertain the best strategy. The first and most important stage is data gathering, which entails obtaining datasets that contain both malicious and benign SQL queries. We will search publicly accessible datasets for pertinent information, such as those found on Kaggle other cybersecurity archives. To create a balanced dataset with a variety of injection patterns, synthetic SQL queries will also be generated. Following collection, each query will be classified as benign or malicious after the data has been cleansed to eliminate any duplicates or unnecessary entries. Queries will be dissected into their component parts using tokenization techniques, and consistency will be ensured by normalization procedures like converting text to lowercase and eliminating unnecessary whitespace.

3.1 Dataset

Dataset that includes queries that are classified as malicious or benign, denoted by the labels 0 and 1, respectively, in a CSV file. 33000 queries make up the file, which is utilized for testing and training the models we employed to obtain precise answers.

3.2 Data Preprocessing

Making sure the input data is clean and appropriate for training the machine learning model depends on the data preparation stage. Using thepandas package, the datasetwhich consists of SQL queries classified as benign or maliciousis first loaded from a CSV file. Finding any missing numbers and comprehending the label distribution are made easier with the first investigation of the data. To preserve the dataset's integrity, data cleaning is done by eliminating rows that have missing values in the "Sentence" or "Label" columns. Following their extraction, the SQL queries are transformed into a list of text features. These text inquiries are converted into numerical sequences via tokenization, in which each distinct word is mapped to an integer. Thekeras Tokenizer class makes this step easier. The sequences are then padded in order to provide a consistent input size, which is essential for reliable model training. By standardizing the length of the input sequences, this padding phase enables the model to handle SQL queries of different durations with efficacy.

3.3 Feature Engineering

The goal of feature engineering is to convert SQL queries into numerical representations so that machine learning models can process them. Tokenized searches will be transformed into dense vector representations of the tokens called embeddings. These embeddings might be specially trained for the particular domain of SQL queries, or they could employ pre-trained models like Word2Vec or GloVe. Padding will be used to handle variable-length sequences in order to guarantee that all input data adheres to a set length and promote consistent model input.

3.4 Model Building

In order to create a model, a neural network tailored for sequence categorization must be built and refined. The suggested architecture for this project is a sequential model with a Gated Recurrent Unit (GRU) layer. Sequential dependencies in text data can be captured by GRUs, which is useful for deciphering SQL queries and identifying possible injections. To enable the network to learn word representations, the model starts with an Embedding layer that transforms integer sequences into dense, dense vectors of a fixed size. These embedded sequences are processed by the GRU layer, which comes next, in order to identify patterns suggestive of SQL injection attacks. In the GRU layer, dropout is used to prevent overfitting. The last layer is a dense layer that produces probability for binary classification (malicious vs. benign) using a sigmoid activation function. The binary cross-entropy loss function and Adam optimizer, which are appropriate for the current binary classification problem, are used to create the model. Feeding the preprocessed training data to the model and verifying it against an independent test set are necessary steps in the training process to monitor performance and make sure the model performs well when applied to new data (Fig. 1).

LSTM and GRU model creation and implementation form the basis of the technique. Tokenized sequences will go into the input layer of the LSTM model, which will also have an embedding layer for vector representation, LSTM layers for capturing sequential dependencies, and an output layer for classification that comes after a dense layer. The GRU model will have a similar architecture, but GRU layers will be utilized in place of LSTM layers. To maximize model performance, hyperparameter tuning strategies will direct the selection of hyperparameters, including dropout rates, learning rates, and the number of units in the LSTM or GRU layers. Refining the models requires both validation

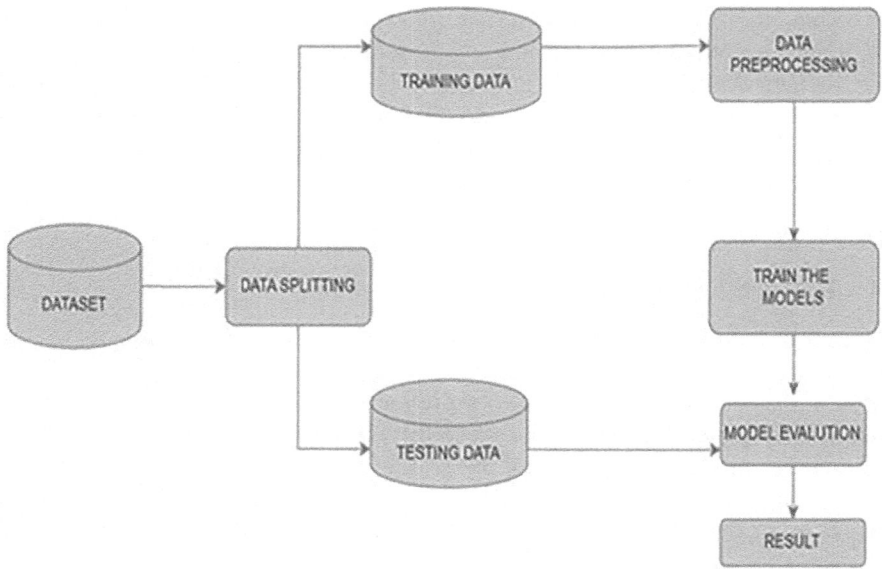

Fig. 1. Model building

and training. Typically, 80 dataset will be used for training, 10 will be divided into training, validation, and test sets. The models will be trained with suitable optimizers (like Adam) and loss functions (such binary cross-entropy). To prevent overfitting, hyperparameters will be changed during training based on validation set performance. The integration of the trained models into a simulation or real-world application will be the main goal of the implementation phase. This involves modifying the models to identify SQL injection in real-time when browsing active websites. The integration procedure will provide interoperability with current security frameworks and systems. The outcomes of model evaluations will be presented in the results and discussion section, with an emphasis on the advantages and disadvantages of the GRU and LSTM models. A thorough examination of errors will be done in order to identify frequent misclassifications and possible reasons for them. Future research will examine ways to improve model performance, such adding more layers or sophisticated embeddings. Model robustness can be further increased by adding more diverse samples to the dataset or by creating more synthetic queries. Furthermore, the models' generalizability to different kinds of web application attacks.

3.5 Design

A specific kind of recurrent neural network (RNN) called a Long Short-Term Memory (LSTM) network is made to identify long-term dependencies in sequential input. An LSTM model can handle SQL query sequences efficiently in the context of SQL injection detection by picking up on the complex patterns and structures linked to both benign and malicious requests. Sequences where SQL injection patterns may occur can be identified thanks to the long-term information retention of memory cells in the LSTM architecture. Usually, the model begins with an embedding layer that turns SQL query tokens into dense vectors. These vectors are then processed sequentially by one or more LSTM layers. The ability of the LSTM layers to recognize intricate connections in the query sequences is essential for spotting subtle and advanced SQL injection tactics. A dense layer is typically used for classification after the LSTM layers, yielding a final output that identifies whether a query is benign or malicious. In order to reduce overfitting and enhance the model's capacity for generalization, dropout layers may be added.

Another type of RNN that can handle sequential data with fewer parameters than LSTMs while still capturing crucial dependencies in the input sequences is called a gated recurrent unit (GRU). GRUs provide a simplified, potentially shorter training time and less computing overhead than LSTMs for SQL injection detection. By integrating the forget and input gates into a single update gate, the GRU architecture reduces the number of gates and parameters required, hence simplifying the complexity of LSTMs. Similar to LSTMs, GRUs begin with an embedding layer that creates dense representations from SQL query tokens. After processing these sequences, the GRU layers look for patterns that could indicate SQL injection attempts. A dense layer that comes after the GRU layers makes the last classification by separating benign and harmful requests. When there are limited processing resources or a need for quicker inference, GRUs can be especially helpful. To increase the model's resilience and stop overfitting, regularization techniques like dropout can be used, guaranteeing dependable performance in practical applications. There are a few things to take into account while deciding between LSTM and GRU models for SQL injection detection. Because of their more intricate gate mechanisms, LSTMs are often better at capturing long-term dependencies, which can be useful for identifying complex injection patterns that change over time. But because of their more straightforward architecture, GRUs can be faster and more effective to train, which makes them a good fit for applications requiring real-time processing or with limited computational resources. To get the best results, both models need to have their hyperparameters, like the number of layers, units per layer, and dropout rates, carefully adjusted. In the end, the decision between LSTM and GRU may be based on particular project requirements, such the computational resources available and the intricacy of the injection patterns. It can be useful to test both strategies and evaluate how well they perform on the validation set to determine whether model is more appropriate for the job.

3.6 System Architecture

The SQL injection detection project's system architecture is painstakingly created to use a multi-layered, structured method to meet the challenges of spotting malicious SQL queries. The data preparation layer, which is its fundamental component, converts unprocessed SQL query data into an organized format that is appropriate for analysis. This step entails a number of crucial procedures, including tokenization—the process of turning textual SQL queries into numerical sequences using programs like Keras's Tokenizer—and data cleaning, which deals with incorrect or missing items. Next, by using padding to standardize the length of these sequences, all input data is made to follow the same format, which is essential for efficient model training and assessment.

Tokenized sequences are converted into numerical representations that the machine learning models can understand by the feature extraction layer. In this step, embeddings are created, in which a dense vector in an embedding space represents each token. By capturing the semantic links between characters, this approach improves the model's capacity to spot patterns suggestive of SQL injection.

A variety of neural network designs are used at the model building layer. For example, because they can capture sequential dependencies in SQL queries, models like Gated Recurrent Units (GRU) and Long Short-Term Memory (LSTM) networks are used. Given their proficiency with sequences and its ability to understand temporal patterns, GRU and LSTM models are well-suited for identifying intricate SQL injection assaults. An embedding layer is usually used in the architecture to turn token sequences into dense vectors. These vectors are then processed by recurrent layers, such as GRU or LSTM, and finally, a final dense layer with a sigmoid activation function is used for binary classification (malicious vs. benign requests).

4 Results

The models' performance will be evaluated using measures including accuracy, precision, and recall, as indicated in Table 1. True positives, false positives, true negatives, and false negatives can all be seen with the use of a confusion matrix. To find out which model is better at detecting SQL injections, the performance of the LSTM and GRU models will be evaluated.

Accuracy: The LSTM and GRU models both have extremely high accuracy, however the LSTM model's is little lower at 99.61 suggests that both models perform a very good job of identifying SQL queries as valid or SQL-injected.

Precision: Precision gauges how well the model predicts favorable outcomes. When predicting a SQL injection attack, LSTM (99.60 exceptionally high precision, meaning they are nearly always right.

Recall: Recall is a measure of how well the model can identify all positive instances, in this case SQL injection assaults. While GRU obtains a slightly better recall of 99.30 LSTM only manages a recall of 99.26 bit more adept at catching every occurrence of a SQL injection attack.

Comparative Analysis: Both the LSTM and GRU models perform admirably, with a slight bias in favor of GRU's accuracy and recall. Both models have remarkably high precision, meaning there are few false positives.

Practical Implications: These models have such high recall, accuracy, and precision that they can be used in practical situations where identifying SQL injection threats is essential to preserving database security. Deployment considerations could include things like the amount of computing power needed for training and inference, where GRU's possibly superior performance could be useful.

Table 1. Results for models

Model	Accuracy	Precision	Recall
LSTM	99.61%	99.60%	99.26%
GRU	99.69%	99.78%	99.30%
Existing System	94.00%	95.00%	90.00%

In terms of accuracy, precision, and recall, the LSTM and GRU models perform noticeably better than the current system. With 99.69 outperforms the LSTM, which comes in second at 99.61 accuracy of the current method is substantially lower at 94.00 LSTM and GRU are equally good at generating accurate predictions. With a precision score of 99.78 false positives. With a precision of 95.00 LSTM, which follows closely at 99.60 models deliver insightful outcomes. Strong recall is demonstrated by both LSTM and GRU, with scores of 99.26 proficient in spotting real positives. The 90.00 significantly lower, suggesting a larger false negative rate (Figs. 2, 3 and 4).

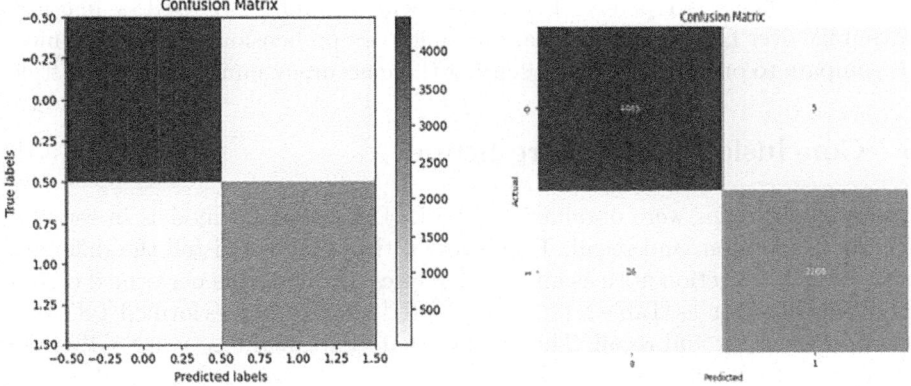

Fig. 2. Confusion matrix for model LSTM

Fig. 3. Confusion Matrix for model GRU

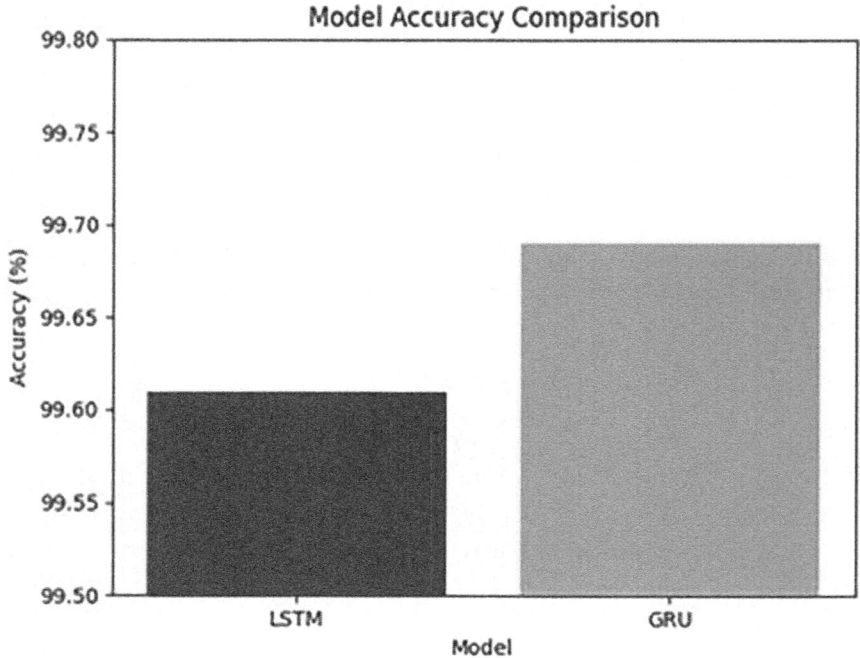

Fig. 4. Model accuracy comparison

The comparative accuracy of two sophisticated models, LSTM (Long Short-Term Memory) and GRU (Gated Recurrent Unit), is well shown by the bar chart. The models have remarkably high accuracy, which is indicative of their strong performance in the assigned task. The graph indicates that the GRU model performs somewhat better than the LSTM model, with an accuracy of 99.69 the LSTM model. The meticulously calibrated y-axis boundaries, which span from 99.5 discrepancy. The figure, which emphasizes GRU's marginal advantage over LSTM, gives a clear and quick comprehension of how these models compare to one another by presenting these accuracy numbers in a bar style.

5 Conclusion and Future Scope

Excellent outcomes were obtained by the LSTM and GRU models in terms of accuracy, precision, and recall. They showed that they could tell the difference between SQL injection attacks and valid queries. Both models performed incredibly well, however as Table 1 illustrates, GRU slightly outperformed LSTM in terms of accuracy and recall. This implies that GRU might be marginally more successful in catching every SQL injection attack instance. Both models have high precision and recall values, accuracy rates above 99.6 scenarios where SQL injection detection is essential for database security. When deciding between LSTM and GRU, factors like computing efficiency and resource constraints should be taken into account. GRU might be better in this situation due to its possible superior performance, particularly in situations where quick detection and action against SQL injection threats is essential.

Performance might be further enhanced by more model optimization and fine-tuning. Furthermore, investigating group techniques or adding different kinds of neural networks could improve SQL injection detection systems' robustness and dependability.

5.1 Future Scope

Even with the project's successes, there are still a number of areas that might be improved in the future to increase the system's efficacy and versatility. The use of hybrid detection techniques, which fuse machine learning with more conventional techniques like heuristic and rule-based approaches, is one important area that needs improvement. By combining the advantages of several detection techniques, this hybrid strategy may improve overall accuracy and lower the number of false positives and negatives. Furthermore, extending the model to include dynamic attack vectors via ongoing learning processes can strengthen its resistance to novel and advanced SQL injection methods. By using reinforcement learning, the system might be able to adjust and improve its detection tactics in real-time in response to attacks that are still happening.

Improving the feature engineering process is another area that will be developed in the future. More complex characteristics, such context-aware embeddings and semantic analysis of SQL queries, could enhance detection skills and offer deeper insights into query patterns. Furthermore, using transfer learning to leverage trained models from related domains could accelerate training and improve performance with little amounts of data.

Future improvements can focus on scalability to manage large quantities of queries in distributed systems and lowlatency prediction optimization of the model to meet the issues related to real-time deployment. By using edge computing solutions, the system may be able to detect events in real time nearer to the data sources, which would decrease latency and increase responsiveness.

Finally, expanding the project's scope to include new platforms like mobile apps, cloud-based systems, and Internet of Things (IoT) gadgets will guarantee thorough protection in a variety of settings and increase its applicability. Achieving effective security in an increasingly linked environment will require building customized detection algorithms for each platform and incorporating cross-platform interoperability.

References

1. Paul, A., Sharma, V., Olukoya, O.: SQL injection attack: detection, prioritization & prevention. J. Inf. Secur. Appl. **85**, 103871 (2024)
2. Alenezi, M., Nadeem, M., Asif, R.: SQL injection attacks countermeasures assessments. Indon. J. Electr. Eng. Comput. Sci. **21**(2), 1121–1131 (2021)

3. Shahnaz, R.U., Hasan, S.: Methods for SQL injection prevention using static and dynamic code analysis. Comput. Appl. Eng. Educ. **28**(4), 764–7779 (2020)
4. Muhammad, T., Ghafory, H.: Sql injection attack detection using machine learning algorithm. Mesopotamian J. Cybersecur. **2022**, 5–17 (2022)
5. Kumar, P.S., Nair, V.A.: Analysis of SQL injection detection machine learning techniques. Secur. Comput. **109**, 102387 (2022)
6. Muslihi, M.T., Alghazzawi, D.: Detecting SQL injection on web application using deep learning techniques: a systematic literature review. In: 2020 Third International Conference on Vocational Education and Electrical Engineering (ICVEE). IEEE (2020)
7. Lee, J., Park, S.K.: SQL injection detection with LSTM networks. IEEE Access **9**, 14532–14540 (2021)
8. Rao, A.B., Singh, M.L.: Comparing the SQL injection detection models for GRU and LSTM. J. Mach. Learn. Res. **23**(55), 1–19 (2022)
9. Gupta, N.C., Sharma, R.A.: Improving GRU models for SQL injection detection. Int. J. Digital Forens. CyberSecur. **9**(1), 34–45 (2020)
10. Johnson, L.T., Miller, E.D.: Comparing SQL injection detection models: LSTM vs GRU. Data Sci. Secur. **5**(2), 115–130 (2021)
11. George, T.K., James, R., Jacob, P.: Proposed Hybrid model to detect and prevent SQL Injection. Int. J. Comput. Sci. Inf. Secur. **14**(6), 441 (2016)
12. Jaradat, M., Rattrout, A., Jayousi, R.: Improving ML accuracy in SQL injection detection using NLP and feature engineering (2023)
13. Patel, P.S., Sharma, A.T.: Applications of machine learning for SQL injection detection in the real world. J. Secur. Appl. Int. **15**(1), 12–25 (2021)
14. Moore, R.L., Roberts, J.K.: Deep learning-based real-time SQL injection detection. Inf. Syst. Secur. J. **16**(4), 50–65 (2020)
15. Davis, C.M., Zhang, L.R.: A machine learning perspective on SQL injection detection case studies. Comput. Secur. **97**, 101936 (2021)
16. Thompson, A.P., Harris, R.C.: Machine learning perspective on trends in SQL injection detection. J. Priv. Cybersecur. **4**(1), 45–60 (2021)
17. Demilie, W.B., Deriba, F.G.: Detection and prevention of SQLI attacks and developing compressive framework using machine learning and hybrid techniques. J. Big Data **9**(1), 124 (2022)
18. Gupta, A., Patel, N.: SQL injection detection via deep reinforcement learning. J. Mach. Learn. Appl. **1**(1), 20–35 (2023)
19. Kim, S., Park, J.: Assessment of SQL injection prevention techniques. J. Netw. Secur. **2020**(5), 44–58 (2020)
20. Johnson, M., Lee, T.: Behavioral detection techniques for SQL injection vulnerabilities. Int. J. Inf. Syst. **37**(3), 103–118 (2021)
21. Smith, R., Brown, D.: Network traffic analysis for SQL injection detection. J. Cybersecur. Res. **15**(1), 35–50 (2022)
22. Gogoi, B., Ahmed, T., Dutta, A.: Defending against sql injection attacks in web applications using machine learning and natural language processing. In: 2021 IEEE 18th India Council International Conference (INDICON). IEEE (2021)
23. Zhang, H., Liu, F.: Comparing traditional and machine learning techniques for SQL injection detection. Int. J. Inf. Secur. **20**(6), 387–402 (2021)
24. Moore, K., Thompson, C.: Identification of SQL injection in cloud computing settings. Adv. Syst. Appl. Cloud Comput. J. **9**(1), 1–15 (2020)
25. Kim, M.Y., Lee, D.H.: Data-mining based SQL injection attack detection using internal query trees. Expert Syst. Appl. **41**(11), 5416–5430 (2014)

26. Patel, N., Sharma, A.: Problems with mobile application SQL injection detection. Mobile Netw. Appl. **25**(4), 1256–1267 (2020)
27. Patel, R., Gupta, A.K.: Techniques for identifying anomalies in SQL injection threats. J. Secur. Priv. **4**(2), 112–127 (2021)
28. Rao, N., Singh, P.: Group learning methods for SQL injection recognition. J. Mach. Learn. Secur. **5**(3), 67–82 (2021)
29. Kumar, S., Sharma, R.: Hybrid methods for SQL injection detection: merging static analysis and machine learning. Comput. Appl. Int. **975**, 14–28 (2021)
30. Patel, A., Brown, M.: Identifying SQL injection attacks in distributed systems presents difficulties. J. Distrib. Comput. **30**(2), 45–60 (2022)
31. Lee, T., Kumar, K.: Dynamic methods for SQL injection detection. J. Comput. Secur. **29**(3), 77–92 (2021)
32. Yeole, A.S., Meshram, B.B.: Analysis of different technique for detection of SQL injection. In: Proceedings of the International Conference & Workshop on Emerging Trends in Technology (2011)
33. Wilson, N., Patel, S.: SQL injection detection in internet of things contexts. J. Internet Things **8**(4), 500–515 (2021)
34. İlker, K.A.R.A., Aydos, M.: Detection and analysis of attacks against web services by the SQL injection method. In: 2019 3rd International Symposium on Multidisciplinary Studies and Innovative Technologies (ISMSIT). IEEE (2019)

Quantum Cryptography

A Quantum Public Key Cryptographic Scheme Using Entangled States and Grover Operator

Soumen Bajpayee[✉], Sarbani Sen, Prithwish Dey, and Imon Mukherjee

Computer Science and Engineering, Indian Institute of Information Technology Kalyani, Kalyani, India
{soumen_phd22,sarbani_phd22,cse22065,imon}@iiitkalyani.ac.in

Abstract. Quantum cryptography is used to enhance data security measures through the use of quantum mechanics. Our proposed Quantum Public Key Cryptographic (QPKC) system employs entangled states and the Grover operator to repel against any form of quantum attacks including Shor's algorithms that are aimed at breaking some classical cryptosystems. In terms of key generation, we design the basis on entangled states to assure privacy-protected relationships between these keys and instant notifications on data snooping efforts by eavesdropping. This strategy gets rid of the weaknesses of tensor product-based systems while ensuring proper security. On the other hand, Grover operator increases efficiency in encrypting and decrypting data by making use of the quantum search feature hence much better compared to the classical methods. Our method employs the inherent advantages of entanglement - enhanced key correlations and dependable eavesdropping detection. By eliminating both classical and quantum threats, this approach strengthens cryptographic protocols, ensuring security against advanced attacks.

Keywords: Quantum public key cryptography · Grover iteration · Entangled states · Cryptanalytic security · Secure communication

1 Introduction

Asymmetric key or public key cryptography [8] solves the problems that are present in symmetric key primitives. In symmetric key cryptosystems, use of the same key for both encryption and decryption requires a secure key interchanging method which poses notable security concerns and challenges. These problems are solved by public key cryptography, utilizing a pair of keys, public key to encrypt and private key to decrypt without loss of security and ease in handling keys since the secret key is never disclosed.

The advent of quantum computing [2,13] has dramatically transformed the field of cryptography [5]. Powerful quantum algorithms now enable diverse attack strategies against symmetric and asymmetric key systems, while unique quantum properties are also essential to improve various cryptographic primitives.

The massive computational ability of quantum computing enables the cracking of strong cryptographic ciphers, both symmetric and asymmetric, which classical attacks can not break in polynomial time. Quantum algorithms [11] leverage useful properties such as superposition and measurement to gain significant speedups over classical algorithms. Grover's algorithm [4], for example, finds a target element in an unstructured database in $O(\sqrt{n})$ time, imposing threats to symmetric key primitives by making brute-force key search attacks faster by a quadratic factor. Simon's algorithm [12] is another one that poses threats to some symmetric key ciphers by finding the hidden period in the key stream, while Shor's algorithm [10] makes the important classical asymmetric key cryptosystems vulnerable.

Quantum algorithms, if run in error-free devices [1], not only threaten different security primitives, but also strengthen them through aspects of quantum mechanics [9]. Grover's algorithm, which affects the security of symmetric key primitives, can also be used to enhance the efficiency and make stronger asymmetric key primitives. This research focuses on using the Grover operator and the strength of quantum entanglement to define a quantum public key cryptographic mechanism that provides robust cryptanalytic security against different attacks.

1.1 Prior Works

In the existing literature, the authors present several attempts to define the structure of Quantum Public Key Cryptosystems (QPKC). On this basis, Okamoto et al. [7] propose an illustration of a QPKC model based on the subset-sum problem, utilizing Quantum Polynomial-Time Turing machines (QPT), quantum trapdoor one-way functions and classical channels. However, there is absence of evidence for the presence of such one-way functions within the QPT model. Additionally, the authors recommend investigating the possibility of Grover's search algorithm for public key cryptosystems. While addressing the issue of the absence of a quantum one-way function, Nikolopoulos [6] presents the use of single qubit rotations for the trapdoor quantum one-way function. In this approach, a quantum public key is used for encryption, while decryption is performed with a classical secret key. Although this scheme offers various levels of security against classical cryptanalytic attacks, it remains vulnerable if the decryption process is carried out through a quantum channel. Considering the application of single qubit rotation, Zheng et al. [18] propose two public key encryption schemes in a work, but both exhibit decryption errors. To address these errors, Wu et al. [15] present a QPKC model that does not rely on single qubit rotation. Here, the model uses Bell states, where the first n qubits of the Bell states combined with generic Pauli operations provide the public key and the last n qubits with the inverse of the Pauli operations serve as the secret key. Although this model eliminates decryption errors, the authors recommend exploring quantum solutions for various public key cryptographic schemes in practical applications.

Several significant works with promising results have emerged in the search for quantum solutions to various public key cryptosystems and the exploration of Grover's algorithm in this context. Gong *et al.* [3] establish a quantum homomorphic encryption scheme for ciphertext recovery using Grover's search algorithm. Here, the authors apply Grover's quantum search algorithm to the superposition states of ciphertexts and it returns the retrieval result after measurement. However, this framework does not reduce computational load and the circuit design is not optimized. Yoon *et al.* [17] address the sustaining issues in the previous QPKC schemes with a novel one that employs Grover's iteration for both encryption and decryption purpose, aiming to resolve security vulnerabilities, encryption and decryption errors. This scheme ensures proper confidentiality of the plaintext while not becoming vulnerable to the attacks performed by Shor's algorithm. However, the last work in QPKC utilizes tensor product structures for secret key generation. Although this approach offers a level of security due to quantum-mechanical principles, it remains susceptible to certain quantum attacks due to the separability of the states of the tensor product. The security of these systems can be compromised if an adversary can exploit the independent nature of individual quantum states. This finding motivates the work carried out in this paper:

- The need to develop more secure QPKC system that can handle advanced quantum threats drives this research. Key generation by using entangled states aims to improve the robustness and dependability of quantum cryptographic mechanisms.
- This development addresses the possible drawback sustaining in the tensor product-based QPKC systems, paving the way QPKC model with upgraded security.
- Capitalizing the unique advantages offered by entanglement, like enhanced eavesdropping detection and stronger key correlations, making it a dependable solution for future quantum public key cryptographic applications.

1.2 Contributions

Keeping the above possibility in mind, this work contributes to the following:

- Our work addresses this scope by proposing the use of entangled states for key generation. The advantage lies in their non-separable nature, which provides a stronger correlation between the components of the key. The inherent phenomena of the entangled states guarantees that any effort by the attacker to intercept the key generates detectable disruption, thereby significantly enhancing the security of the system.
- After key generation using the entangled states, the encryption of the secret message is done using the Grover operator. On the other hand, the decryption process is also successfully carried out without any error.
- Justification of the proper confidentiality achieved through the process is discussed along with other security related analysis.

- A comparison is conducted against various state-of-the-art QPKC schemes to establish the higher security of the proposed method.

1.3 Organization

The rest of the paper is organized in the following manner. Section 2 sheds light on the fundamental concepts of public key cryptography, entanglement and Grover iteration. Section 3 details the steps involved in proposing the QPKC method. Security analysis and comparative discussion is carried out in Sect. 4. Finally, Sect. 5 brings us to the conclusion of the paper.

2 Preliminaries

In this section, the necessary concepts of public key cryptography, entangled states and Grover operator are discussed.

2.1 Public Key Cryptography

Public key cryptography or asymmetric cryptography [8], is a cryptographic system that uses a pair of keys: a public key and a secret key. These keys are mathematically related but computationally infeasible to derive the secret key from the public key. This system allows secure communication between parties without sharing the secret key in advance.

In a public key cryptographic system, each user generates a key pair consisting of a public key (K_{pub}) and a secret key (K_{sec}). The public key is distributed widely and shared with anyone, while the secret key is kept secret by the communicating parties. The sender then files encryption for sending a message (m) using the public key of the receiver (K_{pub}^R): Ciphertext$(c) = Enc(K_{pub}^R, m)$. In contrast, upon receiving the ciphertext c, the receiver decrypts it using the private key (K_{sec}^R) to recover the original message m: $m = Dec(K_{sec}^R, c)$. The security of public key cryptosystems depends on the computational hardness of certain mathematical problems. Examples include the integer factorization problem (used in RSA), the discrete logarithm problem (used in ElGamal), etc.

The security of the secret key can be at risk if a cryptanalyst uses quantum algorithms to attack the system [16]. To safeguard the entire cryptographic infrastructure, it is essential to develop quantum-safe models. In this context, leveraging the advantages of public key mechanisms in the quantum realm becomes important. Quantum public key cryptosystems harness the properties of quantum mechanics to generate cryptographic keys that are resistant to quantum threats, thereby ensuring the confidentiality of the message between the communicating parties.

2.2 Entangled States

Quantum entanglement [14] is a phenomenon where the quantum states of two or more particles become interdependent, such that the state of one particle cannot be described independently of the others. This is crucial for applications in quantum computing and quantum cryptography. Mathematically, an entangled state of two quantum bits is represented by the Bell states, which are: $|\Phi^+\rangle = \frac{1}{\sqrt{2}}(|00\rangle + |11\rangle)$, $|\Phi^-\rangle = \frac{1}{\sqrt{2}}(|00\rangle - |11\rangle)$, $|\Psi^+\rangle = \frac{1}{\sqrt{2}}(|01\rangle + |10\rangle)$ and $|\Psi^-\rangle = \frac{1}{\sqrt{2}}(|01\rangle - |10\rangle)$. An entangled state cannot be expressed using the tensor products of two vectors because their quantum states are inseparably linked, creating correlations that independent states cannot represent for each particle. This interdependence means the overall state cannot be factored into separate components.

Entangled states are vital in quantum cryptography as they enable secure key distribution through protocols like Quantum Key Distribution (QKD), where any eavesdropping attempt disrupts the entanglement and is detectable. In quantum public key cryptography, entangled states strengthen the confidentiality of the message, create of quantum digital signatures, ensuring robust authentication and non-repudiation. They also enable the implementation of quantum key exchange protocols, leveraging quantum correlations to enhance the security of public key schemes beyond what is possible with classical methods.

2.3 Grover Operator

Grover's algorithm provides a quadratic speedup for searching $N = 2^n$ unsorted data by reducing the time complexity from $O(N)$ to $O(\sqrt{N})$ using quantum entanglement. In the work [17], the authors explain the use of the Grover iteration for their scheme.

$|Q\rangle$ expresses the unsorted database:

$$|Q\rangle = \frac{1}{N} \sum_{i=0}^{N-1} \sum_{j=0}^{N-1} |i,j\rangle.$$

The target state in the unsorted database $|Q\rangle$ is:

$$|\tau\rangle = |i_1, j_1\rangle.$$

Below, the rotation operators used in the process are expressed:

$$U_{R_1} = I - N|\tau\rangle\langle\tau|, \quad U_{R_2} = C|Q\rangle\langle Q| - I.$$

The target key is retrieved from the unsorted database using these operators as shown below:

$$\begin{aligned}
U_{R_2}U_{R_1}|Q\rangle &= (C|Q\rangle\langle Q| - I)(I - N|\tau\rangle\langle\tau|)|Q\rangle \\
&= (C|Q\rangle\langle Q| - I)(|Q\rangle - |\tau\rangle) \\
&= C|Q\rangle - |Q\rangle - \frac{1}{N-1}|Q\rangle + |\tau\rangle) \\
&= |\tau\rangle.
\end{aligned}$$

Here, $\langle \tau | Q \rangle = \frac{1}{N}$, $C = \frac{N}{N-1}$. This calculation justifies that after using the above operators U_{R_1} and U_{R_2}, the desired state $|\tau\rangle$ is successfully recovered from $|Q\rangle$.

In the next section, the proposed QPKC scheme is defined with the help of entangled states and Grover operator to establish a more secure mechanism.

3 Proposed QPKC Scheme Using Entangled States and Grover Operator

In this section, we focus on discussing the various phases involved in defining the proposed QPKC method. The proposed QPKC model (depicted in Fig. 1) goes through three different phases to perform the jobs of key-initialization (both secret and public), encryption and finally decryption to recover the message.

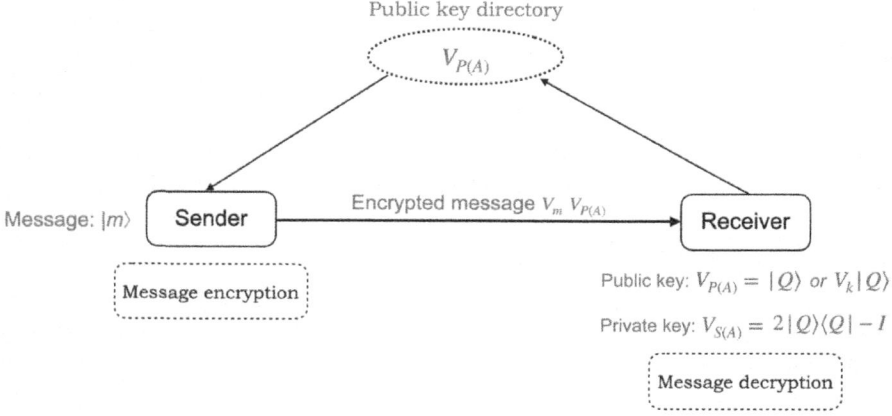

Fig. 1. Block diagram of the proposed QPKC model.

3.1 Initiation Phase

In the first step, the receiver creates a secret quantum state $|Q\rangle$, which is an entangled state of four arbitrary states $|\alpha_1\rangle$, $|\alpha_2\rangle$, $|\beta_1\rangle$ and $|\beta_2\rangle$ (usually taken from $|+\rangle$ and $|-\rangle$). In quantum public key systems, using entangled states to initialize keys guarantees better security because of the unique features found in quantum entanglement as it detects when one tries to tap information from them. Hence, these states make it possible for cryptographic keys to be created with links stronger than those in traditional methods, thereby attaining strong protection from attacks by quantum computers.

Next part of the initiation phase defines the operators $V_{S(A)}$ and $V_{P(A)}$ for private and public keys respectively as given below:

$$|Q\rangle = |\alpha_1\rangle \otimes |\alpha_2\rangle + |\beta_1\rangle \otimes |\beta_2\rangle.$$

The receiver chooses an arbitrary two-bit key k_1, which serves as the basis for the public key. Subsequently, the following operator is constructed:

$$V_k \triangleq I - 2\left|k_1\right\rangle\left\langle k_1\right|.$$

Public Key:

$$V_{P(A)} \triangleq \begin{cases} V_k\left|Q\right\rangle, & \text{if } V_k > 1; \\ \left|Q\right\rangle, & \text{if } V_k = 1. \end{cases}$$

Private Key: $\quad V_{S(A)} \triangleq 2\left|Q\right\rangle\left\langle Q\right| - I.$

The next phase of the process focuses on encrypting the message by the sender using the generated public key.

3.2 Encryption Phase

In encryption phase, the message $\left|m\right\rangle$ is encrypted by the sender using the operator V_m. The public key $V_{P(A)}$ of the receiver is used for encryption which is done at the sender's end. The mathematical description of the process is explained in the following:

$$V_m \triangleq I - 2\left|m\right\rangle\left\langle m\right|.$$

The encryption operator is defined as:

$$V_m\ V_{P(A)} \triangleq \begin{cases} V_m V_k\left|Q\right\rangle, & \text{if } V_k > 1; \\ V_m\left|Q\right\rangle, & \text{if } V_k = 1. \end{cases}$$

This encrypted state is the intended state that the sender wants to send to the receiver. The encrypted message qubit is sent to the receiver for decryption. At this stage, the qubit is secure against quantum threats. The main goal of securing the secret message is successfully done at this step.

3.3 Decryption Phase

The decryption phase $D\bigl(V_m\ V_{P(A)}\bigr)$ occurs at the receiver's end using the secret key operator, $V_{S(A)}$, which is expressed as follows:

$$V_{S(A)} \triangleq 2\left|Q\right\rangle\left\langle Q\right| - I.$$

Reapplying V_k on public key (if it is used during the encryption process) and the application of the private key operator, $V_{S(A)}$, over the encrypted message qubit, $V_m\ V_{P(A)}$, gives back the original message $\left|m\right\rangle$, as shown below:

$$D\bigl(V_m\ V_{P(A)}\bigr) \triangleq \begin{cases} V_{S(A)} V_k V_m V_k\left|Q\right\rangle, & \text{if } V_k > 1; \\ V_{S(A)} V_m\left|Q\right\rangle, & \text{if } V_k = 1. \end{cases}$$

Detailed derivation is shown in Appendix A.

The next section discusses the confidentiality achieved through the process and testing of the proposed QPKC model for various security parameters along with its comparison with the state-of-the-art quantum public key schemes.

4 Security Analysis and Discussion

The previous section details the QPKC method applying Grover operator and entangled states. This part examines the potential security of the proposed mechanism and its higher security compared to other quantum asymmetric key methods.

4.1 Attaining Confidentiality

The goal of confidentiality is successful if the receiver is able to decrypt the ciphered state and retrieve the message $|m\rangle$. Even if there is an attack by a third party to get the message, that attempt must be useless.

- If the attacker attempts to measure the quantum state, it will collapse and prior to that the secret state is not known to the attacker, thus confidentiality remains due to the quantum-mechanical property of the system.
- Moreover, accurate measurement of the state can not be done without knowing the operators V_k and $V_{S(A)}$.
- An attempt to attack a quantum cryptographic system is generating entanglement for stealing information from the system. However, in this scenario, that attempt can only lead to the information retrieval of the public key component. It will not help anyway in an asymmetric key infrastructure as without the secret key component the message $|m\rangle$ can not be revealed.

4.2 Higher Security Because of Entangled States

The proposed model for QPKC ensures higher security than the tensor product-based system for key generation.

- The secret entangled state $|Q\rangle = |\alpha_1\rangle \otimes |\alpha_2\rangle + |\beta_1\rangle \otimes |\beta_2\rangle$ used in this work exhibits non-local correlations between the qubits that cannot be distinguished into individual states. This phenomenon assures that an attempt to measure the result of the key in evident disturbances, thus providing a stronger safety against eavesdropping approach compared to separable states $|\psi\rangle = |\psi_a\rangle \otimes |\psi_b\rangle$ that are purely based on tensor products.
- An eavesdropper disrupts the entanglement between any two components of the system if one of them tries to measure it. The disturbance could be revealed on a pairwise correlation check but is not inherent in states that result from a tensor product.
- The continuous correspondence of the entangled states in a system results in a whole and inseparable state. As a result, it eliminates the feasibility of quantum attacks such as Grover's search for performing brute-force attacks.

The singular characteristics of entanglement make unique quantum states very resilient to attacks, making them perfect for key generation in quantum cryptography systems. In an entangled system, it is impossible to describe the state of one particle without considering its partner. Any trial to measure or interfere with one location leads to a collapse of the complete quantum state, which can be straight away known by the lawful parties. This inbuilt protection guarantees that it is not feasible to get information from a single quantum state without affecting the scheme. On the other hand, the independent nature of the individual quantum states can not be exploited as they are secret to the receiver who generates the key pair in the proposed quantum public key cryptographic system.

4.3 Security Against Shor's Algorithm

Shor's algorithm [10] is a notable one that threatens classical public key cryptographic mechanisms by factorizing the large integers efficiently. This formidable algorithm can endanger cryptographic primitives that depend on computational complexity. However, cryptographic systems built on the principles of quantum mechanics remain intact against the attacks caused by this algorithm.

As the proposed QPKC model is completely based on quantum-mechanical principles, this scheme is safe against Shor's algorithm. No attack model using Shor's factorization algorithm can put an admissible threat on the proposed mechanism.

4.4 Comparison with the State-of-the-Art QPKC Models

As discussed above, the proposed scheme uses the benefit of entangled states to define a QPKC model that provides higher security than existing ones while attaining the proper confidentiality of the secret message. Here, in Table 1 the proposed model is compared to the state-of-the-art QPKC schemes to justify its effectiveness.

Table 1. Comparison with the Existing QPKC Schemes.

Sl. no.	QPKC models	Principle used	Decryption Error	Security level
1.	Nikolopoulos [6]	Single qubit rotation	No	Vulnerable if the quantum channel is used to decrypt
2.	Zheng et al. [18]	Mixed state	Yes	Decryption error is present
3.	Gong et al. [3]	Grover's search and homomorphic scheme	No	Higher computational load and not optimized
4.	Yoon et al. [17]	Grover iteration	No	Possibility of decoupled tensored states used in key generation
5.	Proposed Approach	Entangled states and Grover iteration	No	Entangled states lead to non-separation for the secret state units and detectability of the eavesdropping and preventing individual state manipulation

Ensuring that any eavesdropping attempts are detectable and maintaining robust correlations that prevent independent manipulation, while also enhancing the overall integrity and security of the cryptographic system is what results from the use of the entangled states.

5 Conclusion

Our proposed quantum public key cryptographic scheme using entangled states and Grover operator represents an advancement in securing the system. Using quantum-mechanical properties such as entanglement, we enhance secure key generation with stronger correlations and improved eavesdropping detection than the existing approaches. The proposed method also eliminates possible vulnerabilities in traditional cryptographic systems, particularly against quantum attacks such as the Shor's algorithm. Furthermore, the integration of Grover operator enhances efficiency in encryption and decryption processes, marking a notable improvement over classical ones.

The proposed approach to establish a quantum digital signature scheme for authentication and non-repudiation can be considered an aspect of future research.

A Appendix

In this appendix, we provide the explicit decryption calculations that form the basis of our quantum protocol for public key cryptography. These calculations are essential in order to appreciate the strength and operational efficiency of our method. By exposing the underlying arithmetic theory and operational aspects related to each other, our objective is to explain how decryption takes place in full detail.

A.1 Layout and the Detailed Calculations

The decryption process in the receiver end is performed in the following way:

– The secret key operator $(V_{S(A)})$ is utilized for the decryption process.
– If V_k is applied during encryption, it is reused during decryption and the private key operator, $(V_{S(A)})$ is applied over the encrypted message qubit $(V_m\, V_{P(A)})$ for recovering the original message $|m\rangle$, as shown below (δ_{m,k_1} represents the inner product of m and k_1):

$$D(V_m\, V_{P(A)}) \triangleq \begin{cases} V_{S(A)} V_k V_m V_k \,|Q\rangle, & \text{if } V_k > 1; \\ V_{S(A)} V_m \,|Q\rangle, & \text{if } V_k = 1. \end{cases}$$

Case $V_{S(A)}V_k V_m V_k |Q\rangle$:

$= (2|Q\rangle\langle Q| - I)(I - 2|k_1\rangle\langle k_1|)(I - 2|m\rangle\langle m|)(I - 2|k_1\rangle\langle k_1|)|Q\rangle$
$= (2|Q\rangle\langle Q| - I)(I - 2|k_1\rangle\langle k_1|)(I - 2|m\rangle\langle m|)(|Q\rangle - |k_1\rangle)$
$= (2|Q\rangle\langle Q| - I)(I - 2|k_1\rangle\langle k_1|)(|Q\rangle - |m\rangle - |k_1\rangle + 2\delta_{m,k_1}|m\rangle)$
$= (2|Q\rangle\langle Q| - I)(I - 2|k_1\rangle\langle k_1|)(|Q\rangle - |k_1\rangle + (2\delta_{m,k_1} - 1)|m\rangle)$

$$\left[\langle k_1|Q\rangle = \langle m|Q\rangle = \frac{1}{2}\right]$$

$= (2|Q\rangle\langle Q| - I)(|Q\rangle + (2\delta_{m,k_1} - 1)|m\rangle - 2(2\delta_{m,k_1} - 1)\delta_{m,k_1}|m\rangle)$
$= (2|Q\rangle\langle Q| - I)(|Q\rangle - |m\rangle) \quad [\because \delta_{m,k_1} \approx 1]$
$= |m\rangle.$

Case $V_{S(A)}V_m |Q\rangle$:

$= (2|Q\rangle\langle Q| - I)(I - 2|m\rangle\langle m|)|Q\rangle$
$= (2|Q\rangle\langle Q| - I)(|Q\rangle - |m\rangle)$
$= 2|Q\rangle - |Q\rangle - |Q\rangle + |m\rangle$
$= |m\rangle.$

References

1. Bajpayee, S., Mukherjee, I.: Analysis of the effects of crosstalk errors on various quantum circuits. In: 2024 37th International Conference on VLSI Design and 2024 23rd International Conference on Embedded Systems (VLSID), pp. 408–413. IEEE (2024)
2. Bennett, C.H., DiVincenzo, D.P.: Quantum information and computation. Nature **404**(6775), 247–255 (2000)
3. Gong, C., et al.: Grover algorithm-based quantum homomorphic encryption ciphertext retrieval scheme in quantum cloud computing. Quantum Inf. Process. **19**, 1–17 (2020)
4. Grover, L.K.: Quantum mechanics helps in searching for a needle in a haystack. Phys. Rev. Lett. **79**(2), 325 (1997)
5. Mmaduekwe, U., Mmaduekwe, E.: Cybersecurity and cryptography: the new era of quantum computing. Curr. J. Appl. Sci. Technol. **43**(5), 41–51 (2024)
6. Nikolopoulos, G.M.: Applications of single-qubit rotations in quantum public-key cryptography. Phys. Rev. A **77**(3), 032348 (2008)
7. Okamoto, T., Tanaka, K., Uchiyama, S.: Quantum public-key cryptosystems. In: Bellare, M. (ed.) CRYPTO 2000. LNCS, vol. 1880, pp. 147–165. Springer, Heidelberg (2000). https://doi.org/10.1007/3-540-44598-6_9
8. Paar, C., Pelzl, J.: Understanding cryptography: a textbook for students and practitioners. Springer, Heidelberg (2009)
9. Portmann, C., Renner, R.: Security in quantum cryptography. Rev. Mod. Phys. **94**(2), 025008 (2022)
10. Shor, P.W.: Polynomial-time algorithms for prime factorization and discrete logarithms on a quantum computer. SIAM Rev. **41**(2), 303–332 (1999)

11. Shor, P.W.: Introduction to quantum algorithms. In: Proceedings of Symposia in Applied Mathematics, vol. 58, pp. 143–160 (2002)
12. Simon, D.R.: On the power of quantum computation. SIAM J. Comput. **26**(5), 1474–1483 (1997)
13. Sood, S.K., Pooja: Quantum computing review: a decade of research. IEEE Trans. Eng. Manag. 1–15 (2023)
14. Wong, H.Y.: Introduction to Quantum Computing: From a Layperson to a Programmer in 30 Steps. Springer, Cham (2023)
15. Wu, W., Cai, Q., Zhang, H., Liang, X.: Quantum public key cryptosystem based on bell states. Int. J. Theor. Phys. **56**, 3431–3440 (2017)
16. Yan, S.Y.: Quantum Attacks on Public-Key Cryptosystems, vol. 207. Springer, Heidelberg (2013)
17. Yoon, C.S., Hong, C.H., Kang, M.S., Choi, J.W., Yang, H.J.: Quantum asymmetric key crypto scheme using grover iteration. Sci. Rep. **13**(1), 3810 (2023)
18. Zheng, S., Gu, L., Xiao, D.: Bit-oriented quantum public key probabilistic encryption schemes. Int. J. Theor. Phys. **53**, 116–124 (2014)

An Efficient and Secure Quantum Group Signature with Applications to Vehicular Ad Hoc Networks

Vikas Srivastava[1], Tapaswini Mohanty[2]($\boxtimes$), and Y. Sreenivasa Rao[3]

[1] Department of Mathematics, Indian Institute of Technology Madras, Chennai 600036, Tamil Nadu, India
[2] Department of Computer Science and Engineering, Indian Institute of Technology Roorkee, Roorkee 247667, Uttarakhand, India
mtapaswini37@gmail.com
[3] Department of Mathematics, National Institute of Technology Warangal, Warangal 506004, Telangana, India
ysr@nitw.ac.in

Abstract. A group signature scheme enables members of a group to sign messages on behalf of the group in a manner that conceals the identity of the individual signer. The identification of the member responsible for a particular signature is exclusively within the authority of a designated group manager. Existing state-of-the-art group signatures are based on number-theoretic hardness assumptions such as the integer factorization problem and the discrete logarithm problem. These protocols are not secure in the presence of quantum computers because quantum algorithms like Shor's algorithm can be utilized to undermine the security of these schemes. In this paper, we present a quantum cryptography-based group signature (namely qGroup) protocol. Our design achieves all the security properties of a group signature. In addition, it is secure against attacks by quantum adversaries. qGroup performs better than the existing quantum cryptography-based group signature in the literature as qGroup employs only single qubits, simple measurement operators, and single-qubit quantum gates. We also present an application of qGroup to Vehicular Ad Hoc Networks (VANETs).

Keywords: Group signature · Quantum cryptography · Vehicular Ad Hoc Networks

1 Introduction

A group signature [3] is a cryptographic protocol that allows a group member to sign a message anonymously on behalf of the group. While the signature confirms that the message comes from a group member, it does not reveal which specific member signed it. Thus, a group signature ensures the privacy of the signer. They are used in scenarios where it is important to authenticate messages while preserving the signer's identity, such as in voting systems or secure communications. Despite the anonymity, a designated group manager or an authorized entity can trace and revoke a member's anonymity if misuse is suspected. Therefore, group signatures balance anonymity with accountability. The first group signature was proposed by [5]. In the following years, research on the design and analysis of group signatures has seen tremendous growth. Existing state-of-the-art group signatures are mostly based on number theoretic hardness assumptions such as integer factorization and discrete logarithm problems. Unfortunately, these classical group signatures are vulnerable due to advancements in quantum algorithms. Quantum computers, utilizing principles such as superposition and entanglement, have the potential to break many of the cryptographic assumptions on which current group signature schemes rely. In particular, Shor's algorithm [8,12] can efficiently factor large integers and compute discrete logarithms, which are foundational to the security of many of the currently used group signatures. This means that group signature schemes based on these problems can be compromised by quantum attacks. It can lead to the potential exposure of the signer's identity or unauthorized access to sensitive information. Additionally, quantum algorithms for solving the hidden subgroup problem [4,6,11] and other complex problems could further challenge the security of existing post-quantum group signatures. As quantum technology advances, there is an urgent need to develop a group signature that can withstand such threats in the quantum era. Quantum cryptography (QC) [10], founded on the principles of quantum physics, has become a promising area of research for addressing the aforementioned issues. The security of quantum cryptography is based on the laws of quantum mechanics and information theory rather than the hardness of certain computational problems. As a result, QC-based primitives remain secure indefinitely unless quantum mechanics is proven incorrect.

Related Works. To the best of our knowledge, only three state-of-the-art works have been proposed in the context of designing and analyzing group signatures in the quantum domain. The first QC-based group signature was proposed by Wen et al. [13]. The authors presented a group signature scheme using quantum teleportation. Xu et al. [16] identified several flaws in the design of [13] and proposed an improved group signature protocol. The design in [16] avoids the usage of entangled states and is thus very efficient. Jiang et al. [7] designed a quantum group signature scheme based on a set of orthogonal product states that are not perfectly distinguishable. In this scheme, different particles of the product states encode important information. In the following, these particles were distributed into separate quantum sequences. As a result, it was ensured that an attacker could not reconstruct the product states corresponding to the signed message.

1.1 Our Contribution

The major contribution of this paper is listed below.
- We design a simple, efficient, and secure quantum group signature (namely qGroup) that can resist attacks by quantum algorithms. The security of our design is based on the laws of quantum physics. Detailed performance anal-

ysis shows that our design qGroup is superior to the existing state-of-the-art quantum group signature protocols.
- We show that our proposed design qGroup satisfies all the security requirements of a group signature.
- We also propose a probable application of qGroup in Vehicular Ad Hoc Networks (VANETs). In VANETs, vehicles communicate wirelessly with each other (Vehicle-to-Vehicle or V2V communication) and with roadside infrastructure (Vehicle-to-Infrastructure or V2I communication). The goal is to enhance road safety, manage traffic, and provide other services like navigation and accident alerts. For these communications to be effective, vehicles should be able to authenticate the messages they receive. We provide a possible application of qGroup to achieve this goal.

1.2 Paper Organization

The paper is organized as follows. Section 2 contains the preliminaries. The design of proposed quantum group signature qGroup is provided in Sect. 3. Security analysis of qGroup is given in Sect. 4 followed by the efficiency and performance analysis in Sect. 5. Paper is concluded with an application of qGroup to Vehicular Ad Hoc Networks in Sect. 6.

2 Preliminaries

2.1 Quantum Gates

A 2×2 unitary matrix denotes a quantum gate functioning on a single qubit, sometimes referred to as a single qubit gate. Matrix representation of single qubit gates $I, X, Y,$ and Z are given below.

$$I = \begin{pmatrix} 1 & 0 \\ 0 & 1 \end{pmatrix}, X = \begin{pmatrix} 0 & 1 \\ 1 & 0 \end{pmatrix}, Y = \begin{pmatrix} 0 & -i \\ i & 0 \end{pmatrix}, \text{ and } Z = \begin{pmatrix} 1 & 0 \\ 0 & -1 \end{pmatrix}.$$

2.2 Key-Controlled Quantum One Time Pad

Key-Controlled Quantum One Time Pad is an encryption mechanism proposed in [15]. On input the quantum message $|m\rangle = \otimes_{i=1}^{n}|m_i\rangle$ with $|m_i\rangle = \alpha_i|0\rangle + \beta_i|1\rangle$ and $|\alpha_i|^2 + |\beta_i|^2 = 1$, and the key k, the message $|m\rangle$ is encrypted as

$$E_k(|m\rangle) = \otimes_{i=1}^{n} X^{k_{2i}} Z^{k_{2i-1}} W_{k_i k_{2n-i+1}} |m_i\rangle.$$

Here, the quantum operator $W_{k_i k_{2n-i+1}}$ is defined in Table 1.

Table 1. Key-Controlled Operators

$k_i k_{2n-i+1}$	Encryption Operators
00	$W_{00} = \frac{1}{\sqrt{2}}(X+Z)$
01	$W_{01} = \frac{1}{\sqrt{2}}(Y+Z)$
10	$W_{10} = \frac{1}{2}(I+iX-iY+iZ)$
11	$W_{11} = \frac{1}{2}(I+iX+iY+iZ)$

3 Proposed Quantum Group Signature Protocol

This section describes the construction of the proposed qGroup scheme. qGroup comprises of four algorithms, namely, qGroup.KeyGen, qGroup.Signature, qGroup.Verification, and qGroup.Open. The system has three parties: signers, a verifier Bob, and a trusted third party Trent. Let $\mathcal{G} = \{A_1, \ldots, A_l\}$ denotes the set of group members. The identity of A_i is denoted by ID_i and it is known only by Trent and A_i himself. Any member of the group $\mathcal{G}$ can sign the message on behalf of the group. Trent is the group manager who is trusted by each group member A_i and the verifier Bob.

Let T_1, T_2 be two public, mutually independent substitution functions, where $T_j : \{0,1\}^n \to \{0,1\}^n$, $j = 1, 2$, and T_3, T_4 be $T_j : \{0,1\}^{2n} \to \{0,1\}^{2n}$, $j = 3, 4$. The detailed algorithms are mentioned below:

qGroup.KeyGen: On input the identity $ID_i \in \{0,1\}^{2n}$ of a group member A_i, Trent generates the corresponding secret key of A_i by executing the following steps.
- All group members A_i, $i = 1, 2, \ldots, l$ share a common key $K_{TS} \in \{0,1\}^{2n}$ with group manager Trent.
- Uses the master secret key G to calculate $k_i = G(ID_i)$ where G is a one-way function $G : \{0,1\}^* \to \{0,1\}^{2n}$.
- Shares k_i with A_i using a quantum key agreement protocol.

qGroup.Signature: On input the message m of bit length n, A_i produces the signature σ in the following manner:
- Randomly chooses bit strings $a, b \in \{0,1\}^n$ and $c, d \in \{0,1\}^{2n}$
- Computes

$$e = (e_1, e_2, \ldots, e_n) = a \oplus m \quad (1)$$
$$g = (g_1, g_2, \ldots, g_n) = T_2(a) \oplus b \oplus m \quad (2)$$
$$h = (h_1, h_2, \ldots, h_{2n}) = c' \oplus m' \quad (3)$$
$$l = (l_1, l_2, \ldots, l_{2n}) = d' \oplus m' \quad (4)$$
$$r = (r_1, r_2, \ldots, r_{2n}) = T_3(k_i \oplus m' \oplus ID_i) \quad (5)$$
$$t = (t_1, t_2, \ldots, t_{2n}) = T_4(k_i \oplus m' \oplus ID_i) \quad (6)$$

where $m' = m || T_1(m)$, $c' = c \oplus ID_i$, $d' = d \oplus ID_i$

- Performs the Key-Controlled Quantum OTP on e_j and g_j to obtain

$$|u_j\rangle = X^{h_{2j}} Z^{h_{2j-1}} W_{h_j h_{2n-j+1}} X^{r_{2j}} Z^{r_{2j-1}} W_{r_j r_{2n-j+1}}(|e_j\rangle) \qquad (7)$$

$$|v_j\rangle = X^{t_{2j}} Z^{t_{2j-1}} W_{t_j t_{2n-j+1}} X^{l_{2j}} Z^{l_{2j-1}} W_{l_j l_{2n-j+1}}(|g_j\rangle). \qquad (8)$$

Let $|u\rangle = \{|u_1\rangle, |u_2\rangle, \ldots, |u_n\rangle\}$ and $|v\rangle = \{|v_1\rangle, |v_2\rangle, \ldots, |v_n\rangle\}$.
- Randomly inserts δ randomly chosen single photons in $|u\rangle$ from the set $\{|0\rangle, |1\rangle, |+\rangle, |-\rangle\}$. Also, randomly inserts another δ randomly chosen single photons in $|v\rangle$ from the set $\{|0\rangle, |1\rangle, |+\rangle, |-\rangle\}$. The resulting sets are denoted by $|\bar{u}\rangle$ and $|\bar{v}\rangle$ respectively. A_i also notes the position and initial state of each inserted photons.
- Converts ID_i into $|ID_i\rangle$ using K_{TS} as follows:
  - Let θ be the integer corresponding to K_{TS}.
  - Define a quantum basis $B_\theta = \{|0'\rangle, |1'\rangle\}$ by setting $|0'\rangle = \cos\theta |0\rangle + \sin\theta |1\rangle$ and $|1'\rangle = \sin\theta |0\rangle - \cos\theta |1\rangle$. If the ith bit of ID_i is 0, we encode it by the qubit $|0'\rangle$; otherwise, the qubit is $|1'\rangle$.
- Produces $\sigma = \{m, |ID_i\rangle, b, c', d', |\bar{u}\rangle, |\bar{v}\rangle\}$ as the signature.

qGroup.Verification: A message-signature pair can be verified by Bob with the help of Trent. The detailed verification algorithm is provided below.
- On receiving $|\bar{u}\rangle$ and $|\bar{v}\rangle$, Bob first queries for 2δ inserted photon positions and corresponding measurement bases, and then announces the measurement results of each of those inserted photons in the correct bases. In the following, Bob checks the eavesdropping by comparing these measurement results with the initial states of these 2δ inserted photons. If the error rate is less than or equal to the predetermined threshold value, they proceed to the next step; otherwise, they abort the process.
- Bob obtains $|u\rangle$ and $|v\rangle$ after discarding the inserted photons from $|\bar{u}\rangle$ and $|\bar{v}\rangle$ respectively.
- He calculates h according to Equation (3). For each $|u_i\rangle$, he performs the operation $W^\dagger_{h_j h_{2n-j+1}} Z^{h_{2j-1}} X^{h_{2j}}$ on $|u_j\rangle$ and obtains

$$|\lambda_j\rangle = W^\dagger_{h_j h_{2n-j+1}} Z^{h_{2j-1}} X^{h_{2j}}(|u_j\rangle). \qquad (9)$$

Let $|\lambda\rangle = \{|\lambda_1\rangle, |\lambda_2\rangle, \ldots, |\lambda_n\rangle\}$.
- Bob transmits the sequences $\{m, |ID_i\rangle, |\lambda\rangle, |v\rangle\}$ to the Trent.
- Trent utilizes K_{TS} to obtain B_θ. Next, he measures $|ID_i\rangle$ using the basis $B_\theta = \{|0'\rangle, |1'\rangle\}$ and obtains ID_i. From ID_i, it can calculate the corresponding secret key k_i. In the following, Trent calculates r according to Eq. (5). Then, for each $|\lambda_j\rangle$, performs the operation $W^\dagger_{r_j r_{2n-j+1}} Z^{r_{2j-1}} X^{r_{2j}}$ on $|\lambda_j\rangle$ and gets

$$|e_j\rangle = W^\dagger_{r_j r_{2n-j+1}} Z^{r_{2j-1}} X^{r_{2j}}(|\lambda_j\rangle). \qquad (10)$$

- Measures each $|e_j\rangle$ with its basis. If the measurement result is 0, lets $e_j = 0$, otherwise, puts $e_j = 1$. As $e = (e_1, e_2, \ldots, e_n)$, then Trent calculates

$$a = (a_1, a_2, \ldots, a_n) = e \oplus m. \qquad (11)$$

- Obtains t according to Eq. (6), and performs the operation $W^\dagger_{t_j t_{2n-j+1}} Z^{t_{2j-1}} X^{t_{2j}}$ on each $|v_j\rangle$ to obtain

$$|\gamma_j\rangle = W^\dagger_{t_j t_{2n-j+1}} Z^{t_{2j-1}} X^{t_{2j}}(|v_j\rangle). \tag{12}$$

Let $|\gamma\rangle = \{|\gamma_1\rangle, |\gamma_2\rangle, \ldots, |\gamma_n\rangle\}$.

- Trent randomly inserts δ randomly chosen single photons in $|\gamma\rangle$ from the set $\{|0\rangle, |1\rangle, |+\rangle, |-\rangle\}$. In the following, it transmits the sequence $\{|\bar{\gamma}\rangle, T_2(a)\}$ to the Bob.
- On receiving $\{|\bar{\gamma}\rangle, T_2(a)\}$, Bob checks eavesdropping with the help of Trent and discards all δ decoy particles from $|\bar{\gamma}\rangle$ to obtain $|\gamma\rangle$. In the following, according m and d', Bob calculates l by Eq. (4). Then, for each $|\gamma\rangle$, Bob performs the operation $W^\dagger_{l_j l_{2n-j+1}} Z^{l_{2j-1}} X^{l_{2j}}$ on $|\lambda_j\rangle$ and gets

$$|\zeta_j\rangle = W^\dagger_{l_j l_{2n-j+1}} Z^{l_{2j-1}} X^{l_{2j}}(|\gamma_j\rangle). \tag{13}$$

Following that, Bob measures each $|\zeta_j\rangle$ with its basis. If the measuring result is 0, Bob lets $\zeta_j = 0$, otherwise he lets $\zeta_j = 1$. Given $\zeta = (\zeta_1, \zeta_2, \ldots, \zeta_n)$, Bob compares ζ and g. If $\zeta = g$, then Bob accepts the signature. Otherwise, Bob discards the signature.

qGroup.Opening: Bob transmits the sequences $\{m, |ID_i\rangle, |\lambda\rangle, |v\rangle\}$ to the Trent. Trent utilizes K_{TS} to obtain B_θ. In the following, Trent measures $|ID_i\rangle$ using the basis $B_\theta = \{|0'\rangle, |1'\rangle\}$ and obtains ID_i. From ID_i, Trent can obtain the information about the actual signer.

4 Security and Correctness Analysis

Verifiability: If A_i, Bob and Trent correctly follow the protocol, the correctness of the message-signature pair can be established. Bob verifies the validity of the message-signature pair $\sigma = \{m, |ID_i\rangle, b, c', d', |\bar{u}\rangle, |\bar{v}\rangle\}$ with the help of Trent. At the end of verification if Bob finds that $\zeta = g$, he concludes that σ is the valid signature for the message m. On receiving σ from A_i, he checks eavesdropping and discards all decoy particles to obtain $|u\rangle$ and $|v\rangle$. Bob has c', m, thus, using Eq. 3 he obtains h, and correctly computes, $|\lambda\rangle$ from $|u\rangle$. In the following, he transmits the sequence $\{m, |ID_i\rangle, |\lambda\rangle, |v\rangle\}$ to Trent. Trent utilizes K_{TS} to obtain ID_i from $|ID_i\rangle$. Trent calculates r, t using Eq. 5,6 and 1 to obtain $|\gamma\rangle$, $T_2(a)$. Notice that,

$$\begin{aligned}|\gamma_j\rangle &= W^\dagger_{t_j t_{2n-j+1}} Z^{t_{2j-1}} X^{t_{2j}}(|v_j\rangle) \\ &= W^\dagger_{t_j t_{2n-j+1}} Z^{t_{2j-1}} X^{t_{2j}} X^{t_{2j}} Z^{t_{2j-1}} W_{t_j t_{2n-j+1}} \\ &\quad X^{l_{2j}} Z^{l_{2j-1}} W_{l_j l_{2n-j+1}}(|g_j\rangle) \\ &= X^{l_{2j}} Z^{l_{2j-1}} W_{l_j l_{2n-j+1}}(|g_j\rangle)\end{aligned}$$

and $|\gamma\rangle = \{|\gamma_1\rangle, |\gamma_2\rangle, \ldots, |\gamma_n\rangle\}$. According m and d', Bob calculates l by Eq. (4), and then for each $|\gamma\rangle$, performs the operation $W^\dagger_{l_j l_{2n-j+1}} Z^{l_{2j-1}} X^{l_{2j}}$ on $|\lambda_j\rangle$ to get

$$|\zeta_j\rangle = W^\dagger_{l_j l_{2n-j+1}} Z^{l_{2j-1}} X^{l_{2j}} (|\gamma_j\rangle) \tag{14}$$

$$= W^\dagger_{l_j l_{2n-j+1}} Z^{l_{2j-1}} X^{l_{2j}} X^{l_{2j}} Z^{l_{2j-1}} W_{l_j l_{2n-j+1}} (|g_j\rangle) \tag{15}$$

$$= |g_j\rangle \tag{16}$$

Bob measures $|\zeta_j\rangle (= |g_j\rangle)$, for each j, and obtains $\zeta = g$.

Anonymity. We know that the identity of A_i is known only to A_i and Trent. ID_i is encoded into $|ID_i\rangle$ before it is transmitted through the open channel between A_i, Bob, and Trent. Since ID_i is encoded into $|ID_i\rangle$ using the secret key K_{TS}, nobody outside the group can recover ID_i from $|ID_i\rangle$. Although group members can obtain ID_i, it is not possible to know who the signer is as identity of A_i is known only to A_i and Trent. Hence, qGroup provides anonymity.

Unforgeability. Let another group member $A_j, j \neq i$ wants to create a forged signature on the message m with signature $\sigma = \{m, |ID_i\rangle, b, c', d', |\bar{u}\rangle, |\bar{v}\rangle\}$. A_j doesn't know the position and initial states of the decoy particles, therefore, any changes to $|\bar{u}\rangle, |\bar{v}\rangle$ will be caught by Trent in the verification phase. In addition, k_i is a secret, thus, A_j can not forge the signature on the behalf of A_i. Let an outside attacker $\mathcal{A}$ wants to create a forged message-signature pair on the behalf of A_i. As $\mathcal{A}$ doesn't know the decoy particles, therefore it can't obtain $|u\rangle, |v\rangle$. Similarly, in this case also, Trent can catch forgery if any changes are made by $\mathcal{A}$. In addition, $\mathcal{A}$ is unaware of k_i. Therefore, qGroup provides unforgeability.

Undeniability. If a group member A_i signs a message then later she can not deny that she is the actual signer. Bob can verify this with the help of Trent. If A_i denies that $\sigma = \{m, |ID_i\rangle, b, c', d'|\bar{u}\rangle, |\bar{v}\rangle\}$ is her sign, then in the verification phase, Trent checks this by measuring $|ID_i\rangle$ using the basis $B_\theta = \{|0'\rangle, |1'\rangle\}$. Therefore, qGroup provides the undeniability property.

Traceability. When a dispute arises, Bob sends the obtained message-signature pair $\sigma = \{m, |ID_i\rangle, b, c', d', |\bar{u}\rangle, |\bar{v}\rangle\}$ to Trent. In the following, Trent measures $|ID_i\rangle$ using the basis $B_\theta = \{|0'\rangle, |1'\rangle\}$ to obtain ID_i. From ID_i, Trent can obtain the information about who the actual signer is.

5 Efficiency and Comparison

In this section, we first compute the quantum computation and communication overheads of our proposed design. In the following, we provide a detailed comparative analysis of qGroup with the existing state-of-the-art quantum group signature. Let κ_1 denote the cost for one single qubit quantum operation.

Computation Cost: qGroup.KeyGen phase requires $8n\kappa_1$ quantum computations for quantum key distribution (QKD) protocol and quantum conference key agreement (QCKA), where n is the size of the message. In the qGroup.Signature phase $2n$ single qubits are needed to be prepared and at most $20n$ quantum operations are required. Thus, the total quantum computation cost required is $22n\kappa_1$. 2δ qubits are required to be prepared for checking eavesdropping. Therefore, the cost is $2\delta\kappa_1$. The identity ID_i is converted into $|ID_i\rangle$, and the cost needed to perform this operation is $2n\kappa_1$. In the qGroup.Verification phase, $23n + 4\delta$ quantum operations are needed. Therefore, the total quantum computation cost of qGroup is $(56n + 6\delta)\kappa_1$.

Communication Cost: In the qGroup.KeyGen phase, $4n$ single qubits are transmitted. In the qGroup.Signature phase $4n + 2\delta$ single qubits are needed to be communicated. $5n + \delta$ single qubits are transmitted during qGroup.Verification phase. Therefore, a total of $13n + 3\delta$ single qubits are needed to communicated in qGroup (Table 2).

Table 2. Comparison with existing quantum group signature

	Quantum Communication Cost	Quantum Computation Cost	Using Bell states	Using higher dimensional qubit	Using SWAP test
Wen et al. [13]	$6n$ single qubits	$40n\kappa_1 + 35n\kappa_2$	Yes	Yes	No
Xu et al. [16]	4 (n-qubit)+4 ($2n$-qubit)	$52n\kappa_1 + 2\chi$	No	Yes	Yes
Jiang et al. [7]	$\frac{26}{3}n$ single qubits	$(\frac{50}{3}n + 16\delta)\kappa_1 + n\kappa_4$	No	Yes	No
qGroup	$13n + 3\delta$ single qubits	$(56n + 6\delta)\kappa_1$	No	No	No

n: length of the message, δ: the total number of decoy particles, κ_1 is the cost for single qubit quantum operation, κ_2 is the cost for quantum operation on Bell states, κ_4 is the cost for quantum operation on (4-qubit), χ: cost of quantum swap test

Comparative Analysis: To the extent of our knowledge, there are only three quantum group signature protocols in the current state-of-the-art. Wen et al. [13] designed the first quantum group signature. Xu et al. [16] improved the design of [13] by proposing a quantum group signature that does not employ entangled states. In 2021, Jiang et al. [7] designed a quantum group signature based on orthogonal product states. The design in [13] is inefficient as compared to qGroup because it uses Bell states and Bell measurement. On the other hand, qGroup only uses single qubits, simple measurement operators, and single-qubit quantum gates. Thus, qGroup is more efficient than [13]. Although [16] avoids the usage of entangled states, it involves the transmission of higher dimensional quantum states in n or $2n$ dimensional Hilbert space. In addition, [16] also utilizes complicated quantum operators such as the SWAP test. Therefore, qGroup is more efficient when compared to [16]. Similarly, in [7], higher dimensional qubits are used, i.e., the preparation and measurement of product states are required. Thus, qGroup is simple and efficient as compared to existing state-of-the-art quantum group signature protocols [7,13,16].

6 Application to Vehicular Ad Hoc Networks

Vehicular Ad Hoc Network (VANET) [2,9,14] refers to a dynamic and self-organizing network of vehicles to exchange information with each other and with roadside infrastructure. This communication occurs through two primary channels: Vehicle-to-Vehicle (V2V) communication [1] and Vehicle-to-Infrastructure (V2I) [1] communication. Refer to Fig. 1 for an illustration. The primary goal of VANETs is to enhance road safety, optimize traffic flow, and provide additional services such as real-time navigation and accident alerts. V2V communication enables vehicles to share information directly with one another. For example, if a vehicle detects a sudden stop ahead, it can instantly warn the vehicles behind it, allowing them to slow down and avoid a collision. V2V communication is also essential for cooperative driving applications, such as platooning, where multiple vehicles travel closely together at high speeds. V2I communication involves data exchange between vehicles and fixed infrastructure, such as traffic signals, toll booths, and road signs. This communication allows vehicles to receive updates on traffic conditions, road hazards, or changes in traffic light statuses. V2I can also support more advanced applications, such as intelligent traffic management systems that dynamically adjust traffic signals based on real-time data.

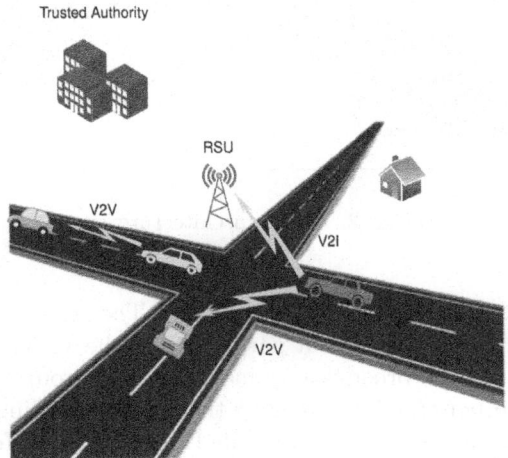

Fig. 1. Vehicular Ad Hoc Networks: V2V and V2I Communications

For VANETs to be effective, the information exchanged must be reliable and trustworthy. Vehicles must be able to authenticate the messages they receive to ensure they originate from legitimate sources. It is crucial because malicious messages could lead to dangerous situations, such as false traffic alerts or incorrect navigation instructions. Therefore, secure cryptographic mechanisms are needed to secure communications within VANETs. While authentication is essential, exposing the identity of the vehicle (or the driver) during every communication can lead to significant privacy concerns. For instance, if the identity is always revealed, it might allow for tracking the movements of a particular vehicle, which could be exploited for surveillance. It is required that messages can be verified without compromising the privacy of individual drivers. We present a possible application of our proposed design qGroup to address the aforementioned security challenges.

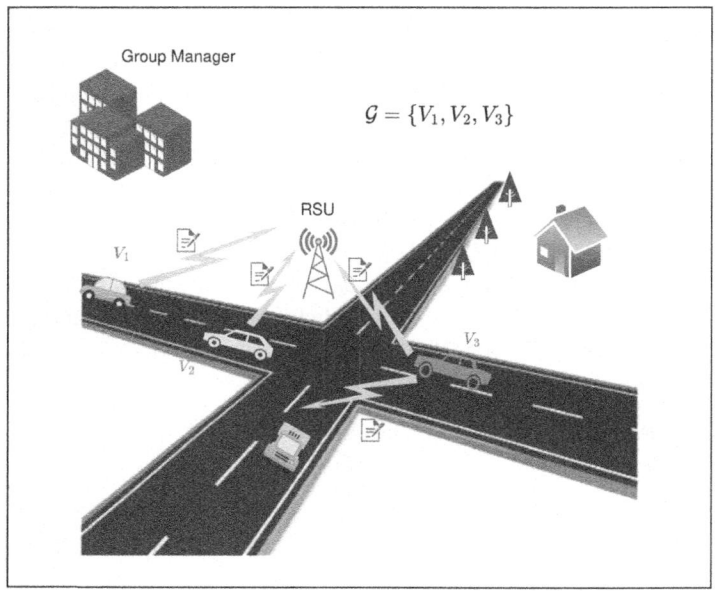

Fig. 2. System architecture

The system architecture is presented in Fig. 2. The system comprises the following entities: (1) Vehicles (V_i) that participate in the VANET. These vehicles are capable of signing and broadcasting messages. (2) Group Manager (GM), a trusted authority responsible for managing the group, including issuing keys and revealing identities if necessary. (3) Roadside Units (RSUs), infrastructure nodes that help verify messages and possibly relay them to other vehicles. (4) Verifier: Any vehicle or RSU that receives a signed message and needs to verify its authenticity. Each vehicle V_i is a member of a group $\mathcal{G}$, say the vehicles manufactured by a particular company or those authorized by a transportation authority. When a vehicle V_i sends a message (e.g., "Heavy traffic ahead" or "Accident reported on the next intersection"), V_i signs the message using qGroup.Signature to obtain the signature σ. The σ ensures the message is valid and comes from a legitimate vehicle, but it does not reveal which specific vehicle sent the message. In the following, by utilizing qGroup.Verification, other vehicles or infrastructure receiving σ can verify that it was indeed signed by an authorized member of the group $\mathcal{G}$. Since the group signature is used, they know it is from a legitimate vehicle but do not know which one. If a vehicle starts misbehaving, such as spreading false information or performing malicious activities (e.g., sending false alerts to cause traffic jams), there needs to be a way to hold it accountable. The group manager GM can revoke anonymity and reveal the identity of the misbehaving vehicle by employing the qGroup.Opening. This feature of qGroup deters malicious behavior while preserving privacy for well-behaved vehicles.

Thus, qGroup may be used in VANETs to provide a way to ensure secure and reliable communication among vehicles while protecting the privacy of drivers. This balance between privacy and accountability is crucial for successfully deploying VANETs.

7 Conclusion and Future Works

This paper presented a quantum group signature namely qGroup. The security of our design is based on the physical laws of nature. qGroup is efficient and provides security in presence of quantum adversary. We also provided a probable application of qGroup to VANETs. Our design can be utilized to ensure secure and reliable communication in vehicular networks. As a future work, development of an efficient quantum-secure ring signature protocol is an interesting direction of research.

References

1. Al-shareeda, M.A., Alazzawi, M.A., Anbar, M., Manickam, S., Al-Ani, A.K.: A comprehensive survey on vehicular ad hoc networks (vanets). In: 2021 International Conference on Advanced Computer Applications (ACA), pp. 156–160. IEEE (2021)
2. Al-Shareeda, M.A., Anbar, M., Hasbullah, I.H., Manickam, S.: Survey of authentication and privacy schemes in vehicular ad hoc networks. IEEE Sens. J. **21**(2), 2422–2433 (2020)
3. Bleumer, G.: Group Signatures, pp. 526–528. Springer US, Boston (2011)
4. de Boer, K., Ducas, L., Fehr, S.: On the quantum complexity of the continuous hidden subgroup problem. In: Canteaut, A., Ishai, Y. (eds.) EUROCRYPT 2020. LNCS, vol. 12106, pp. 341–370. Springer, Cham (2020). https://doi.org/10.1007/978-3-030-45724-2_12
5. Chaum, D., van Heyst, E.: Group signatures. In: Davies, D.W. (ed.) EUROCRYPT 1991. LNCS, vol. 547, pp. 257–265. Springer, Heidelberg (1991). https://doi.org/10.1007/3-540-46416-6_22
6. Hallgren, S., Russell, A., Ta-Shma, A.: The hidden subgroup problem and quantum computation using group representations. SIAM J. Comput. **32**(4), 916–934 (2003)
7. Jiang, D., Yuan, F., Xu, G.: Novel quantum group signature scheme based on orthogonal product states. Mod. Phys. Lett. B **35**(26), 2150418 (2021)
8. LaPierre, R., LaPierre, R.: Shor algorithm. In: Introduction to Quantum Computing, pp. 177–192 (2021)
9. Malhi, A.K., Batra, S., Pannu, H.S.: Security of vehicular ad-hoc networks: a comprehensive survey. Comput. Secur. **89**, 101664 (2020)
10. McMahon, D.: Quantum Computing Explained. John Wiley & Sons, Hoboken (2007)

11. Perepechaenko, M.: Hidden subgroup problem: about some classical and quantum algorithms. Ph.D. thesis, University of Ottawa (2021)
12. Shor, P.W.: Algorithms for quantum computation: discrete logarithms and factoring. In: Proceedings 35th Annual Symposium on Foundations of Computer Science, pp. 124–134. IEEE (1994)
13. Wen, X., Tian, Y., Ji, L., Niu, X.: A group signature scheme based on quantum teleportation. Phys. Scr. **81**(5), 055001 (2010)
14. Xia, Z., Wu, J., Wu, L., Chen, Y., Yang, J., Yu, P.S.: A comprehensive survey of the key technologies and challenges surrounding vehicular ad hoc networks. ACM Trans. Intell. Syst. Technol. (TIST) **12**(4), 1–30 (2021)
15. Xin, X., He, Q., Wang, Z., Yang, Q., Li, F.: Security analysis and improvement of an arbitrated quantum signature scheme. Optik **189**, 23–31 (2019)
16. Xu, G.B., Zhang, K.J.: A novel quantum group signature scheme without using entangled states. Quantum Inf. Process. **14**, 2577–2587 (2015)

Author Index

A
Arock, Michael   79

B
Bajpayee, Soumen   171
Bera, Padmalochan   127
Bopche, Ghanshyam S.   79

C
Chandra, Harish   3
Curcudel, Teodor-Cosmin   94

D
Das, Priyanka   109
Dey, Prithwish   171
Dutta, Suman   62

J
Jaiswal, Aarav   62
Joshi, Piyush   127

K
Kumar Ch, Narendra   142
Kumar, Dinesh   142
Kumar, Gatram Sravan   127

L
Lakshmy, K. V.   47

M
Maitra, Subhamoy   62
Mandal, Mriganka   13
Maurya, Rahul   79
Mishra, Dheerendra   28

Mohanty, Tapaswini   183
Mukherjee, Imon   171

N
Namdeo, Kuldeep   28

P
Pandit, Manish Kumar   109
Prabhaker, Nilin   79
Prakash, Amit   142
Prasanna Kumar, Y.   154

R
Rana, Saurabh   3
Rao, Y. Sreenivasa   183
Ray, Sangram   109
Roy, Debasish   62

S
Sahai, Utkarsh   13
Sarkar, Ramprasad   13
Sen, Sarbani   171
Sethi, Kamalakanta   127
Singh, Akanksha   3
Srinivasan, Chungath   47
Srivastava, Namita   28
Srivastava, Vikas   183

V
Valli Kumari, V.   154

Z
Zeenath, A. U.   47

The manufacturer's authorised representative in the EU is Springer Nature Customer Service Centre GmbH, Europaplatz 3, 69115 Heidelberg, Germany. If you have any concerns regarding our products, please contact ProductSafety@springernature.com

Printed and bound by CPI Group (UK) Ltd, Croydon, CR0 4YY
25/03/2026
02078191-0010